# 1001 MORE THINGS TO DO
## WITH YOUR KIDS

## OTHER BOOKS
## BY
## CARYL WALLER KRUEGER

*Single with Children,* Abingdon Press, 1983

*Six Weeks to Better Parenting,* Pelican Publishing, 1985

*1001 Things to Do with Your Kids,* Abingdon Press, 1988

*Working Parent—Happy Child,* Abingdon Press, 1990

*The Ten Commandments for Grandparents,* Abingdon Press, 1991

*101 Ideas for the Best-Ever Christmas,* Dimensions for Living, 1992

*365 Ways to Love Your Child,* Abingdon Press, 1994

*The Family Party Book,* Abingdon Press, 1995

*222 Terrific Tips for Two,* Abingdon Press, 1995

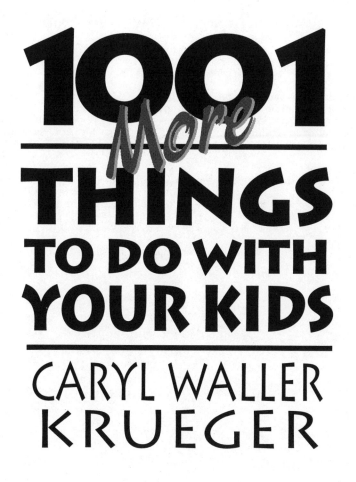

# 1001 *More* THINGS TO DO WITH YOUR KIDS

## CARYL WALLER KRUEGER

ABINGDON PRESS/ NASHVILLE

# 1001 MORE THINGS TO DO WITH YOUR KIDS

*Copyright © 1997 by Caryl Waller Krueger*

All rights reserved.

Scripture quotations, unless otherwise noted, are from the New Revised Standard Version Bible, Copyright © 1989, by the Division of Christian Education of the National Council of the Churches of Christ in the USA. Used by permission.

*This book is printed on recycled, acid-free paper.*

Application has been made for Cataloging in Publication Data.

The author has made every effort to make the information and suggestions in this book practical and workable, but neither she nor the publisher assumes any responsibility for successes, failures, or other results of putting these ideas into practice.

97 98 99 00 01 02 03 04 05 06 — 10 9 8 7 6 5 4 3 2 1

MANUFACTURED IN THE UNITED STATES OF AMERICA

790.192
K

# TO

*Chris, Carrie, and Cameron*
*who were the guinea pigs for*
*many of these ideas and who now*
*pass them on to the next generation*

# CONTENTS

# ACKNOWLEDGMENTS

In collecting this second book of 1001 kid-tested ideas, many good friends have been helpful. My appreciation for their creative suggestions goes to:

Linda Bargmann, Debi Brewster, Gloria and Robert Brewster, Mildred Corruccini, Clifford Douglas, Marty Fraser, Lynne Grantham, Nancy Gruber, Piper and Bruce Hunter, Diana Jackson, Barbara Kerbox, Melissa Kinder, Sheila Kinder, Connie King, Carrie Krueger, Diane and Cam Krueger, Robin Brewster Okun, Elieth Robertshaw, Judy Strachan, Cathy Turrentine, Diana Usrey, and Donna Walker.

# DEAR READER

**H**ow exciting to be spending time with your youngster, having fun, but also learning together! Being a good parent, a creative parent, isn't a painful process when you take a little time each day to be WITH your child.

Ten years ago when I started to write *1001 Things to Do with Your Kids,* friends wondered how I could ever come up with so many ideas. With our own youngsters, nieces, nephews, plus input from my lectures at schools and parent groups, it was easy! And the book became a best-seller for my publisher and was a book club selection.

A few years later, a woman spoke to me after one of my lectures and showed me her dog-eared copy of the book in which she had checked off every idea! "More, please" is what she said. And as other readers echoed her request, I knew it was time to start collecting new ideas. And so, this time with the help of friends, relatives, children—and now grandchildren, too—I created and tested the next 1001 ideas. There are a few of the same subjects, but always with a unique twist. So here's an all-new collection for you and your family.

While this book is loaded with fun things to do together, it also has a serious side. You'll find things to do with your child in order to get chores done, to discipline thoughtfully, to support education and culture, and to teach virtues—those important traits that comprise an intelligent, responsible, and caring youngster.

You may think I have left out certain topics. That's because they have been fully covered in the first book (or in another of my ten books). I do suggest that you have a copy of the first *1001 Things to Do with Your Kids* as a handy cross-reference.

This is not a book that tells you what you must do, but rather what you can do. We didn't do all these fun things in a short space of time—and neither will you—so pick and choose the ones you think you and your kids will enjoy. But remember, you have just a few years before your kids leave home, so get started!

In front of each of the 1001 ideas is a little box. It's mainly decorative, but you can put a check mark in it as you complete that activity—as my friend with the dog-eared copy did. So, to her, and to the thousands of families who enjoyed and benefited from *1001 Things to Do with Your Kids,* here are 1001 MORE things!

*— Caryl Krueger*

# ONE

# A WONDERFUL DAY

SECTION 1: OH, WHAT A BEAUTIFUL MORNING!

SECTION 2: AFTERNOON CONNECTIONS

SECTION 3: DINNERTIME DELIGHTS

SECTION 4: EVENTFUL EVENINGS

**W**eekdays don't need to be dull! Having fun with your child, as well as working and learning together, doesn't have to wait for the weekend. Here are ideas to give highlights to weekdays, so that you can enjoy every day with your youngster. Even if both parents work away from home, these morning, afternoon, and evening connections are vital.

# SECTION 1:
# OH, WHAT A BEAUTIFUL MORNING!

❑ **1.** WAKE UP TO MUSIC. If most everyone in the family gets up at about the same time, play stirring music to get the family moving. Recordings of marches, Tchaikovsky's *1812 Overture,* rap music, or even yodeling will cover up the groans of, "Do I have to get up?"

❑ **2.** INDEPENDENCE DAY. By the time a youngster is four, she can have an alarm clock and be responsible for getting up on time. (If she doesn't, make her bedtime earlier until she does.) Tell youngsters what you expect them to do independently before they leave for school. If necessary, make a list and put it where they can't miss seeing it.

❑ **3.** TICKLE TIME. Start the day with a smile by giving a quick tickle to another family member as you pass one another during the morning rush.

❑ **4.** UP-AND-AT-'EM FIVE. Encourage kids to shout a number (one through five) as they finish the before-breakfast essentials: (1) the bathroom stop, (2) dressing, (3) bed-making, (4) room-tidying, and (5) their morning chore, such as feeding the fish. When you begin to hear many shouted fives, it's probably time for breakfast.

❑ **5.** THE ABSOLUTE ESSENTIAL. Teachers report that kids who skip breakfast do not learn as readily as others. For this reason, insist on a hearty breakfast at your house. Find out what kids like to eat and see that it is available to them. Make breakfast easy, especially if kids have to prepare it themselves. Save the fancy breakfasts for the weekend. Don't let your youngster suffer academically because his stomach is growling!

# WHAT GOES ON AT BREAKFAST?

Beyond good nutrition, breakfast is a necessary time of connecting after the long separation of sleep and before the long separation of school and work. Breakfast conversation should include: each person's plan for the day, telling when the family will be together again, inspiration, news, confidence-building (especially on test or report days), and expressions of love.

❏ **6.** AVOID CONFUSION.  First, talk about today: getting to school and work, getting home, places to go after school, errands to run, kids to pickup, who will start dinner, and any scheduled evening events. Also go over things that a child needs to take: toy, school project, lunch, money, books, Scout cookies, homework, report, gym shoes, and so forth. It helps if you have a "going shelf" near the door where such things can be placed and easily seen.

❏ **7.** WHEN WE MEET AGAIN.  Because the family is going to be separated for many hours, it's important to establish connections from the present (morning) to the future (when we'll see each other again). This may be after school, at supper, or several days hence after a business trip. Let kids tell you about what they want to do when you are together again. And, in turn, tell them how much you are looking forward to hearing what happened while you were apart.

❏ **8.** GOOD WORDS FOR THE DAY.  Two books that can be helpful at the breakfast table are the Bible and the dictionary. Read a verse from Psalms or another inspirational passage. Then, let a child open the dictionary at random and point to a word. (Word-a-day calendars can also be used.) Read the word and a simple definition. See who can use the word during breakfast. Then see who can use it at supper.

❏ **9.** NEWS OF THE DAY.  Although your TV is definitely off during breakfast (so it won't cut down on family communication), a parent can hear the current news by listening to a radio while dressing. Choose a news tidbit in keeping with your child's age: "The World Series starts today."

"Soccer balls are on sale at the Emporium." "It rained two inches at Grandpa's." "Last night the city council approved money for the new school."

❑ **10. CONFIDENCE-BUILDING.** While the day may be merely challenging for adults, it can be intimidating for kids. Breakfast talk should build confidence so kids set out ready to succeed. Consider your child's activities and use lines such as: "Your friends will like the dinosaur you're taking for show-and-tell." "Your book report sounded great last night and I know you'll give it easily." "I like what you're wearing today." "Take a deep breath before the physics test—you're well-prepared." "The cookies you made for Scouts taste great and they'll love them." These reinforce a youngster's feeling of self-worth.

❑ **11. ALL-IMPORTANT LOVE.** As you part, your love for one another should be the send-off. Don't fail to hug, kiss, and verbalize your love each morning to each family member. One family holds hands around the table and gives three squeezes meaning "I love you," then four squeezes for "Have a great day," and finally two squeezes for "Let's go!" Good parting lines include: "I'm proud you're my kid." "Always remember that I love you." "You're very special."

❑ **12. THE BEST THING.** Even if breakfast is a brief meal, take time for family members to share "The best thing I'm going to do today." (One gradeschooler said "The best thing is coming home!") Listen to these "best things" and do remember to add your own hopes for the day.

❑ **13. BREAKFAST TRANSLATIONS.** Most everyone has learned another language or picked up a few foreign words. Gradually introduce these at mealtimes. Say "danka" ("thank you" in German) or "bon voyage" ("happy travels" in French) or "por favor" ("please" in Spanish). Soon, words such as sayonara, au revoir, and aloha will be common terms at your house.

❏ **14.** SURPRISE MESSAGES. While watching evening television, or at some other time, encourage family members to write little notes on small pieces of paper. (Preschoolers can draw a simple picture.) Keep these in a kitchen drawer and occasionally tuck one in a lunch box or coat pocket. The message can be brief: "I'm looking forward to supper with you and hearing about the Brownie meeting." Or, "Let's play catch." Ask at dinner if anyone got a surprise message and who they think was the author.

❏ **15.** CAR POOL CAPERS. Don't waste driving time—use it for fun and subtle education. Avoid corrections and confrontations. For young children, sing songs, teach rhymes, tell a familiar story and let them be the sound effects. With gradeschoolers, let them add up numbers of license plates or play "I'm going to Mars and I'm taking an APE." (Each person repeats the line and adds something with the next letter of the alphabet.) Use car pool time to listen, too, since you'll learn what kids are thinking.

# SECTION 2:
# AFTERNOON CONNECTIONS

❏ **16.** MYSTERY JAR. For after-school fun, place a jar with a message inside on your kitchen counter. Let kids know they are to check the mystery jar after school. Put in a note that says, "Fruit sticks in the freezer" or "How many doorknobs are there in this house?" or "Graham crackers are yummy in the tummy." This starts the homecoming on a happy note.

❏ **17.** THREE BIG REASONS. If kids will be home alone after school, a working parent should make a phone call home—a short call, but with three purposes. First, it reassures the parent that all is well (the school child has returned home). The second reason is an opportunity to talk with the youngster and inquire about afternoon activities (not TV, but inside or outside play followed by chores or homework). And the third reason is to tell the child how much you care for him and what time you'll be home.

❑ **18.** AN IMPORTANT NUMBER.  Of course parents' work numbers are posted at home and the school also has them on file. But the time a youngster usually needs the number is when she's at a friend's, the library, or an after-school activity. Find a good place to put your business number: on the inside of her notebook, taped inside the lunch box, on a card in a coat pocket, or on something your child is sure to have with her at all times.

❑ **19.** A "COOL" HOMECOMING.  If you pick up your child at school, avoid asking if he behaved himself and what he did that day. Just let the youngster talk as you listen. And if you must ask questions, make them casual ones such as, "What shall we do after supper tonight?" Over a snack, your youngster will probably reveal what you need to know about the day's events.

❑ **20.** TOGETHERNESS SNACKS.  Surprise your youngster by joining her in a snack time held in a different location: her room, your bedroom, porch, under a tree, living room floor, or in the attic.

❑ **21.** CHANGE-OF-PACE.  Kids have spent most of the day sitting down. So, the first after-school activity shouldn't be a sedentary one. The diligent student may want to do homework, but encourage a change-of-pace activity such as playing outside with a friend, bicycling to the park, making brownies, or working on a craft or hobby. With your youngster, make a list of change-of-pace activities and do one for at least thirty minutes each afternoon— together with you or on his own.

❑ **22.** CHORE TIME.  Chores done at nine at night can be miserable, but tasks done in the late afternoon can actually be fun. As your child does a task, do some work yourself and see who finishes first: Can he set the table faster than you can make a salad? Can you open the mail faster than he can provide food and water for the dog? Until doing chores becomes easy for a child, this little competition is a quick way to get them done.

## THE GANG'S ALL HERE

As family members return home for the day, it's time for AIR, a three-step welcoming, so important after the long time apart. Like a breath of fresh air, AIR provides a gentle transition from the busy day and takes just a few minutes. At the same time it rids the family of weary and hungry feelings, omits pestering for attention, and expresses your loving interest.

❏ **23.** *A* IS FOR ACKNOWLEDGMENT.   We all like attention, so let your first moments be ones of joyful acknowledgment complete with a greeting, kiss, hug, lap-sitting— not a torrent of words but a renewal of the parent/child and parent/parent love relationship.

❏ **24.** *I* IS FOR INTEREST.   This important sign of caring need not be a lengthy dialogue. In fact, link the interest to a later time by saying, "Did you go on the field trip? I want you to tell us about it when we have our juice." "Did you get a new piece of music at your lesson? Let's play it together after supper." Such easy questions involve no arguments or judgments, but promise a portion of your time later. Show your interest by being sure that the "later time" truly comes. Kids recognize when "later" means "never," an indication of no interest on the part of the parent.

❏ **25.** *R* IS FOR RELAXATION.   How can you take time to relax when everyone is starved? It may sound elegant, but serve part of the meal and call it the appetizer course. Tailor this food to the age of your child and remember that a small amount can suffice. Consider a banana sliced in milk, crackers and cheese, cucumber sticks in yogurt, juice and a graham cracker, or even a salad. Then sit down in a place different from your dinner location and eat this together. Listen, munch, listen, talk, listen, smile, listen, appreciate.

# SECTION 3:
# DINNERTIME DELIGHTS

## THE SUPER SUPPER SETTING

Dinner is a meal eaten at a table, without the TV on. (When the TV is talking, no one else can talk. Listen to the news on the radio before supper since radio news provides more facts than TV news in the same amount of time.) There are certain elements that make the meal something to look forward to, rather than a boring ritual. Try these to enliven this bonding time.

❑ **26.** NO LITTLE RED HENS.   Supper preparation is a great one-on-one time. While other family members are doing chores, reading mail, tackling homework, one parent and one child can be the supper team. A very young child can set the dining table and then draw at the kitchen table. A parent can stir-fry while testing a child on spelling words. A teen can make a salad while having a heart-to-heart talk with a parent. Don't prepare dinner on your own; let it be a joint event, adding to the happy time you spend with your kids.

❑ **27.** SET THE TIME.   When kids are young, establish the routine of eating dinner together. If commuting and team practices cause a later dinner, give at-home kids part of the meal (such as the salad) early, and then sit down together as a group. Insist on dinnertime together and weekly reaffirm your plan by saying, "Our family will eat together at 6:30!"

❏ **28.** NOT AN EAT-AND-RUN EVENT. Dinner should take about thirty minutes. Young children can be given toys in the high chair or put in a playpen next to the table until they learn to stay seated. Since the cook has taken time to prepare the meal, family members should be appreciative and know that it is rude to leave early.

❏ **29.** TAKE A NUMBER. If the family eats in silence or is one where everyone talks at once, put numbers in a bowl and let family members draw for talking order—just sharing something brief before more conversation later. Parents should be sure to contribute from their day: an interesting work project, a challenge, new things learned. Try to keep dinner talk from getting too serious—if someone has a big problem, make time to discuss it after dinner.

❏ **30.** CURRENT EVENTS. Keep kids informed on important happenings in the world outside the family. Young children may listen and ask questions, while older kids can contribute. Encourage them to bring to the table a clipping from the newspaper—even a picture or cartoon. Play down the negative stuff but talk about an election, a scientific discovery, a new business in town, a sports event, and so forth. Ask questions such as, "What do you think about that?" and "How will it affect us?"

❏ **31.** UPCOMING EVENTS. Early in the week, focus the dinner talk on one event that will take place on the weekend. Let everyone help choose the family activity and be sure to put it on the calendar. (You may want to keep a list of possible activities on the bulletin board.)

❏ **32.** VIOLINS PLAYING? Hardly, but do have a music background for dinner. Let kids choose an all-music station or play their own recordings. To be fair, each family member should have a dinner with his choice of music and be prepared to share a few facts about it. Choose music without intrusive lyrics so as not to compete with your own talking.

## ADDING FUN TO DINNER

❑ **33.** THE CONTINUING BOOK.   At first, kids may think this is a dull idea, but I suggest you try it anyway. Choose a book of interest to kids of varied ages, and one they haven't read. Read for just ten minutes as youngsters finish eating. (Parents read until kids are teens and wish to help.) If you need ideas, look at *The Read-Aloud Handbook* by James Trelease (Penguin: New York, 1985).

❑ **34.** KID AMBIENCE.   Let your child make the dining table a special place with no-iron napkins, a flower or object in the center of the table, and candles. Let the child choose the place: in the dining area, around a family room table, on the patio table, and occasionally on a picnic table.

❑ **35.** MORE THAN "YES," "NO," AND "NOTHING."   Meaningful conversation at the dinner table sometimes needs a boost if it's to go beyond those three words. With preschoolers, you can ask a zany question like "What would happen if we had our mouths on the back of our heads?" Older kids and parents can discuss more serious issues like "What should be done about all the wasted food in the world?" Such impersonal questions will warm up kids to talking and soon they may share more personal topics. And when this happens, all should remember that the purpose of dinner conversation is to learn about one another, not to criticize.

❑ **36.** SEATING ARRANGEMENT.   While it may be customary to sit across from children at the table, sitting next to them is better since it takes away the "teacher is looking at you" feeling. Even if you are a small family, let youngsters make place cards (from painted clay or colorful paper) and then take turns making the seating plan.

❑ **37.** WHERE ARE WE EATING TONIGHT?   A parent or older child looks up the name of a country or city in the encyclopedia. Then as dinner begins, she says "We're eating where it is SO windy, a place where there are Cubs, where a cow perhaps started a fire, where Carl Sandburg wrote a famous poem, and where a main street is called Michigan Avenue. Where are we?" (The answer is Chicago.) Make the descriptions of other countries and cities harder or easier depending on the kid's ages.

❑ **38.** FACE MATS. Like place mats, face mats are placed on the dinner table. Youngsters can use art paper or shelf paper and draw the face of each family member. Although the drawings may not be too accurate, encourage elements that help identify the person (a smile, a missing tooth, a tie, blue eyes, a pony tail). The kids can then place these around the table wherever they choose.

❑ **39.** TORTILLA MESSAGES. A creative mom puts mystery messages on tortillas when they're part of the meal. From a slice of cheese, she cuts out letters or numbers and places a code message on top of each burrito, enchilada, or chimichanga. No hints are given and the family has to guess what the symbolism might be. For example, it might be the age of the youngest child, each person's initials, school grade levels, Dad's age, the telephone area code, the number of pets in the house, the month of the year—sometimes it's easy, sometimes hard, but it's always conversational.

❑ **40.** SEVEN CAN SUPPER. Here's an easy meal that older youngsters can make all by themselves and serve to parents. In a saucepan, put a can of chunk tuna or chicken (can size depends on family size). On top of that add these five canned ingredients (the first three drained): sliced olives, sliced water chestnuts, peas, chicken or mushroom soup, and milk (a soup can full). Heat and gently stir. Just before serving, add a can of Chinese crisp noodles.

❑ **41.** GOOD NEWS. School-aged children hear plenty of bad news from the TV set. Balance that with good news this educational way. Tear the newspaper into single pages (choose a page from various sections). Place one page at each place at the table. During the meal, call a moratorium on talk as each person scans his page for an item of good news. Then resume talking as each shares something positive he's read.

❑ **42. DELIGHTFUL WORDS.** When the family sits down to eat, share a few of these special words to describe the day, the food, or the family: awesome, incredible, bodacious, outstanding, exceptional, spectacular, imaginative, terrific, superb, remarkable, fantastic, marvelous, astonishing, phenomenal. It sounds silly, but "sweet talk" does wonders for those end-of-day attitudes.

❑ **43. AKA.** Those initials stand for "Also Known As" and it's a game you can play at dinner. Explain to kids that they can have a new descriptive name such as Munching Michael or The Queen of the House, or Superkid, or DEE-lightful Dad. Give kids awhile to choose their AKA and then let each announce who he is. Use these AKAs for the remainder of dinner and the evening.

❑ **44. TIRED TODDLER.** When a young child gets bored with the meal and others in the family haven't finished, give him a whipped cream dessert! On his tray, put a big glob of low-fat whipped topping (or yogurt) and let him finger paint with it. Of course, he'll lick his fingers but a busy baby is a happy baby.

❑ **45. AFTER THE LAST MOUTHFUL.** Avoid the stampede from the table through cooperative cleanup. Everyone from toddler on up should have an assignment. Each can carry his own dishes to the kitchen sink. Parents and teens can put away leftovers. The person with the best sense of organization can load the dishwasher, or a teen can wash and a younger child dry the dishes. A toddler can stand on a stool and wipe the counters and table clean. And a young child can sweep the floor. With this joint activity, the cleanup is over in less than ten minutes.

# SECTION 4:
# EVENTFUL EVENINGS

After dinner, parents and kids usually have individual things to do, but first take a short time for a family activity. Whether you spend twenty minutes or an hour, this special time brings family members together before homework and the bedtime routine.

## FOR BABIES AND PRESCHOOLERS

☐ **46.** FINGER GAMES. It's comforting for a parent and child to be close, and for finger games you'll want the child in your lap. Start with "This Little Piggy," "This Old Man," and "Teensie Weensie Spider." Then graduate to "Patty Cake" and learning to count to five. With a marker, make little faces on your fingers and let these tiny people talk to your child.

☐ **47.** EXPLORATORIUM. Surprisingly, many kids don't really know how to play with their toys—they just toss them around. Get down on the floor and explore just one toy—the little train, the doll in the bed, the jack-in-the-box. Illustrate the train sounds, talk to the dolly, act surprised when Jack pops up. Then combine two toys—for example, let Jack surprise dolly. If you use different toys each night, your child will learn creative ways to play.

☐ **48.** LITTLE FINGERS, LITTLE CRAFTS. Don't feel you need to buy an expensive craft kit—make a simple one with your child. Punch big holes in a piece of cardboard and show how to lace string or yarn through the holes. Or, draw together on plain paper with crayons (you don't need coloring books yet). Explore the good feeling of soft clay. Don't try to figure out what a child molds with it; any shape is fine.

☐ **49.** MUSIC MAKERS. Put dried peas into a plastic container and tape it shut. This is the child's instrument. Yours is two wooden spoons to beat time. Make up a short silly song such as "This is our song, so sing along!" After you have the song and instruments going, see if you can march down the hall to your music.

❑ **50.** SIMPLE GAMES.   Put a long string on the floor and see who can walk the length of it without falling off. Have a doorway chinning bar and practice hanging from it. Play with all the balls in the house by sitting on the floor with legs outstretched and rolling the balls back and forth.

❑ **51.** WHERE SHALL WE GO?   Ask questions and let the child show you the answer. A parent may ask, "Where can we read?" (A child leads to the bookshelf and a rocker.) "Where can we find rain inside the house?" (A child leads to the shower.) "Where can we find ice?" (A child leads to the freezer.) Vary this by hopping, skipping, or crawling to the destination, or carrying a child piggyback.

❑ **52.** QUICK PLAYHOUSE.   Throw a sheet over a card table and put a book, toy, dishes, a rattle, and so forth, underneath. Then you and your child move in—except you pretend to be a baby and the child the parent.

## FOR GRADESCHOOLERS

❑ **53.** BOX GAME WEEK.   Uncle Wiggly, Scrabble, dominoes, checkers, chess—you no doubt have a shelf full of games at your house. It only takes fifteen to thirty minutes to play a game (or part of a game such as Monopoly) in the time after dinner. Have a box game week when family members choose six or seven games to be played one each night after dinner. Applaud the winners for their skill and also applaud the losers for their graceful good sportsmanship.

❑ **54.** OUT OF THE HOUSE.   A change of place gives a boost to the upcoming quiet evening activities (homework, chores, reading, bedtime preparations, and TV). So, leave home for an after-dinner walk, a visit with neighbors, a quick trip to the park, bicycling around the block. Some families also work in a visit to the library or a thirty-minute swim at the Y. Don't just drift from dinner table to TV; plan a change of scenery.

❑ **55.** KIDS IN CHARGE.   Start the tradition of letting youngsters be in charge one night a week. One family does this each Thursday when kids take over before supper, choosing what and where to eat, what activities follow dinner, what TV programs to watch, what books to read, and whether bedtime is postponed fifteen minutes for good behavior. Occasionally being in charge helps youngsters to accept supervision when parents are in charge.

❑ **56.** BE A SPORT.   Throw balls in baskets, practice hitting baseballs, and catching footballs. Sink a can in the backyard and practice golf putting. Hit tennis balls against a wall. Do tricks on the jungle gym. Play table tennis. Work out with an exercise video.

❑ **57.** SHARE A CRAFT.   You can work side-by-side on different projects or together on the same project. Consider woodworking, sketching, sewing, porcelain painting, pottery-making, stamp or coin collecting, furniture refinishing, flower arranging, collage making, gourmet cooking, soap carving, model train building. If you don't have any ideas, you'll find lots at a craft store.

❑ **58.** QUICK BAKING.   Don't serve dessert with dinner but prepare something with kid-help that can be eaten later in the evening. Make pudding, brownies, cupcakes, or fruit cobbler. For an unusual treat, mix together nuts, canned mandarin oranges, and vanilla cookie pieces in a little melted butter and brown sugar. Served warm, this ten minute production may become a favorite.

## FOR TEENS

Be realistic! Your after-dinner time with teens is going to be short—perhaps just twenty minutes, but it can be a pleasant change in the hectic schedule. School nights are not usually social nights, so kids should be at home. Of course, they need to complete homework and then they'll want TV and telephone time—but only after a little togetherness with the family. Try these quick ideas.

❑ **59. GET PHYSICAL.** Right after dinner, take just fifteen minutes for something active: jogging, cycling, shooting hoops, or Ping Pong. It's okay if your teen is better than you are!

❑ **60. GAMESMANSHIP.** Spend time playing a game the teen enjoys: backgammon, chess, poker, grown-up card games, and box games. Chess can be played over several nights' duration by just putting a poker chip or coin under the last piece moved.

❑ **61. SPEEDY WORK.** If you work on a project together, you may be able to cut down on Saturday tasks. Change the oil filter in the car, work on constructing a bookshelf, clean a closet, sew on buttons. Such jobs done together increase a youngster's self-esteem because you show that you need him.

❑ **62. POPCORN PROJECTS.** Evenings at home are ideal times for munching popcorn. Make it interesting by working with kids to make a gallon or more of homemade popcorn. Then experiment with toppings: garlic salt with chili powder, or cinnamon and sugar, or powdered sugar with brown sugar. Or, look in a cookbook for how to make caramel corn.

❑ **63. KICKING-BACK TOGETHER.** Read while your youngster reads. Look at a TV show together and comment on it. Listen to music together. Most every teen has some evening kick-back time. Try to coordinate your activities so you can be together. One family has what they call "Ten minutes in the dark" when they just sit outside together— no conversation needed.

❑ **64.** PLOTTING FOR FUN. Discuss family and teen entertaining. Plan parties and discuss foods, games and activities, whom to invite, music, costumes if any, and a time schedule. Including a teen and asking for advice show your respect and confidence in her.

❑ **65.** HOMEWORK SNACK. Don't be a pest, but drop in at least once during the homework session. Bring a tray with juice, cookies, or crackers and cheese to share. Ask if you can be of any help—not doing the homework but proof-reading, testing, finding supplies, hearing a report. This keeps you in touch with both the academics and the teen.

## THE BEDTIME COUNTDOWN

Depending on the age of your children, you may tuck them in bed, or they may kiss you good night as you go to bed. Still, a regular bedtime routine is very important as a loving and calming activity.

❑ **66.** SING THE TOYS AWAY. When it's time to pick up toys, teach youngsters this song (to the tune of "Three Blind Mice") and see if the toys are in their places after two, four, or six times through the song: "Pick up toys, pick up toys. Some are girl's, some are boy's. They all have a home and I'll put them away. That way I can find them the next time I play. Pick up toys, pick up toys."

❑ **67.** BEDTIME TAG. If you have trouble heading young-sters toward their beds, a parent can introduce bedtime tag. It's just like any other game of tag and can be played inside the house in winter and in the yard in summer. Designate an area for the game. The parent will do the tagging and when a child is tagged, she's the first to start getting ready for bed. You can also make it two or three tags before a child is out and must start the bedtime routine.

❑ **68.** THINKING DEEP THOUGHTS. Family members scatter to various parts of the house (the basement, under the dining table, in a box in the garage, in the shower stall) for a quiet five minutes of thinking on just one topic. A parent whistles or rings a bell at the end of the five minutes and all gather in one place to share the mystery of where they've been and what they thought. For example: "I was in the bathtub thinking about summer at the lake." "I was at the desk thinking about paying bills." "I was on the kitchen floor hugging the dog."

❑ **69.** SOOTHING SUDS.   While teens usually prefer a morning shower, younger kids enjoy a warm bath as a prelude to good sleep. Even though soaking in water is delightful, it is also a time for occasional bathing lessons: how to wash ears safely, how to give a good shampoo, how to brush fingernails and toenails, how to carefully wash the tummy button and private parts.

❑ **70.** NO DRIPS.   Kids love popsicles but they can be a sticky mess. Why not let them drip in the bathtub? Give little children their dessert treat in the tub, then scrub them up and get them ready for teeth-brushing and bed.

❑ **71.** BATHTUB BOATS.   Show young children how to fold paper into small boats for floating in the tub and moving with fingers or toes. Add other bathtub toys on top of the boats and see what it takes to sink them. Wring out the wet boats and roll them into tiny balls for tossing into a floating cup. Then, as the tub drains, see who can "score" by tossing them into a nearby wastebasket.

❑ **72.** BATHTUB STORM.   Storms will be less intimidating for little kids if you recreate the storm right in the bathroom. With the youngster in the tub and washed, start slowly with rain (coming from a sprinkling can). Then make "thunder" sounds by knocking on the side of the tub or beating on a toy drum. Make "lightning" by going over to the wall switch and turning the lights on and off. (Of course, never let anything electrical near the tub.) Then tell the child it is time to come in from the storm and safely wrap him up in his towel.

❑ **73.** BODY STICKERS.   Let little kids be nude for awhile before bed and have fun with stickers. Show him how to put a sticker on the end of a finger and wave with it. Then on toes and wiggle them. Hide one on the palm of her hand and play peek-a-boo. Put one on her tummy and tell her to push her tummy in and out. One on a cheek can be puffed in and out. Then remove all stickers (restick them on a favorite stuffed animal) and jump into pj's.

❑ **74.** HOW LONG TO BRUSH?   Good habits start early, so (several times weekly) brush your teeth alongside your kids. Research shows that brushing is less thorough on the side you hold your brush—right-handers do the poorest job on the inside right, lefties on the inside left. While kids think that they know how long two minutes is, a timer will accurately inform them when they should be finished.

❑ **75.** FLASHLIGHT NIGHT.   For the thirty minutes prior to bedtime, give each family member a flashlight. Turn out all other lights. See what fun it is to find the cookie and milk snack, lay out clothes, take a bath, read a story—all by flashlight. It can be reassuring and allay fear of the dark to have a nonlit flashlight on the night table.

❑ **76.** TOO OLD TO READ TO?   How about letting your kids read to you something that interests them? You'll learn more about your child from their choices. And, the reading often leads to good conversation at bedtime.

❑ **77.** LITTLE BAGS HELP.   Thank goodness for plastic bags that zip shut and let us see what's inside! Before bed is a good time to tidy the bedroom and plastic bags can really help. Use them for barrettes and hair bows, jewelry, crayons, puzzle pieces, small toys, game pieces, and even those mystery items that will later find their way to their proper home.

❑ **78.** MY DAY.   Take photos of your child: getting up, dressing, having breakfast, going to school, doing homework, eating dinner, playing a game—whatever activities are most common to his day. With his help, paste the photos onto heavy paper and make into a book called "My Day." Place it on his night table and before bed look through the book to see which activities were part of this day.

❑ **79.** **BEAR BASKETBALL.** When you put a toddler to bed, place many toys and animals in the crib—and one bear. You can teach hand-eye coordination by showing him how to drop the toys into a large basket placed next to the bed. When the game is over, let him choose his three favorite soft toys to go back into the crib.

❑ **80.** **READY FOR A NEW DAY.** Help a youngster get a head start on the next day by preparing the night before. Let youngsters select their clothing from a section of acceptable school clothes in their closet. At the same time, used clothing should be picked up. Encourage kids to gather in one place (your "going shelf") books, homework, projects, show-and-tell items, lunch money, and items for after-school activities.

❑ **81.** **THE CHAIR PERSON.** There's usually a chair in a child's room. Use that as the place to make a chair person: a laid-out collection of clothes for the next day. Let her lay out the underwear, pants or skirt, and top she plans to wear in the morning, placing it like a real person in the chair with socks and shoes on the floor in front. The chair person will remain seated all through the night, waiting for action the next morning.

❑ **82.** **SUMMARY OF THE DAY.** Before tucking kids in, gather the entire family in one bed (kid's or parents'). See if the group can recount the events of the day: "We got up." "We ate breakfast." And so on, right up to "We put on our pj's," "We played this game," and "Now we're going to sleep."

❑ **83.** **60 PERCENT TO 0 PERCENT.** Although a magazine survey showed that 60 percent of children under ten are afraid of the dark and being alone, this can be reduced by parent-child conversation that calmly talks about nonexistent monsters and ghosts, storms and disasters, fierce animals and insects. Talk about darkness being just the absence of light—and permit a night-light if that is comforting. See that activities and stories before bed are calming and not fearsome. Place a bell on the night table and let your child practice ringing it to summon help, but not for trivial needs. Some youngsters like to have a radio on—it makes them feel less alone. Tell your child that you will be close by and check on him regularly—and do so. (These are brief nonconversational checks.) Read poetry and let the soothing rhythms bring sleep. Don't lie down with a little child, but occasionally sit nearby to help a youngster triumph over night fears and grow in independence.

❏ **84.** NO MATTER WHAT. Whatever the age of your child, whatever has happened during the day, animosities should be erased at bedtime. For unsettled problems, set a time to discuss them (tomorrow evening, Saturday morning). With sleep followed by school and work, you are entering a long period of separation from your youngster, so be sure to express your love.

❏ **85.** LOVE LINES. Put your love into words: "I'm so glad you're my kid." "We can do anything together." "Remember, I love you." "I love you no matter what." "You're very special to us." "You were really good today." "Today was better than yesterday, and that's great." "I'm proud of you." "I'll check on you in a little while."

❏ **86.** WHEN PARENTS ARE AWAY AT BEDTIME. Sometimes a parent can't tuck in a child, but there are still ways to connect. Make a cassette of bedtime songs, a story, and prayers so that a child can hear your voice. For a child who reads, a note on the pillow is comforting. Or, name a doll or animal "Daddy's love buddy" or "Mommy's kissing pal." When you are home, include the doll or animal in the bedtime routine and when you're going to be away, be sure the doll or animal is sitting right on the bed pillow. When parents are not present, the sitter needs to follow the traditional bedtime routine, which can be explained as part of the instructions.

❏ **87.** **RELAXED RAG DOLLS.** In preparation for sleep, there need to be relaxing activities—not games of tag or jumping jacks. One family has an interesting ritual. The child lies flat on the bed like a rag doll and the parent lifts one of the "doll's" legs, seeing how limp it is. Then the parent drops it with a thud. Then the other leg and each arm is tested to be sure it is truly a limp rag doll. Finally the covers are pulled up and the parent kisses dolly goodnight.

❏ **88.** **JUST PRETEND.** You can't force sleep, but you can encourage resting time. First, see that bathroom and drink-of-water needs are satisfied. At bedtime (or naptime) suggest that a young child stretch out and hug a favorite toy. Say that it is okay to talk to that toy or sing to it. Grade-schoolers can listen to soft radio music. However, there is to be no getting out of bed (except for emergencies). Be strict on this. Tell the pest that keeps getting out of bed that for each time you have to put him back, he goes to bed ten minutes earlier the next night. Suggest that he just *pretend* to sleep—he doesn't actually have to sleep—and as we all know, pretending sleep usually brings sleep.

❏ **89.** **BEDTIME BLESSINGS.** No matter what the age of a child, bedtime prayers can include blessings for others. One family does it with the notes of a simple scale. On "do" a parent may start by singing "Goodnight and blessings on all." Then a child can go up one note to "re" and sing "Bless Grandpa." Then blessings can be asked for each other family member, a person taking an exam, a sick friend, the dog, and so forth. It's fun to see if you can go from "do" through "re, mi, fa, sol, la, ti" and up to "do."

❏ **90.** **NEW BABY'S PRAYER.** As you put your little one to bed, here is a prayer to say:

Little babe, so small, so dear,
We're so happy you are here.
Now it's time to say goodnight.
Everything will be all right.
I hold you in my arms so tight,
So rest until the morning's light.
Close your eyes and have your rest,
Little one, so sweet, so blessed.

❑ **91.   TODDLER'S PRAYER.**   This new prayer is for a young child: Little girl (or boy), I hold you near. With God you're safe from every fear. My kisses send you on your way, So let sweet sleep now end your day. When morning comes with clouds or sun, You'll be refreshed for happy fun. Now rest secure within our love, And blessings on you from above.

❑ **92.   KINDERGARTNER'S PRAYER.**   Here's a prayer your child can learn: Playing time has been such fun, And book reading now is done. It's time for me to go to bed, Pretty angels round my head. God's messengers are at my side. Safe in His love I now abide.

And don't forget to end your day with a prayer for yourself!

# TWO

## LET'S PLAY!

SECTION 1: THE CHILD-FRIENDLY HOME

SECTION 2: THE INSIDE SCOOP

SECTION 3: RIGHT IN YOUR OWN BACKYARD

**W**hile youngsters can play alone or in a group at school, playtime with just a friend or two can be the best. The shared intimacy, the stress free and casual camaraderie of playing with a friend is an important part of childhood and teaches lessons in how to have fun, be creative, and get along. See that your home is child-friendly—from the toddler years right through the teens.

# SECTION 1:
# THE CHILD-FRIENDLY HOME

❏ **93.** NOW IS THE TIME. Plan to have friends of your youngsters at your house this very week. Of course it's nice when your youngster is invited to another's house but be eager to have kids play at your house. Make the effort, make the time, make the arrangements, even pick kids up or walk over to get them. Urbanization of neighborhoods and more households with both parents working outside the home won't silence the sounds of childhood if you create a comfortable gathering place.

❏ **94.** FOOD AND FUN. Be prepared with snacks—not junk foods, but nutritious and appealing things to eat or prepare. While kids snack, take this opportunity to briefly talk with your child and her friend—then just listen and learn. Hungry teens especially associate a good time with good eats, so be prepared!

❏ **95.** ROTATING TOYS. Play at home can get boring with the same toys, so a month or so after Christmas or a birthday let your youngster select some toys that can be stored in a box on a high shelf for play in a few months. Some parents rotate toys with the start of each season. It's like "Christmas in April" when the stored box is opened.

❏ **96.** PLAY PLACES FOR YOUNGER KIDS. No matter how small your house, create a place where kids can play without worrying about breaking something or being underfoot. The child's own room or family room is ideal, but one dad created a carpeted area in the garage and put a low portable fence around it. This cool spot was a favorite on hot days. Toys should be handy and kept on shelves or in boxes or bins. See-through plastic bins are nicest, "banker's boxes" will do, and one family created a wall of pegboard and hooks with see-through plastic grocery bags for each kind of toy or game.

❑ **97. PLAY PLACES FOR TEENS.** As kids mature, they want more privacy from parents and younger siblings. Help them make a place for listening to music, reading magazines, and talking together. Furnish with big pillows or beanbag chairs, a low table for food, and a radio or CD player. While you may be comfortable with a closed room door when there are kids of the same sex together, when there are boys and girls together this rule should apply: A brick in the door and two feet on the floor!

❑ **98. KID INPUT, PARENT GUIDELINES.** Ask youngsters what you can do to make your house an interesting place for their friends. Keep these points in mind:

- Once you've greeted the friends, don't intrude on play. When a child has a friend over, she doesn't need you as a playmate.
- Ask what time the friend should go home and remind him about fifteen minutes ahead so that there is time for cleanup.
- Don't be a grouch. Loud music or a few crumbs on the floor beats worrying about where your child is and what she's doing.
- Be prepared with ideas, but hold back, giving playmates the opportunity to create their own fun.
- Let kids settle their own disagreements as much as possible. If you think arguments are caused by boredom, suggest a change in activity.
- Never discipline your child in front of a friend. If possible, wait until the friend goes home. If you must say something, call your child into another room and talk quietly.
- Be grateful—your child has a buddy! Be sincerely pleasant to the friend and compliment her on something. Say you hope she'll come and play another day.
- Make play even better. After your youngster has had a friend over, ask him what was good about the time together and what wasn't enjoyable. Talk about how to make play even better the next time.

# SECTION 2: THE INSIDE SCOOP

❑ **99.** MARBLE MANIA. Gather many marbles and many cardboard tubes. You can start with a few, but you'll want lots, so ask friends to save them from gift wrapping paper and kitchen towels and wraps. Your youngster is going to make a tube raceway, starting at a high point (such as a kitchen stool) and going down gradually to the floor. Cut some tubes in half lengthwise so you can see the race course. Connect the tubes using masking tape or duct tape, remembering that the upper tube should always feed into the next lower tube. At first, it's fun to just watch the marbles go down the chutes. But there can also be races, starting two marbles at a time or seeing which one rolls the farthest at the end. If you want to get fancy, create a fork in your racecourse or make a trapdoor hole that some marbles will whiz over and others will fall through. You can even expand your tubing to cover several rooms.

❑ **100.** WRITE ON YOUR BACK? Why not? Back writing can be a fun activity when kids are wearing bathing suits but have tired of the water. Using washable pens, line up kids (and adults) train-style and practice writing a word on the back in front of you. Everyone then tries to figure out what his word is. When you get the knack, write short messages and concentrate harder!

❑ **101.** MIRROR FACES. Sit in front of a large mirror with one or more children (sitting on a bathroom counter in front of a wide mirror works well). Quickly announce an expression such as "happy." See whose face is the happiest. Let that person name the next look: sad, laughing, afraid, sleepy, winking, angry, crying, pouting, ugly, beautiful, dreamy, silly.

❑ **102.** BOISTEROUS BEANBAGS. Play on the floor with your youngster and some beanbags. Throw them at each other's toes. Show how to balance them on the head.

Put one on your stomach and watch it move when you laugh. Lie on your back with feet in the air and balance one on each foot. Stand up with your head back, put one on your nose, and try to walk.

❑ **103.** EGG CARTON FUN.   See who in the family can find the best use for clean egg cartons. Let kids put snacks in them for no-mess eating. For breakfast, soft boil eggs and put one in each carton with toast squares in some of the pockets. A child's desk drawer can use one to hold clips, rubber bands, keys, and so forth. Do the same for kid's stuff in the bathroom: bows, clippers, pins, and so forth. For a teen, the carton can be used in a drawer for holding earrings. In the garage, let kids sort different nails into the pockets. The carton can hold beads or buttons for crafts. Place one in a family room cupboard for all those mysterious little toy parts you find.

❑ **104.** RAINY DAY LIFESAVER.   Can a large trash bag be an interesting toy or gift? Here's how to make a toy in a trash bag. Using a very large disposable aluminum turkey-roasting pan, cover the bottom with sand or cornmeal and place the pan in the bottom of the flattened trash bag in order to catch any spillover. Supply a collection of inexpensive toy soldiers, planes, motorcycles, trucks, cars, animals, and fencing—whatever you can find. Stimulate a child's imagination by helping her to create a situation (a man parachutes into a field and lands on a cow's back . . . . Davy gets a new motorcycle and decides to ride and ride until he runs out of gas). Then see what happens as roads are made and people go into action. When play is over, store everything in the trash bag until next time.

❑ **105.** THE BALL MYSTERY.   This is a game kids of all ages can play. And depending on age, you'll use three to six empty cans of the same size. Remove the lid and label, be sure there are no sharp edges, wash and dry them. Set them out on a table, then hide a small ball under one of them. Quickly move the cans around, then see if the youngster can find the ball. Next, let him hide the ball and you try to find it. It's a game kids enjoy showing to friends.

❑ **106.** HIDE THE TIMER. Younger kids will enjoy this fast-moving game played throughout the entire house. While youngsters stay in one closed room, a parent hides a timer (the kind that continuously rings or buzzes, set for about two minutes). Kids race to find it before it goes off. The one finding it is the next to hide it.

❑ **107.** INVISIBLE WRITING. Place lemon juice in a shallow dish. Cut the point off a toothpick and show a child how to use it to write a secret message on paper: ("Dessert in the refrigerator." "You can stay up late." "Let's play Monopoly.") When the message is thoroughly dry, pass it around the dinner table to see if the mystery message can be read. Then, show how it can be read with a flashlight (or with a parent holding it near a lighted bulb or placing the paper by a heater) as the heat makes the writing appear.

❑ **108.** APPLE PUZZLE. Teens or parents can do the cutting with a sharp knife, going around the apple's circumference in a zig-zag manner, making many similar Z-shaped cuts. Be sure the knife point is reaching the core. Then pull the two pieces apart. A young child can try to make it fit back together. For older kids, cut apart several apples, and using a stopwatch, see who can reassemble the apples the fastest. Be sure to eat the apples afterward.

❑ **109.** PUDDLE JUMPING. Kids will enjoy jumping over imaginary puddles. Using old newspapers or grocery bags, show kids how to rumple them into "puddles"—some flat, some puffed up, some narrow, some very wide. When they've made about twenty, they can deliver them to strategic pathways in the house as well as in front of the refrigerator, toilet, and television. Put some together in a hall to make it nearly impossible to get past without stepping in the puddle. One child is the first leader and he announces that the jumping will be with two feet together, or by stepping backward, or hopping, or swinging arms in circles as you walk. A leader can also give commands such as "Get a grape from the refrigerator." Finally have timed races to see who can leap all puddles the fastest. At night and with all the lights out, see who can avoid the puddles.

❑ **110.** BOX TRAIN. Help a child line up a row of cardboard cartons (without tops or with the tops tucked in). Connect them with duct tape to form a train and attach a rope at one end. Let her collect dolls, animals, trucks and other items that need to be transported by train. The child is the engineer and uses the rope to take the train through the house. It's also a novel way of picking up toys at the end of the day.

❑ **111.** SAME BUT DIFFERENT. A parent thinks of popular books, movies, or television shows and translates the title into other words. For example, "The Three Little Pigs" becomes "The Trio of Small Porkers," "Beauty and the Beast" translates to "Gorgeous and the Creature," and "Sesame Street" is "Seedy Avenue." After challenging kids with a few of these, let them think up some themselves.

❑ **112.** MIGHTY MEGAPHONES. For two children you'll need two gallon-sized plastic milk jugs. A parent can easily cut off the bottom of each. Now they become megaphones so kids can broadcast to one another and to parents, [shouting into the top hole].

❑ **113.** WINDOW WONDERS. Let kids choose used bright colored crayons and remove the paper wrapping from them. On a work surface covered with newspaper, give each youngster a piece of wax paper about eighteen-inches long. Show how to use a grater or peeler to grate one color of crayon onto the wax paper, then another. Push each color of shavings into an area about two-inches square and at least one-quarter-inch deep. Overlapping colors will produce new colors. Place a small hardware "nut" near one edge of the shavings (to be used later for hanging). Cover the shavings with another piece of wax paper and top with a piece of newspaper. Help the youngster run a warm iron over the newspaper for about ten seconds. (Peek under to be sure the shavings are melting.) Remove the newspaper and wait until the crayons are completely cool and hard. Peel the crayon creation from between the layers of wax paper. At this point it can be trimmed if desired. Thread a ribbon through the nut and hang in a window for all to admire.

❑ **114.** IT'S IN THE BAG.   Fill a bag with a dozen ordinary objects such as a key, brush, ball, comb, pencil, toy car, penny, ring, clip, bottle opener, hard candy, or bolt. With two or more participants, let the first one reach into the bag and draw out one item and begin the story, using that item in a sentence. For example if the key is pulled out of the bag, the story might begin: "Once upon a time a bad king locked a beautiful princess in her room and threw away the key." The next person draws out an item (for example, the brush) and must continue the story: "All day long she played with her pet lion and used her own brush on his mane." Continue in the same way and see the imaginative twists and turns in the story.

❑ **115.** DOLL MANNERS.   An easy way to teach children good manners is to have a pretend meal with a doll or animal in attendance. Together with you, set a little table and provide juice and cookies. Let the child teach the doll, with a little help from you. Some Mom lines: "Does Dolly have her napkin in her lap?" "Ask her if she'd like more juice." "What did she say when you offered her a cookie?" "Do you think she's finished eating and has asked to be excused?" In this way, you are not directly teaching or correcting the child, but the message will still come through.

❑ **116.** HOMEMADE PHONE.   Show a child how to put his fingertips lightly on his neck and feel the vibrations when he hums. This is the basis for the homemade phone. You'll need two metal cans with the tops safely removed and a hole made in the center of the bottom. (Be sure the top edge and bottom hole aren't sharp.) Cut a piece of string that will reach the length of the hall or other long area. Draw the string through the can holes and knot it, connecting the two cans with their open ends toward the string ends. Let each youngster take one can and move apart until the string is taut and not touching anything. One child speaks into his can while the other puts the cup to her ear to listen, experimenting with how softly they can talk and still be heard. Point out how different the sound is from normal conversation.

❏ **117.** **SHELLS AND ROCKS.** What youngster doesn't have a collection of miscellaneous rocks and shells! Help him make something decorative by embedding them in plaster of Paris—available at any craft shop. Use pie pans as a form for making an interesting wallhanging (glue a hook to the back), or cut down yogurt containers to make forms for personal paperweights. Prepare the plaster according to instructions, then place the rocks and shells in an appealing arrangement.

❏ **118.** **JUST LIKE REAL LIFE.** Young children enjoy pretending and you can help by providing some supplies. To go along with their toy dishes and cookware, provide an unused picture cookbook and some recipe cards. To add to fun with a toy telephone, give them an outdated phone book. When riding in the car, provide road maps and a small purse with an expired driver's license. For a desk or table, share an old typewriter or adding machine—it's still fun for kids, even if it doesn't work perfectly.

❏ **119.** **ARM WRESTLING.** For kids of about equal strength, arm wrestling can be fun. Sitting at a table and clasping one opposite hand, at the signal the participants try to push each other's arms down to touch the table. Three downs make a win.

❏ **120.** **BACKWARD WRITING.** Let kids try to write a simple sentence backward and then hold it up to a mirror to see the message. It probably won't be readable. Then show the trick: look in the mirror while writing, not at the paper. Then let them write messages to family members or friends.

❑ **121.** MATCHING PAIRS.   This game can teach concentration to kids from age four and up. Using a deck of cards turned face down in several rows on a table, the object is to turn over two matching cards (two fives, two queens, and so forth). If no match, replace them face down. If a match, you keep those cards and take another turn. For older youngsters, use a full deck. For the youngest, start with a total of ten cards (five matching pairs) and when they master it, add more pairs.

❑ **122.** STILTS.   When kids wish to be taller, you can actually show them how to make that happen. For each youngster you'll need a pair of cans (large juice cans or coffee cans) with one end removed. (Be sure there are no sharp edges left.) On each can, make marks on either side one inch down from the closed end. A parent should use a hammer and nail to punch through the can at this point, and then widen the holes with a screwdriver. Now cut two pieces of rope that are three times the length from the child's knee to the floor. Let kids thread the ends through the holes from the outside and tie knots on the inside. Help the youngster (who is wearing rubber-soled shoes) up onto the can top, standing on the ball of the foot. With this mastered, hand her the ropes and steady her as she takes her first straight-legged steps. Soon it will be easy!

❑ **123.** TOOTHPICK TOWN.   A box of round toothpicks and quick-setting glue are all that's needed for a toothpick town. It makes a unique centerpiece for the table. Help a child cut the pointed ends off the toothpicks. Now you're ready for construction. With uprights and cross pieces you can make a fence and then build a miniature log cabin to go inside the fence.

❑ **124.** MYSTERY BOOK.   Let kids cut out magazine pictures that they like, then paste these on every other page of a spiral notebook. On the blank pages, cut out a portion of the page to make a little window—some large, some small. Then when you "read the book" together, see if the youngster can identify the mystery picture by looking through the window.

❏ **125.** WHO'S GOT THE BUTTON? In olden times, button collections were popular, and nowadays they're popular again. Provide kids with a glass jar and a variety of buttons (you can ask friends for some, too). At first kids will find it fun to sort them into colors and shapes and count them. Then, they can make a display by sewing them onto a piece of fabric that can be framed for a wallhanging. Or, they can be glued to a piece of painted plywood and framed. Also teach kids how to play "Tiddledywinks" with buttons.

❏ **126.** MEGATOWN. Who says you must play with just one toy at a time? Some of the most creative play comes when kids combine several toys: train, Hot Wheels, a doll house, small figures and animals, and toy buildings. (Don't be concerned about the relative proportions of cars and figures—it doesn't matter in this kind of play.) Encourage the building of Megatown on a floor area where it can be played with undisturbed for several days or weeks. Create a city, suburbs, park, school, zoo, and so forth. Help kids create Megatown scenarios: a race between cars and trains, the arrival of friendly aliens, a dog elected mayor makes up new laws, the animals escape from the zoo, and so forth.

❏ **127.** LANDSCAPING WITH SHEETS. When kids are playing with cars and trucks, it helps to have roads and highways, hills and valleys. Provide old sheets and show youngsters how to use marking pens to draw roadways on them. To make hills, crumple newspaper into a mound and put it under the sheet, pressing it down firmly. Then cover the mound with uncrumpled newspaper to make a smooth surface and replace the sheet. Now you have a hill that vehicles can roll down on their own. The nice thing about landscaping with sheets is that when play is over, they fold up nicely for another day.

❑ **128.** SING ALONG.   Don't be hesitant about learning the words to kids' favorite songs—as long as the words are acceptable! And do teach kids your favorite songs, or those of your parents and grandparents. Nowadays many schools don't have money for music classes, so it's up to you to teach singing. Borrow a songbook at the library to find the words of old-time favorites and patriotic songs. At the typewriter or computer, let each person key in the words of a song or two. Make sufficient copies and take them along on your next excursion for a car sing-along.

❑ **129.** PILLOW PUPPETS.   When a youngster needs a soft cuddly toy, help him make one out of a pillowcase. Stuff the case with fabric scraps, foam rubber, or anything clean and soft. Then, tie it shut to form the neck. With marking pens, let him draw a face and hair on the case. He then stands behind his big puppet friend and talks for him. The pillow puppet makes a good naptime companion—a child will talk to him and easily fall asleep.

❑ **130.** FABRIC FOLKS.   Let kids draw a figure of themselves on a sturdy piece of cardboard about twelve-inches high. Then, get out your scrap bag, scissors, and glue. Show them how to cut out clothes for the figure and glue them in place: hats, shirts, pants, mittens, shoes. When playtime is over, put the fabric folks in a folder to keep them safe for another day.

❑ **131.** LITTLE HANDS, BIG CARDS.   It's difficult for little children to hold the cards for games—in fact one of our sons always took his cards to another room to sort them. That's when we invented the card fan holder. Cans such as Crisco or some snack foods have plastic lids. Using two lids of the same size, place them with the flat sides together and staple them as near the middle as possible. Put tape or a sticker over the staple. Now cards can be sorted and played easily if the child places them between the two lids.

❑ **132.** BARTER TIME.   Go over the toy shelves with children, selecting good toys they no longer play with. Suggest the same idea to other families in your neighborhood. Then arrange a barter time when each child has a card table of toys on an area of your lawn. Show how two-way and three-way trades work and how to barter for one big toy with three little ones. Bartering doesn't cost anything and teaches good lessons about negotiating and value.

❑ **133.** NO LAUGHING.   With a group of two or more kids, have them sit facing one another or in a small circle. Set a timer for three minutes and see who can sit that long without talking, giggling, or laughing. Participants can make funny faces at one another, as long as they are silent. It's harder than it sounds!

## PAINTING PROJECTS

❑ **134.** CREATING PAINT.   With kid help, make finger paint. In a large pan, mix one cup of cold water with one cup of flour. Let the child stir it until it is smooth. Next, the parent adds three more cups of cold water and cooks the mixture over medium heat, stirring constantly until the mixture bubbles and thickens like gravy. Reduce the heat and cook one minute more. Pour the mixture into four bowls. Let kids add a different food coloring to each bowl and stir. Cover the bowls with plastic wrap until cool. Then paint!

❑ **135.** PAINT PRECAUTIONS.   Paint can permanently stain, so work outside or in a play area. Provide aprons or big T-shirts for artists, and cover surfaces with newspaper. A good first project is making wrapping paper and a matching card. This saves money, and the wrapped gifts look unique and festive.

❑ **136.** MAGICAL WRITING.   Show kids how to use up those white crayons that come in every box. Let a child write a simple message using white crayon on white paper, and then ask someone to read it (which can't be done). The child then presents the reader with any color of watercolor paint. When he paints quickly over the surface of the paper, the mystery message appears, revealed in magical white writing.

❑ **137.** INK SPOTS. This project uses ink and paper and requires a covering to protect the work surface. Fold a piece of white or colored paper in half. Open it, put a drop of ink in the crease, close it, then massage it. When dry, the paper can be refolded as a greeting card or hung as art work on a bulletin board.

❑ **138.** POTATO DESIGNS. Cut a potato in half for each child. Then, with a blunt knife or other safe tool, let the youngster cut a design or letter into the cut end. This becomes a stamp that can be dipped into various colors of paint and printed on paper. By rinsing the potato stamp, you can use it for several colors. With a little guidance, kids can now create artistic note paper and wrapping paper, using the potato stamps, as well as sponges and kitchen tools such as whisks and mashers. Print on paper that can be folded to use for letter writing. Don't throw away large drawings; instead use them to wrap gifts to and from kids. These uses save money and encourage art.

❑ **139.** GLASS DOOR ARTISTS. It's fun for kids to paint sliding glass doors. Cover the ground with newspaper for drips. Let kids use spoons to put the paint on the glass doors and let fingers do the arranging. (When tired of the painting, kids can wash it off with soap and a hose.)

❑ **140.** WHAT SHALL WE PAINT? Walk through the house and let kids find things they'd like to paint such as the bookshelves in their room or an old wagon. Set up an outside painting area. Find all those miscellaneous spray cans you have in the workshop. Show kids how to safely use spray paint and clean the nozzle afterward. Use a light spray of a second color to cover any irregularities.

❑ **141.** ROLL IT ON.   Here's a drip-free way to let kids paint. Save used roll-on deodorant bottles. Pry off the ball at its base (a parent should do this with a screwdriver). Rinse the bottles and fill each with one color of slightly diluted liquid tempera paint. Put the ball back on and let kids roll away. And, when they've finished, replace the caps to keep the paint fresh.

❑ **142.** PUDDING PAINT.   To celebrate the end of a painting project, make pudding paint. Just make a batch of chocolate instant pudding according to the directions. Have kids sit at a table with clean hands and a clean piece of paper in front of them. They then dip their fingers into the pudding and paint away (licking their fingers when they have finished their masterpiece).

## KITCHEN FUN

❑ **143.** WHAT'S GOOD ABOUT LIMA BEANS?   Some kids don't like to eat them, but most all will enjoy growing them. Provide a glass jar and some paper toweling that has been slightly dampened. The paper towels should be stuffed in the jar so they touch the sides. Then, the youngster inserts some lima bean seeds between the towels and the glass and places the jar in a sunny window. The seeds are interesting to watch as they sprout. Keep the paper towels moist until the seedlings outgrow the jar and then plant them in pots or in the garden.

❑ **144.** MAGIC MUD.   Give your youngster a cup of cornstarch in a bowl and also a cup of water. Let her add the water gradually until the mixture is like bread dough. Then, show her how to roll the mixture into a ball. Now, watch the ball carefully as it will magically dissolve to liquid!

❑ **145.** PRETZEL SUCKERS.   Sometimes it's hard to get kids to eat fruit. Work together to make these tantalizing snacks. Insert small pretzel sticks into banana chunks, pineapple pieces, or grapes. You won't be able to make enough!

❏ **146.** IN A PICKLE. Although pickles can be made from many fruits and vegetables, show kids how to make Thunder and Lightning pickles.

THUNDER AND LIGHTNING PICKLES

4-5 large ripe cucumbers
⅔ cup salt
1 tablespoon white mustard
2 teaspoons grated horseradish
2 medium hot red peppers

3 pints of ice water
3 sprigs dill
2½ cups vinegar
⅔ cup water
¾ cup sugar

Let kids peel cucumbers, cut in half lengthwise and scoop out seeds, then cut the halves in thirds lengthwise and then cut the thirds in half. Place in ice water, add salt, cover and let stand overnight. The next day, drain well. Divide the dill, mustard, horseradish, and peppers between two sterilized jars. Heat the vinegar, water, and sugar, add the cucumbers and boil gently five minutes. Then pack the pickles into the jars to an inch from the top. Add the boiling solution to a half inch from the top. Seal for storing, but put some in the refrigerator for immediate eating. This recipe will make two quarts.

❏ **147.** MYSTERY BISCUITS. When it's time to use up leftovers, let one of your kids help you make mystery biscuits. Any refrigerated biscuit dough will work, but the roll-up crescent variety works best. Don't tell others what's inside! It can be a half hot dog, chicken pieces, lunch meat, tuna fish, olives and onions, ground beef and taco sauce, broccoli or other veggies, cheese, even peanut butter and jam if used sparingly in the very center. Roll them up and bake according to package directions.

❏ **148.** MOUSE SALAD. Youngsters can prepare a squeaky salad as you make the remainder of the meal. Give them: canned pear halves, dried apricots, string licorice, whole cloves, mini-marshmallows and toothpicks cut in half. You can pat the pears dry and set them out on the work surface, with the hollow side down. Kids insert toothpicks in dried apricots and attach two at the midpoint of each pear as perky ears. Then, they cut two mini-marshmallows in half and use a clove to push each into the pear as a nose and eyes. Each mouse is then put on the salad plate and a coil of licorice is laid out for the tail.

❑ **149.** TONGS RACE. When you're busy in the kitchen, you can keep young children busy and improve their coordination at the same time. Gather twelve small toys, or use twelve small items found in the kitchen. Show how tongs can pick up these items. Then, place a muffin pan in front of the child and let her put one item in each cup. Once she gets the knack of using the tongs, use the kitchen timer to see if she can put the twelve items into the cups in one minute. Then see if she can take them out and put them back in two minutes. She'll want to do it again and again as she gets faster.

❑ **150.** NOT-HOT HOT DOG. For children too young to work over a hot stove, work together to prepare a not-hot hot dog. Using a long hot dog bun, put peanut butter on one side and jam on the other. Then, instead of the wiener, put a banana inside. It looks like a hot dog and it's a lunch your young child can make with just a little help from you.

❑ **151.** BASTER PLAY. Water and kids go together and your young child will enjoy playing with your baster as you prepare supper. All you need are two bowls of water (put a little gravy coloring, juice, or food coloring in them to make it more interesting). Then, let your youngster go to work squeezing the bulb, watching the colored water come up the glass tube, and then emptying it.

❑ **152.** LITTLE RESTAURANT. Even if your family is small, let one child create a family restaurant. Help him set up the table with a special cloth and napkins. Provide him with an apron and menus (which he letters by hand or on computer). Make family members wait outside the room, and then seat them and present the menu. The first course gives a choice between soup or shrimp cocktail. If anyone orders the shrimp, the waiter goes into the kitchen and returns to say that it isn't available. The main course choices can be stewed buffalo with okra or the dish that you really plan to serve. (You can also use up many one-portion leftovers by putting them on the menu.) While others are eating the soup, the waiter and cook prepare the plates and then remove their aprons and join the others. However, at the end of the meal, the waiter puts his apron back on and offers dessert: a choice of ice creams and toppings.

❑ **153.** MONSTER DOUGH.   Creatures from the deep or outer space are fun to make from this no-cook (and inedible) dough. Combine 1 cup of salt with one and a one-fourth cups water and two teaspoons of cooking oil. Show kids how to knead the mixture until smooth. Then divide it into several small bowls, color each with food coloring, and mix well. If it is sticky, add flour; if it is dry add droplets of water. Use the creations as decorations at the dining table.

❑ **154.** REGULAR PLAY DOUGH.   Make this easy recipe and enjoy modeling fun with your kids. Mix together in a saucepan: one cup of flour, one half cup salt, one half cup water, two teaspoons cream of tartar, one tablespoon of vegetable oil, and a few drops of food coloring. Heat and stir until a ball begins to form. Cool before using or store in an airtight container in the refrigerator until modeling time.

❑ **155.** EDIBLE PLAY DOUGH.   Measure two cups of peanut butter, two cups of powdered milk, and three tablespoons of honey into a large bowl. Let your youngster mix it all together. If it is too sticky, add more powdered milk, one spoonful at a time. You can add chocolate bits, nuts, raisins or other edibles. Next, prepare a clean surface for dough play and be sure all hands are clean. Kids will make interesting objects they can later eat.

# SECTION 3: RIGHT IN YOUR OWN BACKYARD

❑ **156.** AIRBORNE AEROBICS. See who can keep a soccer ball in the air for the longest time without touching it with hands or letting it touch the ground. Count how many times each player bounces the ball off her helmeted head, shoulder, thigh, or feet. Give players three turns and average their scores to determine the best juggler.

❑ **157.** MARVELOUS MUD. When rainy days continue on and on, still permit outside play—in the mud! Establish some clothes that you don't care about and let the kids wear them with boots. Create a mud pond in an old kiddie pool. Set it out on a rainy night and the next day show kids where they can scoop up dirt and take it to the pool. You can be sure they'll want to play in it. Spoons, pails, funnels, and old strainers make slimy fun. With less water, kids can create roads for small cars or mud mansions (like sand castles). Of course, there can always be mud pies created in old pie tins and allowed to dry.

❑ **158.** POPCORN HIDE-AND-SEEK. Kids love finding a person (or a gift) by following a trail of popcorn through your yard or the park. Occasionally make a fork in your trail—one fork being a dead-end so that seekers must go back and follow the other fork.

❑ **159.** AN EASY CATCH. It's discouraging when balls bop kids or pop out of their small hands. Teach the technique of catching by using a partly deflated beach ball. Stand behind the child and guide his arms and hands as you show tossing, as well as catching, by making a cradle to catch the ball.

❑ **160.** WINDMILLS. It's quick and easy to make a windmill or pinwheel. Using sturdy paper, cut a seven-inch square. Draw lines across the square from opposite corners. Cut on the line from each of the four corners to about three-fourths inch from the center. Take one corner of each of the resulting triangles and glue or staple it to the center. Using a short straight pin, make a hole in the center and then push the pin through, affixing the pinwheel to a narrow straight piece of wood or stick. For safety, be sure the sharp end is firmly in the wood. Now a youngster can run with it and watch it twirl.

❑ **161.** **DIGGING TO CHINA.** Create a place for kids to dig in the backyard—some spot that is visible from the house but not too prominent. Small shovels or trowels will encourage digging and the excess soil makes a mountain next to the hole. While kids won't dig straight through the earth to the other side, look at a globe to learn what place is on the other side. A digging area can provide fun with cars, trucks, and boats, and does make bath time a nonarguable event!

❑ **162.** **RELAXING TOY.** When you think that your budding gymnasts need a quiet activity, here's one that is fun and fascinating. Provide each child with a plastic liter-sized soda bottle with the label removed. Let him fill the bottle halfway with cooking oil, then a few drops of food coloring, then the remainder of the way with water. Put the cover on tightly and then take the bottle outside and stretch out on a lounge chair or blanket. Show the youngsters how to slowly tilt the bottles back and forth, watching the tidal wave inside build. It teaches that oil and water really don't mix, and it also provides quiet fun.

❑ **163.** **WHEEL RACE.** Make two racing prods—one for a parent, one for a youngster—by putting a cross piece on the bottom of a three-foot long piece of lath (or other wood the size of a yardstick). The cross piece forms a "T" at the bottom. Now find two large wheels from an old wagon or trike. Using the racing prod, see who can push their wheel the farthest. Kids usually excel over parents.

❑ **164.** **CALL A MOOSE.** With a shoelace and a round can from potato chips, you can create the "call of the wild." (Save up these round cans so a group of kids can each have one.) Discard the plastic top and punch a small hole in the bottom. Tie a knot in one end of the shoelace and thread the remainder through the hole and out the bottom. Dip the lace that hangs out from it in water. Then, run your fingers down the lace as if squeezing the water out. The resulting sound will either bring moose to your backyard or send the dog into hiding!

❑ **165.** GOOP. This wonderful substance is made indoors but best played with outdoors.

GOOP

8 ounces of white glue     food coloring
water           20 Mule Team Borax

Combine glue, three-fourths cup water, and food coloring in one bowl. In another bowl, mix one-fourth cup water with one tablespoon Borax, and add this to the first bowl, stirring until it forms a Goop ball. Remove the ball. Again combine one-fourth cup water with one tablespoon Borax and mix it into the glue mixture, stirring until another Goop ball forms. Keep repeating the process until the glue mixture is gone. Then knead all the Goop balls together. Now you're ready to play by pulling and patting the Goop into strings and unique forms. Store the Goop in an airtight container.

❑ **166.** HOMEMADE RAIN GAUGE. Using a test tube, help a child affix it to a stake. Place it upright in a low traffic but open area of the yard. After a good rain, listen to the radio and find out how much rainfall was measured. If it was five tenths of an inch, mark that spot on the gauge with tape and pen. From this he can figure the markings for less or more rain. See how accurate this gauge is compared to the experts. Find out how much rain is normal for your area and how much rain has fallen thus far in the "rain year."

❑ **167.** WEB WATCHING. Locate a spider web in the yard. Don't disturb it, but observe how it is anchored and how big it is. Look at it each day to see what the spider is catching. What does the spider eat? How fast does it eat? Does the spider ever leave the web? Consider giving your spider a name.

❑ **168.** FACES IN THE CLOUDS.   When kids need a quiet moment in the middle of outside play, provide a blanket for a relaxing activity. Lie down with them and look up at the clouds. Describe what you see in a particular cloud—a face, a mountain, a bus. Everyone will see something different. Look for cloud formations and make up a story, for example: one cloud (perhaps the bus-shaped one) is trying to go up a hill (the mountain-shaped one) and runs out of gas. You can also pretend that clouds are islands and that you are swimming from island to island across the sky. See how fast the clouds change, offering new creative story shapes.

❑ **169.** DOLL BOUTIQUE.   Most little girls like to dress dolls. Help make a doll boutique in the backyard. Invite your daughter's friends to bring fashion dolls to the boutique. Show how flowers and leaves can be made into doll apparel gluing leaves and petals to material. For example, a hollyhock blossom hat, a chain of daisies as an elegant stole, rhubarb leaves as a skirt. Snapdragon blossoms make excellent shoes. Your child's creativity may amaze you.

❑ **170.** GIANT BUBBLES.   Don't cry over spilt expensive store-bought bubble liquid. Make a giant container of your own by mixing two cups of Joy dishwashing liquid (somehow this brand works best) with six cups of water and three-fourths cups of light corn syrup. Pour one cup in a large shallow bowl. Store the remainder, tightly covered. Using a large coffee can or juice can, cut off both ends. Hammer the cut edges until they are smooth. Dip either end in the solution and wave back and forth, forming giant bubbles.

❑ **171.** SLIPPERY SLIDING.   A slight grassy slope and an old shower curtain can provide good exercise and fun. Cut the shower curtain in half lengthwise and lay both pieces on the slope, the upper piece overlapping the lower one. With everyone in swimsuits and a hose for dribbling water on the slide, there can be running, jumping, and sliding fun for all ages.

❑ **172.** **LEAPING BOXES.** You'll want sturdy crates and lightweight kids to enjoy jumping fun. Start with just one small crate and see who can leap the farthest from it. Then, add a second larger one and let kids leap from one to another. Gradually add crates until kids can have a contest to see who can leap the fastest from one to another, off the end one, and back to the first.

❑ **173.** **POTPOURRI.** Show youngsters how to collect the petals from dead rose blossoms at your house (or from neighbors who give permission). Set them on trays until they are completely dry. Then, using a large pail, crush the rose petals with an "essential oil" (available at craft shops). Package the potpourri in squares of net for immediate use in drawers, or in pretty, tightly sealed jars for gifts.

❑ **174.** **TODDLER TUMBLES.** When small children are out playing on asphalt or cement, knees can easily get scrapes. Avoid "Owees" this easy way: buy a pair of tennis wristbands and slide them on the bare knees. They'll also pay for themselves when the toddler wears them over long pants since there will be fewer tears to mend (and fewer tears to shed).

❑ **175.** **HARE AND TORTOISE BIKE RACE.** On a safe driveway or sidewalk, chalk two parallel four-foot wide lanes about twenty-five feet in length. (Older children can have a longer race course.) Two riders start cycling down the lanes as slowly as they can, keeping their feet on the pedals as they stay within the lines. The last cycler to cross the finish line is the winner.

❑ **176.** **TWENTY MINUTE WEED CONTEST.** Using strings, divide the lawn with a section for each youngster and adult. Draw names out of a bag and let each person choose a section. Then, in just twenty minutes, everyone pulls weeds (being sure to get the roots). See who pulled the most, the biggest, the smallest, or the most unusual.

❑ **177.** MANY SPRINKLING CANS. Save gallon-sized milk containers until you have enough for a group of kids. Punch many holes in the bottoms of the jugs. Let kids take them outside and use a hose to fill them with water. Then they can give plants, grass, and their own feet a drink.

❑ **178.** CRAZY CROQUET. If you don't have a croquet set, find one at a garage sale. Of course, the regular game is fun, but crazy croquet can make your yard a neighborhood favorite. Choose objects that the ball must go under, over, around, or through: a lawn chair, a tree, a child's wagon, a plastic container with both ends cut off, a hose, and so forth. Use the wickets (but bent metal clothes hangers are a good substitute) at the entry and exit of each obstacle and number them so that players go in order, one shot at a time, a second shot if mastering the obstacle. If you have a slide, start the game there by having players start their balls at the top, which should then go through a wicket near the bottom.

❑ **179.** GIANT HOPSCOTCH. This is an extended form of regular hopscotch, except make it like a trail, down your driveway, and then along your sidewalk. Mark some squares for the left foot, some for the right foot. Put in plenty of two-foot resting spots. When they tire of it, let kids wash it away with a hose.

❑ **180.** ROLLING RACE. In a yard or park, find a small grassy slope for active fun. (This also works on a sand dune.) Show kids how to lie on one side and start rolling down the hill (you may have to provide a gentle push for little ones and promise to catch them at the bottom). When the fun of rolling begins to fade, have simple races, then a relay where the roller runs back up and tags the next person to start.

❑ **181.** CHALKTOWN. On a safe driveway, help kids sketch out a large transportation system using white chalk. Show how to draw highways, small roads, airports, and railway tracks. Using green chalk, add trees, fields, and mountains. With blue chalk make rivers flowing into lakes with docks. Using red and brown chalk, draw houses, and sky-scrapers. Next, collect many toy cars, planes, boats, animals, and people from toy bins in the house. Place these in your setting with boats crossing the lake, police chasing a car, planes taking off, farmers in the field, families in the houses. Several children will enjoy Chalktown for many days (a car can drive over the chalk)—until the rain washes it away.

❑ **182.** TAKE AIM! Place two foot-long sticks in the ground about a foot apart. Make a line about ten feet back from the sticks. Each player stands behind the line with a frisbee and tries to roll it between the two sticks. Give play-ers five tries and keep score if you wish to select a winner.

❑ **183.** KID GARAGE SALE. Suggest that kids and their friends clean out their rooms and family rooms, gathering clean out-grown clothes and usable unwanted toys, books and games. Set up card tables with signs marked twenty-five cents, fifty cents, one dollar. Let one youngster, who adds well and can make change, be in charge of each table, putting the money in a fanny pack. A parent can oversee one table or the entire project. If you have lots of young participants, consider a table with lemonade and cookies for sale. This event is good training in salesmanship.

❑ **184.** WHAT'S IN THE YARD? From your own garden, gather blossoms from flowers and leaves from trees. Place them carefully between wax paper and then under heavy books. When they are dried (after about two weeks), make a plant identification book. Use a dab of glue to affix them to a page and label the page with the name of the flower or tree. Ask friends and neighbors if you can search their yards for plants not found in yours. See how quickly kids learn the names of the specimens.

❑ **185.** BUGGY GARDEN? You can keep insects off plants without using poisons. Help a child to plant a bug-free vegetable garden by using fireplace ashes around the edge, and planting marigolds and nasturtiums (which repel insects) next to the veggies. Your garden shop can give you other poison-free suggestions.

❑ **186.** **TALK TO THE FLOWERS.** Develop conversational skills by taking a walk with little kids around the yard (or down the street). You set the example by chatting to plants and creatures, and then let the kids take over. "Hello daisy, we're taking a walk and like your yellow flowers." "Hi there ant, where are you going?" "Greetings fence, how many gates do you have?" "Bye grass, sorry I stepped on you."

## BALLOON FUN

Balloons can be fun, providing you follow certain precautions. Keep balloons away from babies and toddlers who might put them to their mouths, break them, and suck them into their throats. The following ideas are such fun that even sophisticated teens and parents will want to join in the action.

❑ **187.** **BALLOON BARBER.** For each participant you'll need an air-filled balloon, a safety razor (or bladeless razor for young kids), and shaving cream (one or two cans for a group). Each person is given a handful of shaving cream, then he sits down on the ground with the balloon between his knees and lathers the cream over the entire balloon. Then the razors are passed out and the "shaving" begins. The aim is to get all the lather off the balloon without popping it.

❑ **188.** **BALLOON VOLLEYBALL.** Divide kids into two teams and place a string or net between two trees or poles. Fill several heavy-duty balloons about one-third full of water and then fill with air. (This makes a balloon that flies erratically.) A balloon is thrown, rather than hit, from one side of the net to the other. The game is played like volleyball and ends when one side has eleven points.

❑ **189.** **LADDER SPLAT.** Everyone loves to see dropped things go "splat." The object is to make the biggest splash. Kids fill many balloons with water to the same size, using a watering can with pointed spout or a small hose nozzle. A ladder is placed on patio or driveway and each player tosses a balloon to the ground with as much force as possible. Scorekeepers quickly outline the splat with chalk and put the youngsters initials inside. (Turn the ladder each time to provide a dry area.) The winner gets to pick up all the balloon fragments!

❏ **190. SPACE BALLOONS.** Help kids to build a giant slingshot to catapult water balloons into space—or at least across the yard. Fill many balloons with water and put them in boxes or bags for easy transport. Establish a firing line and an area beyond with a finish line. (Important: when someone is in that area, no one is permitted to launch a balloon.) Using rubber tubing available at a hobby shop, cut two ten-foot pieces and connect them with a large plastic kitchen funnel. (Drill a hole in each side of the funnel and tie the tubing with a small tight knot inside.) If you don't have a funnel, experiment with other receptacles, such as plastic milk cartons with one end cut off. Two youngsters, standing well apart, hold the ends of the tubing, while a third youngster puts a water balloon in the funnel and pulls it back. When he lets go, the balloon sails toward the finish line. Practice this several times before having a competition.

❏ **191. BALLOON KEEP-AWAY.** Provide each player with a pie pan. The group sits in a close circle and an air-filled balloon is launched. Each player uses her pan to swat the balloon away. If it can be hit again, the game continues. If the balloon hits the ground, the nearest person is out. If it hits a person, the person that hit the balloon is out.

❏ **192. COOL-OFF TIME.** For a wet and wild ending to an afternoon of balloon fun, gather all the surviving balloons and fill them with water. Using a very fine needle, poke a small hole in each balloon so that there is a slow leak. Then let kids start firing them at one another. The object is to keep tossing them at others until the balloons run out of water.

# THREE

# FOUR SEASONS FUN

SECTION 1: SPRING

SECTION 2: SUMMER

SECTION 3: AUTUMN

SECTION 4: WINTER

**T**hese ideas that tie in with specific holidays and the seasonal weather will help to build wonderful year-round family memories.

# SECTION 1: SPRING

❑ **193.** THE FIRST SPRING TREE. Even before spring has sprung, you can help kids make a spring tree right inside your house. Start with a scouting expedition to find a small dead tree or a large branch. Your tree should be pruned into a pleasant shape and then scrubbed. Spray paint the tree in a pale color or with clear polyurethane to give it a shine. Depending on its size, plant it in a basket or pot filled with sand or plaster of Paris. Now it is ready to be decorated with tissue flowers, Easter eggs, felt birds, or other objects that say "Spring is here!"

❑ **194.** READY, AIM, FIRE. On the first day of spring, celebrate by bundling up and eating outdoors. Plan an easy-to-eat meal and let family members sit in a tree or on the jungle gym at home or in the park. Put large paper bags—weighted with a rock—on the ground at varying distances. As the meal progresses, let each person try to fire his refuse into the bags—no prizes, but cheers for good shots.

❑ **195.** JAPANESE DOLL DAY. Early each March, Japanese girls enjoy a centuries-old celebration by displaying their elaborately dressed dolls. Let your daughter also celebrate by inviting friends to a doll party, using paper doll invitations. Have a doll fashion show and tea party.

❑ **196.** APRIL FOOL FOOLERY. Encourage family members to do clever pranks (never mean or dangerous) on this humorous holiday. Get a plastic bug collection at a party store—cockroaches encased in plastic ice cubes will wake up soda drinkers! A fake mouse in the cupboard is fun. Or, put a small paper cup of water on the top of the bathroom door to provide a surprising shower.

❑ **197.** SPRING FLOWER CONTEST Put each family member's name on a popsicle stick or other marker. Then walk around the yard together looking at all the budding flowers, each person putting his marker by the plant he thinks will bloom first. This helps youngsters become aware of the coming of spring.

❑ **198.** **EDIBLE BIRD NESTS.** Let kids make this spring snack for themselves or for a party. First, they crumble three large shredded wheat cereal biscuits into a mixing bowl. Then, stir in a half cup of shredded coconut, two tablespoons of brown sugar, and a half cup of melted margarine. Using a muffin pan, line the cups with small pieces of foil, then press the mixture into the bottoms and up the sides. Bake them for ten minutes in a 350 degree oven (or until toasty crisp). When cool, let kids lift out the foil nests and remove the foil. When ready to serve, add the "eggs": green and red grapes, melon balls, cherries, even jelly beans, and Easter candy.

❑ **199.** **A CELEBRATION OF FREEDOM.** Passover is the Jewish celebration commemorating the Exodus from Egypt. The name comes from a devastating plague that passed over the Israelite homes. Today it is celebrated at a feast called a Seder, which has commemorative foods and the reading of the Passover story. If your family is invited to this feast, certainly go. If not, educate your children by sharing newspaper stories about it.

❑ **200.** **KEEPSAKE EASTER EGGS.** A few weeks ahead of your big Easter party, assign each guest the name of another guest so that a special Easter egg can be made. If guests don't have their own ideas, suggest these: cutting an oval in one side of the egg and drawing a scene inside, covering an egg with thread or fine ribbon, or writing a short letter or poem around the egg. Prepare egg-viewing on a prominent table or shelf by lettering the guest's name on a cardboard collar that holds the egg. After everyone has admired them, put them on the table as place cards.

❑ **201.** **LOOK-ALIKE EGGS.** Exchange names within the family or a larger group. Then, using indelible markers, each person makes an egg to look like that person—match hairstyle, eye color, and so forth. Then have a guessing contest as to the identity of each egg.

❑ **202.** **HAIRY EGGHEADS.** Give everyone in the family a "good hair day" by making eggs with "hair." Using nail scissors, carefully cut off the top of the egg, saving the insides for cooking. Put a pin hole in the bottom. Then wash and dry the eggs. Next, using indelible markers, let family members put facial features on each egg. Fill eggs with soil and a small quantity of quick-germinating grass seed. Use an egg carton as your growing area. Water gently, cover with plastic wrap, and put in a sunny area. When grass sprouts, remove the plastic wrap. In about ten days, the eggs will have a bushy mane, ready to trim, tie in a ponytail, cut Mohawk style, or braid. Make each finished egghead a collar of cardboard on which to stand.

❑ **203.** **SYMBOLS OF EASTER.** No matter what your religion, teach kids the meanings of Easter symbols. White lilies are symbols of purity. Rabbits and chicks represent springtime and new life. The cross is the symbol of Jesus' victory over death and is displayed in Christian churches. It is also recreated on biscuits called hot cross buns. Candles, which are often extinguished on Good Friday to symbolize the darkness of the Crucifixion, are then relighted Saturday evening. The Easter Parade, which originated in New York, highlights springtime clothing and fabulous hats. Egg hunts go back to a German folktale that credits the Easter rabbit with laying eggs for good children. The lamb was the Jews' sacrificial symbol at Passover and later the Christian symbol for Jesus' sacrifice. Colored eggs came from Mesopotamian Christians who used them as symbols of Easter joy.

❑ **204.** **EASTER BREAKFAST.** Using a cookie cutter, cut the center out of a piece of toast—one for each guest. Kids can toast the centers and frost with cream cheese while a parent puts the toast frame on the skillet, breaks an egg into the opening, and then fries toast and egg on both sides. In advance, let youngsters prepare two or three kinds of melon balls and place them in a bowl inside an Easter basket for a festive table centerpiece.

❑ **205.** HELP BUILD A NEST.   In the spring, birds are looking for materials to use in making their nests. On a tree or shrub where you have seen birds, let kids hang colorful bits of yarn, tiny pieces of cotton, and short pieces of thread small enough for birds to carry away. When you see the birds regularly going back and forth to a particular spot (a knot of branches or twigs), you can assume they have a nest there. Do not disturb the nest! When the eggs have hatched and the babies have flown away, only then look at the nest and see which of your materials went into the making.

❑ **206.** PREPARE FOR HALLOWEEN NOW.   Why pay for pumpkins when you can have the fun of growing your own? At the garden shop, look at the pictures on the seed packets and choose the ideal shape for your jack-o'-lantern. Plant the seeds in an area where you don't have other precious plants, since pumpkins have the habit of taking over the territory. Pumpkins don't require much tending—just sun and a little water.

❑ **207.** SPRING TREASURE HUNT.   Make a backyard hunt by drawing simple pictures on pieces of paper (a fence, hose bib, rosebush, garage door, tree, deck, sandbox, and so forth). Retaining the first picture as the first clue, place the others. (For example, give the child the picture of the fence, and at the fence place the picture of the hose bib.) At the last clue, place a little surprise in a plastic bag buried in the ground or well-hidden. Do a different set for each child, or let young kids search together as a group.

❑ **208.** GO FLY A KITE.   Spring breezes make great kite-flying days. (Kite-flying is over 2000 years old and was started by the Greeks and the Chinese.) On a day when you see flags swaying or leaves fluttering, buy inexpensive kits and work together to assemble them. Choose a site away from streets, power lines, and trees. Have your child hold the kite about forty feet downwind of you. As you walk backward letting out string, the child holds the kite high and then lets it go. Now it's time to let the youngster be the pilot as the kite soars.

❏ **209.** BACK FENCE COLLAGE.   With kid help, cut up miscellaneous colored paper, comics, and wrapping paper into various shaped pieces and place them in a bag. Then attach a large piece of paper to the fence. Let kids reach into the bag for one piece and then glue it in place, gradually putting together a collage. When finished, you can lay the paper flat, brush additional glue on it, and shake glitter over the collage.

❏ **210.** MAY BASKETS.   On May Day, honor the old Roman tradition of secretly delivering flowers to friends. Early in the day, or the evening before, collect wildflowers, garden flowers, and assorted greenery. Let them sit in a pail of water for an hour or more. For each bouquet, you'll need a container that can be made ahead of time: fancy shopping bags or colored construction paper cut into a piece at least ten-inches square and twisted into a cornucopia. Decorate the paper with ribbons and glitter. To form a handle, make holes on opposite sides of the cone and run a twenty-four-inch ribbon through the holes, tying it on the inside. Just before delivering, kids arrange the flowers against the greens and tuck them firmly in the cone. Now you're ready to "ring and run" as kids place them on the doorknobs of friends and relatives.

❏ **211.** MAKE A MAYPOLE.   You'll need a sturdy pole in the ground, or you can put a pole through the hole in the center of a heavy umbrella table. Next, cover a long wrapping-paper tube (larger in diameter than the pole) with colorful paper. For each youngster, cut an eight-foot length of crepe paper streamer and staple one end securely to the inside top of the tube. Staple a flower to the loose end and put the tube over the pole. With sprightly music playing, kids pick up the loose ends and move around the maypole. Then divide the group in two and let half go one direction and half the other direction, ducking under or going over the streamers.

❑ **212.** CINCO DE MAYO. In 1862 the Mexicans expelled the French forces, and even today on May 5, there are celebrations of this event on both sides of the U.S. border. (Don't confuse this with Mexican Independence Day that is September 16.) Make your own fiesta, choosing from the huge variety of Mexican foods. The decorations can be red, white, and green streamers (the colors of the Mexican flag). Play mariachi music in the background. Buy a piñata or make one out of cardboard and tissue paper. You can even cover a box with strips of colorful paper. Fill your piñata with candy and hang it by a sturdy rope from a tree branch. Using a bat or pole, blindfolded kids each get one swing. Watch the scramble for candy when it finally breaks!

❑ **213.** MOM'S OWN WEEK. Rather than just a one day celebration, make the Mother's Day celebration last an entire week. Dad, or another adult, can help a youngster make a booklet out of seven envelopes stapled together and each labeled for a day of the week. Inside each envelope is a promised good deed such as: making lunch, reading poetry to her, cleaning out a closet, watching a sibling so she can have a long bubble bath, and so forth. In last of the seven envelopes can be a letter of love to Mother.

❑ **214.** DAUGHTER EXCHANGE. If you're tired of hinting about a Mother's Day gift, this idea lets you go shopping and still be surprised. With a friend who also has a daughter (or son), agree on the amount of money to be spent. Then go to the mall and exchange daughters. It's fun to shop with the other girl and help her buy what her mommy would like.

❑ **215.** MOM'S GARDEN GIFT. Dad helps the kids plan this gift—a garden they will plant and care for, and from which Mom can just reap the rewards. At a garden shop choose one flowering plant for instant beauty, one tool, and a selection of seed packets of vegetables and compatible flowers. Arrange these in colored tissue paper in a basket. Make a card that tells that the family members are giving their time and effort to start and maintain the gift. Each message should be specific: "May planting, love Cliff" or "Watering twice a week, love Mark" or "June weeding, love Jamie." At the back of the basket add a homemade wood sign that reads "Mom's Garden," which she can place in her special garden.

❑ **216.** THE EYES HAVE IT.   As the sun grows brighter, show kids how to glamorize their sunglasses in preparation for summer. You'll need trimmings such as felt and pipe cleaners, beads, glitter, and small buttons. Help kids cut flowers and leaves from felt and glue them onto pipe cleaners that you twist around the ear pieces. Try a row of beads over the top of the frame, or glue glitter all the way around the frames.

❑ **217.** INTERNATIONAL SWING DAY.   This celebration originated in Korea but can be carried on by your children. It's a day of outside fun featuring swings of all sizes, some for two people. If you don't have a swing, consider hanging one from a tree. Hang bells nearby so that swingers can ring them with their toes as they swing.

❑ **218.** WRITE ON!   High school graduates like to collect signatures of friends. Suggest a new way to do this using a light colored T-shirt or light blue denim jacket. Friends sign, using a black felt-tip marker. Back home, the teen can go over the signatures with fabric paint. It's a memorable outfit for informal school events or the last day of school.

❑ **219.** FATHER FLIPS!   Actually it's Dad's pancake breakfast that flips. Help youngsters prepare the batter, then let them be creative about the pancakes for Father's Day breakfast. Make some in shapes (and others must guess what they are) or add strawberries or blueberries to some. One family puts in M&Ms, pushing them in just after flipping them to the second side.

❑ **220.** SURPRISE PARTY FOR DAD.   In advance of Father's Day, go to a T-shirt shop and get a shirt for Dad that says "King for a Day." Then plan a surprise picnic in the park (secretly putting all the party items in the car trunk). On the big day, suggest that the family go for a ride, ending at the park where you have arranged to meet another family. The dads are given their shirts and join in multigenerational games such as egg tossing, two-legged or sack races, and tag using water balloons. Tug-of-war can be the last event before lunch and gifts.

❑ **221.** GIFTS FOR DADS.   Let kids choose their own gifts to give. Present them at a picnic, the ball game, or the intermission of a play. Good ideas are: a new cap, a soda mug, sports equipment, barbecue tools, magazine subscription, electric tool, jazzy socks, or handmade coupons good for a home-style car wash, garage cleaning, lawn-cutting, or other service.

❑ **222.** ROYAL END TO FATHER'S DAY.   Whatever activities you enjoy together during the day, see that the end of the day is royally suitable for the king. Kids can settle Dad into his comfy chair with the Sunday paper or his favorite TV program. Then help kids make a drink called "The King's Ambrosia." In a blender, whip up a small can of drained sliced peaches and add a half cup of orange juice and one teaspoon of vanilla. Just before serving, add two scoops of vanilla ice cream and blend until thick. Serve with two straws just in case Dad wants to share.

❑ **223.** END-OF-SCHOOL HONORS.   Your child may not have received straight A grades, been given a letter for outstanding sports achievement, or been class president. Even so, appreciate progress—no matter how small—and do attend those final assemblies. Start when kids are young to celebrate success—this doesn't mean you reward shoddy work, but you do emphasize an area of improvement. You can do it with words ("Imagine, you're finishing sixth grade—you're halfway to your high school diploma" or

"Wow, your D in math moved to a C!"). Or you can do it with action by planning an end-of-school surprise: a trip to the skating rink, a special movie, a beach picnic.

❑ **224.** END-OF-SCHOOL DISPLAYS. Let your child help to display his best work. Frame a piece of art for the wall. Or cover the coffee table with all those clay pieces made in previous years. Read an outstanding paper at supper. Write or telephone grandparents with some special news or send them an outstanding essay paper or drawing.

# SECTION 2: SUMMER

❑ **225.** JELL-O TOSS. Follow the package directions for making Jell-O Jigglers in a flat baking dish. When the gelatin is set and you're ready to play, cut into one-inch squares. For outside fun, young children can toss squares into a pail, seeing who has the best aim. For older kids, form pairs standing three feet apart. Give each player three cubes and see who can toss the cubes into the other's open mouth. Or, kids can climb a tree or play equipment and aim at various targets.

❑ **226.** MAKE A POND. In just one day, your family can create a scenic backyard pond—a great idea for a family with older kids since it could be a hazard to younger ones. Place the pond (which is not for wading) where there are bushes behind it and where it is easily seen from the house. Obtain a pond liner or a wide piece of heavy duty black plastic. Use a hose or string to "draw" the outline in keeping with the size of your liner. Then everyone digs. Use a plank across the hole to be sure the edges are level. Slope the hole toward the middle that should be at least one-foot deep. Check the pond bottom for protruding rocks, then cover it with damp sand. Next, spread the liner, letting it come up and over the rim. Be sure that excess material is folded down flat. Fill the pond to a desired level and make any rim adjustments. Then, trim the excess liner at the rim, leaving enough to tuck under rocks for a natural appearance. Push some rocks partly into the water for a realistic look and then landscape with small plants. It's a summertime project your family will be proud of year-round.

❑ **227.** FLASHY FIREFLIES. Show children how fireflies communicate by sending blinking signals. An enjoyable outdoor game can be played by all the family on a moonless night in a large yard or a park. Each person will need a flashlight and a partner. With their partner they create a signal consisting of short and long flashes. Partners go to opposite ends of the play area and all flashlights are off until the game begins. At this point, partners start flashing and when they recognize their partner, they run to meet each other. The first partners to find each other are the winners and the game begins again.

❑ **228.** SPONGE TAG. Using string, make a large circle in which players wearing swimsuits must stay. Place a pail of water at the edge of the circle and put a large sponge in it. The person selected to be "it" grabs the sponge and throws it at someone. The person who was hit dunks the sponge in the pail and tries to hit someone else. For rowdy fun, provide several pails of water and every player with a sponge.

❑ **229.** POPCORN RELAY RACE. For a party or backyard fun, let kids make a big batch of popcorn. Next, show each participant how to make a pair of popcorn holders. Poke a hole in the center of a paper cup and push a sturdy rubber band halfway through the hole. Place a paper clip on the end of the rubber band inside the cup and pull the other end until the clip is at the bottom of the cup. The rubber band will hold the cups in place on top of the players' feet. Divide the group into two teams and let the captain fill each player's cups with popcorn. Place a shallow box for each team about fifteen feet from a start line. When the whistle blows, the relay begins with the first member of each team racing carefully to the box and emptying his cups in it, spilling as little as possible along the way. The runner returns to the start line and tags the next team member, then goes to the end of the line to refill his cup. After three minutes, the popcorn in each box is measured (a large measuring cup works well) and the team with the most wins.

❑ **230.** **BUBBLE CIRCLE.** On a nonwindy day, put a thin paving stone in the bottom of a plastic wading pool. Then fill the pool with bubble liquid (see #170 for the recipe) just to the place where the top of the stone will stay dry. Have a youngster stand on the stone as you lower a hula hoop over his head and into the bubble liquid. Raise the hoop and a big bubble circle will form. Don't forget to save the bubble stuff for use another day.

❑ **231.** **POLAR BATH.** At bath time, provide kids with a big bowl of ice cubes. After they're clean, they can float the cubes in the tub until they've cooled down and are ready to get out and dry off.

❑ **232.** **JULY 4 BIRTHDAY.** Since Independence Day marks the birthday of the United States of America, think of a birthday gift that the family could give to the country. Some suggestions are: planting a tree, writing a congressman with a good idea, offering to paint over graffiti, cleaning up the street where you live, or approaching a business that might provide food or funds for a party at a veteran's hospital.

❑ **233.** **NEIGHBORHOOD PARADE.** For Independence Day—or just any day—let kids organize a miniparade by going around the neighborhood and getting volunteers. The parade can consist of decorated bikes and wagons, strollers with pets or babies riding, and kids dressed as clowns or the parade flag bearer. Drummers and other instrumentalists can also march. For a truly big parade that might go to a park, go down the town's main street with decorated golf carts, bikes, and horses with the town fire engine leading the way. The traditional ending is an ice-cream social.

❑ **234.** **COOL KIDS.** On hot days, there can be a constant procession of kids coming to the kitchen for cold drinks. With kid help, fill plastic soda bottles or water bottles with favorite drinks, leaving space at the top. Cap and put these in the freezer. Then, when you head out for fun at a picnic, beach, or park, you have big refreshing drinks that stay cold for many hours.

❑ **235. SQUARE PUMPKINS?** Kids can give a pumpkin a creepy new look by teaching it to grow into a square. When a pumpkin first begins to form, very carefully slide it into a gallon plastic milk carton without breaking it off the vine. As it grows bigger, it will fill the carton. When it's ready to be picked, just cut the carton away, revealing the unique shape.

❑ **236. FREE AT LAST.** Youngsters who have the summer off from school enjoy the initial freedom, but usually, after a few weeks, the novelty wears off. This is the time to talk together about some goals for the summer. These could include a building project such as a sandbox, tree house, fire pit, fence, or bookcase. Or a physical fitness goal such as learning to ride a bike or do a certain number of push-ups. Or it could be a learning goal: how to tie shoes or tell time. Or an educational goal such as reading a specified number of books. After conversation, write up each family member's summer goal (parents included), and post it. Then don't nag, just encourage.

❑ **237. CORN DOLLS.** For each doll you'll need the husks from one ear of corn and some lightweight string. Holding the husks together, turn down the top two inches and tie them to form the head. Halfway down, tie the waist line. Pull out a piece on either side as an arm and tie near the end for a wrist. At the lower end, separate the husks into two legs and tie each ankle. Kids can put a face on the corn doll with markers.

❑ **238. PVC=PRETTY VIGOROUS CHALLENGE.** Gather together leftover lengths of PVC pipe from neighborhood garages. Also collect old Ping Pong balls (or any balls that will fit through the pipe). In a big sandbox or at the beach, kids can create hills and mountains. Lay the pipes on the slopes, some connecting, some with roads between them. Kids will develop their own races as the balls follow the tube tunnels.

❑ **239. BASTILLE DAY PARTY.** On July 14, celebrate the 1789 storming of the French prison that was the beginning of the end of the monarchy. French Independence Day at your house can feature a French cafe supper: French bread served with fruits and cheeses, or cheese fondue. Drink sparkling grape juice and top it all off with crepes (little pancakes) with French vanilla ice cream. Have one person research a few French phrases that can be taught to everyone.

❑ **240. PARENTS DAY.** Traditionally the fourth Sunday in July, this day is unlike Mother's Day and Father's Day because no gifts are involved. It celebrates the spirit of good parenting. At breakfast, talk about the qualities necessary to be a good parent (love, patience, intelligence, humor, honesty, self-worth, creativity, responsibility) and the qualities necessary to be a good child. (Are they the same? Are there some that a youngster can do without?) You'll no doubt come up with a few more. Then celebrate together by switching roles for the day.

❑ **241. COOL JUMPING.** While jumping rope is great exercise, it can also make you hot. Cool down by adding a little splash and dash to the game. All you'll need is a long (about twelve foot) cotton clothesline, plus large plastic glasses. Fill each glass to the top, then players (each holding a glass) jump into the turning rope and make four jumps before jumping out. After all players have done this, compare the glasses—the youngster with the most water left is the winner. You can also play with teams, the second player on the team jumping in with the first and taking the cup as the first jumper goes out.

❑ **242. SAND CANDLES.** Let kids collect sand from the beach or the sandbox—about one quart per youngster. Place the sand in bowls and mix in just enough water so that an interesting hole, about the size of a cup, can be made in the sand. In a double boiler, the parent melts paraffin or old candles and a crayon for color. Suspend a wick or string from a dowel placed across the bowl top. Pour cooled wax into the sand mold to about a half inch from the top. (If you don't have a wick to suspend over the mold, you can wait until the wax is setting and then place a candle in the center.) When the wax is completely cool, remove the free-form candle from the sand.

❑ **243. KIDDIE KORRAL.** What do you do with a wading pool that's sprung a leak in the bottom? If it's beyond repair, it can become a safe play area for a baby. With a comfy blanket on the bottom and an interesting collection of toys, it provides a play place as parents garden or do other tasks. And, it moves easily from place to place.

❑ **244. CAMP WILDERNESS.** There's no need to drive to a campsite when you can create "Camp Wilderness" right in your own backyard. With other parents, choose a day when all the neighborhood kids can sleep out together in your secure backyard. For supper, invite the other parents to bring food for the grill and help set up tents and games. After eating together, the host parents take over for twilight fun and bedtime snacks. Don't count on a lot of sleep as there will be screams and laughter as stories are told. Insist that no one leave the area and that emergencies or other problems are reported to you. In the morning, mix up a big bowl of blueberry pancake batter and let the campers prepare their own on a griddle on the outside grill. Afterward, let everyone pitch in to clean up and then send the happy (but sleepy) campers home.

❑ **245. BORED PETS.** Veterinarians say that pets who learn new things stay young longer. And on long, warm summer days, pets can get just as bored as kids. Suggest Pet School and let kids see how to improve the life of their pets. Fish can have a larger bowl and more interesting landscaping. Hamsters and guinea pigs can "go free" in a tiled bathroom for awhile (close the lid). Cats will benefit from a homemade carpeted maze to play in and scratch. Dogs can learn a new trick, practiced each day with praise and rewards.

❑ **246.** SUMMER STORMS. Power outages and fierce storms won't upset your family if you prepare for them in advance. In a sturdy box, let kids pack the supplies and place them in the basement or other safe place (such as the car trunk in case you are caught away from home). Supplies can include a flashlight and a radio with extra batteries, a first-aid kit, sweaters, blanket and pillow, some long-lasting well-sealed snacks, water, a book containing many stories, and a deck of cards for various games. Check and update the contents yearly.

❑ **247.** NIGHTTIME PICNIC. On a night when kids can sleep late the next morning, plan a picnic supper after the sun has set. Young children may require a cracker and cheese snack at their usual eating hour, but save the main dish and dessert for a candlelight supper. Kids can make the plainest backyard look wonderful with a colorful table cloth, a few flowers, and candles on the table and in far corners of the yard. The cozy atmosphere is conducive to good conversation.

❑ **248.** METEOR SHOWER. Watch your newspaper in August for the annual Perseid meteor shower—usually a three-day event that peaks in the early morning hours. Choose a night with the least moon and pick a place in the yard free from other lights. Get comfortable on lounge chairs or blankets, face northeast, and start counting. Sometimes you'll see dozens in just one minute—a display that appears near the constellation Perseus. And don't forget to wish on these "falling stars."

❑ **249.** MINIATURE GOLF. Create your own miniature golf course in your backyard. Yes, you will have nine round holes in the ground, but they'll fill in or grow over quickly when you tire of the game. You'll need at least two putters (available at thrift shops), balls, eighteen poker chips, and nine sixteen-ounce cans to be sunk in the ground. Place two poker chips on the ground to show the starting place— from between the chips—for each hole. Here are some of the obstacles: a shoe box with a hole on either side, a sand trap made by piling some sandbox sand around one hole, a bunker made of rocks with just a few openings through them, a hula hoop laid flat that must be shot into and out of, a series of coffee cans to go through, a hole (the can) elevated with soil so that one must play up to it, a series of five wire "doors" (made from hangers) to shoot through, small branches and leaves to serve as the rough, and a water hole made by sinking a very large container of water into the ground immediately in front of a hole.

❏ **250. NATURE PAINTS.** In your own backyard there are natural colors just waiting to be used. Let kids draw a picture outside, using just a black marking pen for the outline. Then, go hunting for colors to rub on and fill in. Use grass for green, geranium blossoms for red or pink, and dandelions for yellow.

❏ **251. MINI-MEALS.** In hot summer weather, appetites may need a little less food and more encouragement. The answer is minimeals, foods kids will enjoy helping to prepare. For breakfast, make tiny pancakes, just one and a half inches across. Alternatives are mini-muffins, mini-sausages (cocktail size), and doughnut holes. For lunch, cut sandwiches into fourths or sixths and watch them disappear. Serve with bite-sized cheese cubes and small crackers, tiny pickles, grapes, or cherries. For dinner, serve chicken wings or drumettes. Vegetables can be peas and panfried new potatoes. Dessert can be mini-sundaes served with just one mini-marshmallow or chocolate chip on top.

❏ **252. TREASURE BOXES.** A good project for a summer day is to make a treasure box—a private place for a youngster to keep that special bird feather, rock, or baseball card, safe from curious siblings and parents. Help a youngster select a sturdy carton such as the kind that envelopes or copy paper come in. Or use a plastic container with a lid. Get a padlock at a hardware store. Collect small magazine pictures, photos, wrapping paper, stickers, stars, beads, orphan earrings, nuts or small nails, and a penny. Then with glue, affix the paper items first, then the dimensional ones. For a final touch, line the inside of the box with a soft fabric. If you wish, a clear lacquer finish will make the outside surface more durable.

❏ **253.** **WATERMELON LANTERNS.** Kids can make watermelon lanterns for an inviting nighttime table setting. Cut the top of a melon and let younger children use a melon ball tool to scoop out the insides. Next, older youngsters who can handle knives make the lanterns by carving small designs into the sides. Place small candles in jars and put inside. Serve bowls of summer fruits topped with sherbet along with kid baked cookies for a very special dessert for family and friends. The lanterns can be saved for another night by wrapping and refrigerating them.

❏ **254.** **SOLAR SNACK.** On a hot day, show kids how to use the sun's rays to cook a snack. Glue a big piece of black construction paper to a big piece of heavy-duty aluminum foil. When the glue is dry, roll up the paper like an ice-cream cone, foil side in. Now you're ready to cook. In a small glass dish that will fit inside the cone, crack an egg and top it with cheese. Or, cover a few slices of apple with cinnamon sugar. Put plastic wrap tightly over the top and put it in the "oven." Prop the cone with the open end of the oven toward the sun and let your snack cook for about twenty minutes.

❏ **255.** **COOL SAILING.** Making boats of ice is fun; sailing them in a tub or wading pool is even more fun. Make ice boats this easy way (all should be identical in size for fairness). Use a pint-sized milk carton filled with one and three-fourths cups of water with a little food coloring in it. Push the "mast" made of a wood chopstick into the water through the carton opening. Place the carton in the freezer for next day fun. When ready to race, make a sail out of colored paper, then cut the carton away and staple the sail to the mast. Now, place the boats in the water and see how they sail. As the ice melts, some may tip over, sails may fall off, but the winner is the one to outlast the others.

❑ **256.** NEW SCHOOL YEAR, NEW ROOM. While you can't give a youngster an entirely new room, together you can give it a new look. Consider what the needs will be for the new school year—a bigger study area, storage for sports equipment or an expanding hobby, or some new clothes. Give the room a new arrangement, bag up outgrown clothing and toys for charity giving, expand the work area with board-and-brick shelves or a desk wing made of a piece of wood with file drawers underneath. Consider new window coverings that you can make together. And, if the carpet is worn, cover it with a bright area rug. Let youngsters hang interesting things on the wall: posters, sports equipment, a bulletin board, a full-length mirror. Make a sign for the door announcing whose room it is.

❑ **257.** FASHION WARDROBE. Don't just set out to the mall to buy kids clothes without a plan. Let them first search a week's worth of newspapers and cut out ads for clothes they'd like to own. Encourage them to compare the prices. Is there a style that looks especially good on their body shape? What colors do they like? How much money can be spent? From this information make a shopping list and, when you return home, see how your purchases compare with the pictures.

❑ **258.** LABOR DAY SURVEY. While enjoying the picnic or barbecue on this holiday, talk about labor—different kinds of work. Let one youngster make a list as each person tells about his or her job and the jobs of relatives. See if jobs held by one generation affected the professions of the next generation. Do any of those present have the same profession? What careers do the adults think would be best for each youngster? What do the kids think of these suggestions?

❑ **259.** LABOR DAY STREET PARTY. Bring all the parents and kids together for a potluck party. With your kids, hand deliver the invitations and when folks RSVP, ask them to bring a casserole, salad and rolls, or dessert. Play these three games. *(1) Target practice.* Hang a series of targets such as pie pans, hula hoop, and metal cowbell from a clothesline or tree branch. Everyone gets a chance to hit the targets with three tennis balls. *(2) Guess your weight.* Make one person Professor Guesser who whispers his guestimate to each person stepping forward to be weighed on bathroom scales. If the professor isn't within five pounds, the person gets a candy prize. *(3) Tug-of-war.* Put a knot at the middle of a sturdy twenty-foot rope. Divide everyone into two teams at opposite ends, with kids at the front and adults at the rear. Draw a line on the ground and start the game with the knot above the line. Now everyone starts to pull and when one whole team is pulled across the midline, the other team has won.

# SECTION 3: AUTUMN

❏ **260.** **NEW BEDTIMES.** Although it's technically still summer, Labor Day signals the start of fall. Let this day also remind you that your youngsters are starting a new school year and deserve new bedtimes. (Bedtimes should be thoughtfully set and strictly enforced since teachers complain that many students are too sleepy to function in the morning.) Discuss a bedtime with each youngster and take into consideration her ideas as well as how quickly she fell asleep under the old schedule. Kids that can't get going in the morning definitely deserve earlier bedtimes. Don't let the end of a TV show influence the decision. It may be easier to put several children to bed at the same time, but unless you have twins, each should have her own special time.

❏ **261.** **HARVEST MOON.** Each autumn there is one moon that is very special. Called the harvest moon, it occurs nearest the autumnal equinox of the sun, about September 23. The moon rises at the same time for several nights and shines with such brightness that farmers in northern climates can work late into the night to bring in the harvest. Check to see when it will be harvest moon in your area and sit outside to watch it. Let kids make Swiss cheese sandwiches in honor of the moon, and corn on the cob to honor the harvest.

❑ **262.** APPLE TIME.   Autumn apples can be made to last by including the family in a project to dry them. (They make tasty treats for lunch boxes or snacks.) Everyone peels and cores the apples and one person slices them into rings about an eighth-inch thick. A younger child can dip each ring in a mixture of three parts water to one part lemon juice so the apple doesn't turn dark. Another youngster can lay them out on paper towels and cover them with another towel, patting them dry. Now they can be strung through the holes and hung in a sunny window for seven to ten days until dry and chewy. Or, they can be put on a cooling rack placed on a baking tray and dried in a 150 degree oven for four hours.

❑ **263.** BIKE DAY.   Before the weather changes, choose a weekend day when all activities are done with bicycle transportation: marketing, errands, team practices, and excursions. You will need helmets for all and safe child seats for those too young to peddle. Plan a safe route to a picnic location and let everyone carry part of the load: food, blanket, hats, and so forth. In advance, call a friend who lives along the way and stop there for liquid refreshment. If you make Sunday a bike day, think how smashing you'll all look cycling in to church!

❑ **264.** SANTA'S WORKSHOP.   Before the garage gets too cool for comfortable work projects, set up Santa's workshop—a garage area where the family can work together on craft gifts. Find a project that can involve all ages. A good one is making candleholders from wood stairway spindles—something easily available at a lumber store. These will need to be cut in segments, sanded, drilled to hold a candle, painted or lacquered, then wrapped along with an appropriate candle, and tagged for giving.

❑ **265.** AUTUMN WALK BRACELET OR BELT.   Before going on a walk or hike with kids, provide them with an adhesive bracelet or belt. Use adhesive-backed paper (such as Contac) and make a strip about two-by-eight inches for a wrist or a strip long enough to go around the child's waist. On the nature walk, collect and affix only fallen items—leaves, blossoms, bark, seeds, and sand or dirt. Back home, they can go on the bulletin board or dining table as a remembrance of your autumn walk.

❑ **266.** SIGNATURE PUMPKINS.   In early September while pumpkins are still growing, show your youngster how to write her name on a pumpkin with a ballpoint pen. Then, with a sharp pen tip or letter opener, go over the writing, breaking the pumpkin skin. As the pumpkin gets bigger, so will the signature.

❑ **267.** DENIM NOTEBOOK.   School notebooks take on a new look when you and your child dress them in jeans. Using an old pair of jeans, cut a piece that is two inches larger than each dimension of the notebook. Wrap the book in its new covering, fold the extra material inside, and glue it down.

❑ **268.** SCHOOL LUNCH SEMINAR.   Stifle brown bag boredom by having a conference with kids concerning a school lunch that goes beyond peanut butter and jelly. Consider these alternatives and let kids vote on which ones to try. Fruits: a melon scored for easy eating and a container of cottage cheese, cherries with yogurt dip, grapes frosted with egg white and dusted with sugar. Veggies: tomato stuffed with tuna fish, carrots with low-fat salad dressing dip, lettuce spread with peanut butter and tightly rolled. Main dish: chili or soup in a thermos, triple decker sandwich, chicken legs, precooked meatballs, hard-boiled egg with salsa dip, and that peanut butter sandwich with sliced banana or bacon inside. Dessert: oatmeal cookies and a small container of frosting with spreader.

❑ **269.** PIE-PLEASER DAY.   Honor pies of all kinds on one special day planned by the kids. It can be apple or peach pie for breakfast, lunch of triangle-shaped fruits and sandwiches served in a pie pan, pizza pie for dinner, and a light custard pie for dessert.

❑ **270.** **COLUMBUS QUIZ.** On Columbus Day, see who can answer these five questions correctly. (1) What was his native country and what country did he sail for? (Answers: Italy, Spain.) (2) How did he navigate? (Answer: By dead reckoning—he knew just enough celestial navigation to measure the latitude from the North Star.) (3) Was he trying to prove the world was round? (Answer: No, educated people already knew that. He was trying to find a short route to the Orient.) (4) How did King Ferdinand and Queen Isabella help him? (Answer: She did not give her jewels; the royal treasurer advanced $14,000.) (5) What were the names of his three ships? (Answers: Nina, Pinta, Santa Maria.)

❑ **271.** **AUTUMN LEAVES.** Show kids how to turn green leaves red. Cut about five green leaves into pieces and place in a jar. Cover with rubbing alcohol and then mash them a bit with a spoon. Seal the jar with plastic wrap and a lid. Then fill a large bowl with hot tap water and swirl the jar in it until the alcohol turns dark. Cut a strip about an inch wide from a white coffee filter, placing one end in the mixture and the other end over the jar lip. In a few hours, you'll see the autumn colors that are normally hidden by the green chlorophyll.

❑ **272.** **AUTUMN MAZE.** When there are leaves covering the lawn, use a leaf rake to make a pathway like a maze (with dead ends) for kids to follow. For each child, hide a wrapped granola bar or other snack for them to find under a pile of leaves at the end of the maze.

❑ **273.** **PUMPKIN TOWER.** Kids carve three pumpkins (one small, one medium, one large) using any design they choose. Set aside the tops of the large and medium ones. Place a large candle in each and then stack them, largest on the bottom, where they can be seen and appreciated indoors or out. They can also be carved to make a pumpkin man: the top one as the head, the middle one the body with carved buttons, and the bottom one with carved legs and feet.

❑ **274.** **TRICKS TO MAKE A TREAT.** Of course there is always pumpkin bread, but there is another treat that can be made when it's pumpkin time. Let kids take out all the seeds from a moderate-sized pumpkin, rinse them, and then dry them on paper towels. In a bowl, mix three table-spoons of salad oil and one-fourth teaspoon of salt or garlic salt. Toss the seeds and then spread them on a cookie sheet. Bake at 250 degrees for an hour, but be sure to stir them every ten minutes. When cool, kids will gobble them up!

❑ **275.** **NONSPOOKY HALLOWEEN AT HOME.** Increas-ingly, families are getting together for nonscary home-style parties rather than encouraging candy-begging in the neighborhood. Decorate with bales of hay (or corn shocks) and pumpkins. Have a costume contest. Along with the usual pumpkin carving contest and apple bobbing, have a pumpkin relay race. Divide the group into two teams and give each a similar-sized small pumpkin. Participants crawl to a designated line and back, pushing the pumpkin with their foreheads. Also hang sugar cookies (instead of apples) on strings from the ceiling. (Poke holes for the strings as soon as cookies come out of the oven.) Kids must eat an entire cookie, keeping their hands behind their backs. Serve hearty country food such as chili, and end the evening with simple square dances or line dances.

❑ **276.** **PROGRESSIVE HALLOWEEN PARTY.** Preteens will enjoy a neighborhood costume party when four fami-lies within walking distance share the work. Each neighbor and youngster prepares food and a game. The first house: a punch bowl cauldron (dry ice makes it smoke) and a selec-tion of board games. The second house: chips and dips with sodas, then bobbing for apples in a kiddie pool. The main course can be at the next house with hot dogs in pita bread plus a salad of orange Jell-O containing black raisins.

Then all can also play the dance game called limbo. The final stop can be decorating prebaked round cookies to look like pumpkins, followed by music and dancing.

❑ **277.** AUTUMN PARTY GAMES. Younger kids can play "Witch's Broom" in which they are blindfolded and walk on a broom from bristle end to handle. Gradeschoolers might enjoy dancing with apples tucked under their chins, passing them on to one another. Or, light just one candle in each room of the house. Divide the group into pairs, each thinking of a trick as they hide. One couple doesn't hide but goes trick-or-treating. They look for hidden pairs and when they find one, the hidden pair demands the trick they've thought of. Then, the four start out looking for another pair, and when they find them, all four must do that next trick. And so it goes until the last couple is found—and they are given the prize.

❑ **278.** SAME COSTUME, DIFFERENT LOOK. Each invitee to the party is told to dress as a pumpkin. Some will make a big orange bag out of inexpensive fabric with holes for neck, arms, and legs. The bag will be stuffed with newspaper. Another may paint her face like a pumpkin and wear an orange hat with a green felt stem. Remember to take a photo of all the various pumpkins and give each one a prize (fattest, funniest, most original, seediest, skinniest, and so forth).

❑ **279.** PUMPKIN PRINTING. After Halloween and before your jack-o'lantern turns moldy, use the rind to make stamps. A parent can cut the rind in squares, circles, moons, diamonds—whatever shapes kids want. Next, provide tempera paint for dipping and paper to print on. The pumpkin stamp can be used many times, rinsed, and used in another color to make pictures, designs, note paper, and wrapping paper.

❑ **280.** LEAF PRINTS. Show kids how to sponge paint on the underside of a freshly picked leaf that has distinctive veins. Then place the leaf on a piece of paper and cover with a second piece of paper. Apply gentle pressure and then remove the top paper and leaf. The remaining leaf print can be used as a place card or for writing paper, or made part of a book of prints.

# SECTION 4: WINTER

You'll find many winter holiday ideas in my books *101 Ideas for the Best-Ever Christmas,* as well as in *1001 Things to Do with Your Kids.*

❑ **281.** STRESS-FREE HOLIDAYS. There are many components to the holiday season: traditions, family gatherings, connecting with friends, gift giving, personal reflection, and spiritual renewal. Allow time for your children to enjoy each aspect of the holidays. Plan fewer but more meaningful events. Talk about your family traditions—keep some, throw out some, establish new ones. Let each family member light a candle at dinner each night and follow this with a moment of thoughtful silence. Make the days ones of excitement, caring, fun, and wonder.

❑ **282.** FIRESIDE FUN. Teach kids how to lay and light a fire as well as what to do if a fire gets out of hand. Demonstrate the use of a fire extinguisher and how to call 911. Enjoy an outdoor campfire (perhaps after a wintry hike) with everyone in warm clothes. Show how to safely extinguish both indoor and outdoor fires.

❑ **283.** GOOD DEEDS. Without any advance hints, bring up the subject of good deeds. At dinnertime, ask family members if they can suggest some good deeds and then jot down their ideas. Continue the discussion by asking what good deeds tie in to Thanksgiving, Hanukkah, Christmas, or New Years. When you have a fairly good list, discuss which ones might be meaningful to do as a family.

❑ **284.** FIRESIDE SUPPER. Save on heating bills by eating an occasional supper by the fire. Start with a bowl of fruit soup (pineapple, peaches, raisins, pears, cinnamon, and nutmeg in juice) served warm. Next have a "pile on" potato. This is a baked potato that you top with cheese, sliced hot dogs, sour cream, chili, and so forth, and serve in foil surrounded by a napkin. In between bites, place it in your lap and it will keep you warm. Serve cookies, warm from the oven, to end the meal. This menu can also be popular for a teen party. You'll find that winter fireside suppers are conducive to warm feelings and good conversation.

❑ **285.** WISH LISTS. Each family member writes out a list of things he would enjoy receiving as gifts. Of course, he won't receive all the things on the list, but some suggestions can be saved for birthdays. Post the lists on the bulletin board so that family shoppers can get some good ideas and also share some with grandparents.

❑ **286.** ROLL THOSE CANDLES! At a craft store, let each child choose a sheet of beeswax. Also purchase candlewick cording. Cut the sheet into four rectangles. Next, the youngster lays a wick (about an inch longer than the beeswax) across one side. Roll up the beeswax tightly, starting at the side with the wick. A cluster of candles makes an attractive decoration for the table or mantel.

❑ **287.** GRATEFUL CHAIN. Starting early in November, family members share at supper what is meaningful to them as well as especially good things that happened during their day. Cut construction paper into strips and write the remembrance briefly on the paper. Then, make it into a link, using glue or a staple. Attach the next one to the first and gradually your "grateful chain" will grow so that it can be hung above the table, down the hallway, or up the stairway.

❑ **288.** GRATEFUL TREATS. A parent makes a gift tag for each person who will attend the Thanksgiving dinner. Then kids prepare a two-part treat for each guest: along with a piece of candy, they add a note that says "I'm thankful for you because . . . ." The note and candy are wrapped, the tag put on the outside, and then distributed during dessert.

❏ **289.** ALPHABET BLESSINGS. This familiar game has a new twist when each letter represents something for which the family is grateful. Go around the table from A to Z. It might start: "I'm grateful for applesauce . . . babies . . . candy." See who can recite all twenty-six!

❏ **290.** WILDERNESS FEAST. While you're cozy indoors enjoying a huge meal, there are birds outside who would enjoy a feast of their own. Help youngsters prepare seeds and bread, placing them off the ground so as not to attract rodents. If it is freezing outdoors, place a pan of warm water nearby to provide a quick drink.

❏ **291.** COUNT-YOUR-BLESSINGS CAKE. For holiday dessert, make and frost a cake. The family gathers around to finish trimming the cake with M&M-type candies, adding one as they name a blessing. You'll be surprised at how many candies adorn the cake!

❏ **292.** FANTASY CANDLES. Here's a craft that kids will enjoy making and giving. You'll need two pounds of paraffin or that same quantity of candle stubs, a quart milk carton, a long taper (narrow candle), and plenty of ice cubes. First, let kids put the ice cubes in a sturdy bag and hit them with a hammer, turning them into midsized chunks. An adult or teen should supervise melting the paraffin (carefully over water or in the microwave) since wax can be flammable. One child holds the taper in the center of the carton, another scoops the crushed ice around it, filling the carton. Next, the adult pours the melted wax into the carton and as it runs down through the ice it makes a crackling sound. (You can make the candles in various heights and colors if you choose.) When the wax is hard, tip the carton to drain away the water, then carefully peel away the carton. When you light the taper, the show begins since the ice has caused unique pockets in the paraffin, revealing imaginative light.

❏ **293.** **GINGERBREAD HOUSE.** From sturdy cardboard, fashion a small house with windows, door, and a roof. Using a mix, make gingerbread in a loaf pan, then slice it and let it dry overnight. Next, kids affix the gingerbread to the house with frosting. Provide decorator frosting tubes to fashion shutters, roof shingles, and a sidewalk. Use coconut for snow around the house. Tiny candy canes set in frosting or marshmallows make a fence, and other candies can be used as colorful decor. Use it as your holiday table centerpiece.

❏ **294.** **HAPPY HOLIDAY SHOPPING.** Divide the list between adults and teens and let younger kids decide with whom they wish to shop. Go to special stores featuring sports equipment, computers, jewelry, clothing, or hardware, and let kids see what treasures and bargains they can find. Punctuate the shopping with a stop for yogurt or a cookie. Ask youngsters what they see that they'd like for themselves (and pass along these ideas to those shopping for them). For wrapping, use the colored comics with red ribbon—letting each shopping team work in a separate room. Kids are proud to have input in shopping rather than just being told what they are giving.

❏ **295.** **GREETING CARD MAGIC.** Don't just toss incoming Christmas cards in a heap. Talk with your family on how best to display them. Here are ideas that your youngsters can carry out with a little basic help from you. Hang a sheet on a wall and then pin the cards to the sheet. Or, place an attractive hook in the ceiling (you'll use it each year) and attach to it about seven wide ribbons reaching to the floor plus about two feet more. Attach a weight to each ribbon and then move it outward so that the ribbons form a conical tree. As cards arrive, pin them to the ribbons.

❏ **296.** **AUTOMOTIVE PICNIC.** Go for a wintry ride to see all the outdoor Christmas decorations in your area. Plan a special car picnic to eat along the way. Let kids make hot cheese-filled biscuits as parents cook skewers of cubed meat, small onions, boiled potatoes, and brussels sprouts. (Wrap these in individual foil packages.) Prepare individual thermos bottles of hot soup. And, of course, provide a small bag of Christmas cookies for each child. Let kids observe the creativity of the displays and see what ideas they'd like to use next year.

❑ **297.** WHAT'S INSIDE CHRISTMAS? Play this word game with children about age eight and up, or you can form teams of an adult with a child. How many words can you make using the letters of CHRISTMAS? For example: mist, cat, this, chair. (You can also play using other holiday words such as mistletoe or fireplace, and other holidays such as Halloween, Independence Day, and Valentine's Day.)

❑ **298.** POPCORN SNOWMEN. Everyone loves marshmallow treats so let kids make these for decorations, table favors, gifts, or family munching. In a large mixing bowl, put fifteen cups of popped popcorn. In a saucepan, melt one stick of butter and twenty ounces of marshmallows, stirring until melted. Pour over popcorn and mix well. Making the balls for the snowmen is easy if you coat your hands with butter and work on wax paper. Make three sizes of balls and stack one on another. Give them pretzel stick arms, also eyes, mouth, and buttons made of colored candies. Add a scarf made of red string licorice or fruit leather. If trimmings aren't sticking, affix them with a little white frosting.

❑ **299.** FAREWELL CIRCLE. At the end of a Christmas party, family reunion, or other large gathering, close the evening with a candlelight song. Use short candles and put a foil collar around them to take care of drips. Form a circle in the dark and let each person light the candle of the one next to him. Then sing a closing song ("Silent Night," "Goodnight Ladies," "Auld Lang Syne"). At the end, go around the circle, each person blowing out his candle until it is dark.

❑ **300.** TRAVELING DINNER. Most everyone knows someone who can't get out, yet would appreciate a home-made holiday dinner. Make it a nice gift by purchasing a large inexpensive tray and letting youngsters make a place mat and favor. When preparing your holiday meal, share generous helpings of everything plus a sampling of Christmas cookies. Place a small wrapped gift on the tray (note cards, aftershave, silk flower, and so forth). Let kids deliver the tray.

❑ **301.** RECYCLING GREETINGS. Sit around on the floor and look at all the cards received. Separate the photo cards and put them on your bulletin board to remind you of those friends. Let each family member choose a card he thinks is most beautiful and then write a note to the sender. Cut illustrations off cards, thread them with yarn, and save for next year's gift tags. Finally, cut in half the picture from twenty cards and shuffle them. See who in the family is fastest at matching the two halves.

❑ **302.** A FAMILY NEW YEAR'S EVE PARTY. Make it a potluck event with guest families bringing foods tied in with the time zones: chowder for the East Coast, salad and corn for the Midwest, a beef dish for the mountain states, and lemon pie for the West Coast. Kids and adults can play the resolution game. Each person writes a resolution including the word "because": "I plan to go on a trip to Paris . . . because I adore French men." Or, "I plan to lose weight . . . because my wife says I'm starting to resemble Santa." Collect the resolutions and cut them in half just before the word "because." Then, put the halves in separate bowls. Each person takes a turn drawing one from each bowl and then reading them together as a unique and often humorous sentence.

❑ **303.** END OF THE YEAR STORY. Each January, start a very simple diary of family highlights in a small notebook kept at the dinner table. Note two or three highlights each month, for example: January 5—snow is two-feet deep; February—Molly is second in speech contest, Dad gets a new office; March—Grandpa visits. Then, as the year ends, make a final December entry, perhaps what you'll do New Year's Eve. Then on New Year's Day, read it together and marvel at all the accomplishments of the previous year.

❑ **304.** **POLAR PICNIC.** Let kids gather the trappings for an indoor winter picnic on the living room floor: ice chest, thermos, paper plates, checkered tablecloth, and a big blanket. Everyone should wear shorts and sunglasses. Tasty food can be prepared with kid-help: hot dogs, hamburgers, fried chicken with side dishes of potato salad, cole slaw, or fruit salad, and apple pie. Fill the thermos bottles with pink lemonade. To complete the theme, toss rubber horseshoes, have indoor relays, and an obstacle race.

❑ **305.** **LOVE LETTERS.** A love letter from one family member to another makes a novel Valentine's Day gift. Provide kids with special paper and help them construct a simple sincere letter. There are six parts. *(1) Place and date in the upper right corner might say:* "Written while watching you play," or "written while sitting by the fire." The date can also be whimsical: "February—St. Valentine's month" or "Ten days before THE day." *(2) The salutation.* This can be more sentimental than just "Dear Max." How about: "Dear Marvelous Max," or "To my first precious child," or "To someone who changed my life." *(3) The first sentence.* Share a reason for writing: "I know you'll get lots of silly Valentines, but this is a serious one." Or, "Sometimes I don't tell you how much you mean to me." *(4) Give an example of something that happened between the two of you:* how a youngster tidied the kitchen when you were tired. Or something a person said you'll always remember— whatever links you together. *(5) The reiteration.* Say it again: "I'll always love you." "You've made me happy." "I'm glad you're my kid." *(6) The close and signature.* Get poetic: "You're forever-lovin' Mom." "Your number one fan, Dad." "Still in love after twenty years." A few stickers, an envelope filled with glitter and sprayed with after-shave, and you've got a real love letter!

❑ **306.** GIVE A HAND TO GRANDMA. Little kids can make Valentine cards by tracing around their hands with red markers on white paper. A parent can draw a large heart around the hand print. Mount the paper on cardboard and put the child's name and year on it. Grandmas will save these each year, seeing how the hand prints get larger.

❑ **307.** SECOND CHRISTMAS. Keep the spirit of the holidays alive. Celebrate again in February or March when spirits need lifting. Enlist kid-help to plan a festive one-day event, complete with a few decorations and an inexpensive gift for each person. Stuff a turkey and teach kids how to carve. Play holiday music as you eat Christmas cookies.

❑ **308.** LEAP DAY. Every four years you get an extra day—February 29. Make it unique by discussing with the family something special to do. Encourage your child's school to have a special Leap Day discussion on how to make the time at school better and safer. At home, suspend most rules and routines. Don't cook. Put bowls of chili in the refrigerator for family members to heat and eat when they please. Place a bowl of fruit on the counter along with crackers and cheese and a plate of cookies or brownies.

# FOUR
# AFTER SCHOOL FUN

SECTION 1: GOOD SPORTS

SECTION 2: EXTRACURRICULAR, NOT EXTRA STRES

# SECTION 1: GOOD SPORTS

❑ **309.** NO EXCUSES. Living in a small apartment, the lateness of the hour, no one to exercise with—those are just excuses that can be overcome. Get a chinning bar and install it in a doorway so that the family can always enjoy a healthy stretch. Before kids' bedtimes, flip off the TV and do somersaults, handstands, and jumping jacks in the living room or hall. Have hand weights for all to use and get an aerobics video (suitable for kids and parents) as "someone" to exercise with.

❑ **310.** THE TERM GAME. See who in the family can explain the meaning of these sports terms: balk, free throw, bunker, cast, slalom, sinker, double axel, pirouette, left hook, eight ball, audible, Fosbury flop, mogul, formula one, wedge, touchback, spike, lure, suicide squeeze, and forehand drive. Could anyone identify all twenty?

❑ **311.** GO FOR THE GOAL. In a large yard, make a playing field about twenty by fifty feet with a chalk goal at each end. Play like a regular soccer game but make the rule that for goal attempts the ball must enter the goal area on the ground. The first team with five goals wins.

❑ **312.** JOIN UP. Membership in a "Y," sports club or gymnasium will encourage your family to be more active. Ask friends about facilities they enjoy. Visit them with your youngsters. See which appeals to the majority. Then join up and vow to really get your money's worth.

❑ **313.** SPORTS NIGHT. If you have trouble finding time to get out to walk daily or play tennis, set aside one night a week for an hour of active sports with the family. Write it clearly on the calendar so that everyone will take part. It can be going to your gym or club, or it can be fun in your own backyard (playing catch or doing tricks on the jungle gym) or in your driveway (shooting hoops or hitting balls against the garage door) or walking, jogging, skating, or cycling around the neighborhood.

❑ **314.** THE FAMILY THAT PLAYS TOGETHER. As kids get older, investigate the many "togetherness" options available in the sports field so the family can enjoy active time together. The top rated all-family sports are: bowling, in-line skating, mountain biking, tennis, and horseback riding. Talk with youngsters about going water rafting together, or taking golf lessons. These joint activities can be excellent bonding experiences.

❑ **315.** SPORTS CHALLENGE. Issue an invitation to another family with youngsters of similar ages to yours. Divide into fair teams but not along family lines. Let each team create a name for themselves (Mason Street Monsters, Awesome Olympians, and so forth) and select a team captain. Plan six to eight events in keeping with kids' ages. Some might be: around-the-house team relay, dodge ball, croquet, shooting baskets (have a ladder for short kids), obstacle race, or rope climb. Play in the morning, serve hot dogs and lemonade for lunch, and then relax in the shade.

❑ **316.** SOCCER BALL STEALING. Make two teams of two. One team stands in the center of a double chalk circle (two rings, two feet apart) with the other team between the chalk circles. These players pass the ball between themselves while staying between the chalk lines. The two in the center try to reach out and steal it. With a stopwatch, determine the pair who can steal it the fastest.

❑ **317.** EASY FISHING. Take kids to a trout farm or other fishing farm and let them see what it's like to catch a fish. Teach them how to bait a hook, cast, reel in the fish, remove the hook, even clean the fish. If they aren't turned off by this process, take them out for a real fishing trip and afterward, teach kids how to cook the catch.

❑ **318.** BACKYARD VOLLEYBALL. Of course there are official rules, but you don't have to heed them for backyard volleyball as long as the game is fair. All you need to start is a rope between two trees and a ball. Set the rope a suitable height for the players. You may eventually graduate to a net and even take the game to the beach for sandy fun.

❑ **319.** INTRODUCING TENNIS. Draw a chalk line on the driveway about fifteen feet from and parallel to the garage door. With racket and ball, play a game with your youngster, taking turns hitting the ball to the door and returning it. Then move the line back ten feet more and show the backhand stroke and how to serve. When your youngster has some confidence, take her to the park for a real game.

❑ **320.** OKAY CROQUET. While backyard croquet may not flex many muscles, it does teach strategy and helps to perfect aim. It's a great after-supper all-family game in the summer. If children are young, make it just a two-ball game with a parent teamed with a child.

❑ **321.** FORE! You can't play golf until you can connect with the ball. Start by taking the family to a driving range at a time when it isn't too busy and you can all be next to one another. Show how to hold the club, swing, follow through, and of course "keep your eye on the ball." When a youngster gets a good feel for the swing and is consistent with his aim (and doesn't keep missing the ball), enjoy golf at a par three course. For truly interested beginners, buy used clubs at a sports store. Golf is no longer an elitist game and it's good exercise.

❑ **322.** MINIATURE GOLF. While this game is mostly for fun, it does have value in teaching putting skill. Make teams of an adult or teen with a younger child so that everyone has a chance to win. Miniature golf courses are often part of fun centers that also feature batting cages, bumper boats, and video arcades. So, if you go, take along lots of quarters!

❑ **323.** CUSTOM SPORTS GIFT. When there's a golfer in the family, let kids customize golf balls as a special occasion gift. Purchase a package of balls and a bag of tees. Next, cover the work surface with newspaper and decorate the balls with permanent marking pens, adding names, pictures, and short encouraging lines. Then, go to work on the tees, adding colorful stripes to them.

❑ **324.** HOME BATTING CAGE. Many recreation areas have a batting cage that lets players safely hit balls. You can make one in your own backyard by purchasing a large amount of inexpensive fish netting and hanging it from trees to form a barrier for balls. And, when parents are busy, it is a good one-person activity.

❑ **325.** ICE RINK. Flood and freeze part of your backyard as an ice rink. With kid-help, shovel snow into a barrier around an area and then use a hose to fill it. Do this on a calm night so that the ice freezes smoothly. This also works on a vacant lot with neighbors pitching in to do the work.

❑ **326.** OUR TEAM. Choose a spectator sport that's of interest to the entire family (football, baseball, soccer, basketball) and attend some games. Read the daily newspaper columns that detail the team's successes or failures. Get to know the players. Take an interest in trades. Enjoy a game via TV or radio so as to keep up-to-date every day. At a sports shop, purchase a team shirt or cap for each family member.

❑ **327.** TWIRL THAT TOWEL. The newest sign of enthusiasm by sports spectators is towel waving. At a sports event when there is an occasion to celebrate, it is waved high and twisted in the air. There's no need to buy a costly team logo towel for this occasion. With youngsters, select older hand towels and dye them the team color. Make a sufficient number so that they can share them at the game with their friends.

❑ **328.** TRIATHLON. Athletic activity within the family should promote good sportsmanship and personal achievement as opposed to mere competition. A family triathlon is fun and can accommodate kids of varying ages. Start on bikes, riding in a safe area to a predetermined destination where there is a red ribbon for each to claim and return home. (Young children can be given a head start.) Participants go immediately to event number two, which is the obstacle course: climbing through a tube or box, up a rope, and then running around the outside of the house to a table. On the table is event number three: guzzling a can of pop or juice.

## BICYCLE EXERCISE—
## WITH HELMETS OF COURSE!

❑ **329.** BICYCLE RELAY. Divide cyclers into teams of two. For a flag relay, make a wide straight course of at least 100 feet with a start and finish line. Place a team member at each end, standing next to his bike. Give the rider at the start line a "flag" (handkerchief or colorful piece of fabric). At "Go," she starts for the opposite end. As she crosses the line, she hands the flag to her teammate who then mounts and rides back. The first one to across the line is the winner.

❑ **330.** BARREL RACING. You may not have barrels or cones, but find good-sized objects such as cardboard boxes and place them on your race course, close enough together that it takes skill to cycle around each one. With a stopwatch, make it a race against the clock.

❑ **331.** CURVY CYCLING. This competition is for teen cyclers—wearing helmets and knee pads. Make a race course with start and finish lines. Using chalk, draw two parallel curving lines the length of the course. Being timed with a stopwatch, each participant tries to see how quickly she can negotiate the curvy course. You can also make a race course with obstacles to cycle around or over: crumpled newspaper, cones, pails of water, a hose placed across the course, or a series of boxes.

❑ **332.** RIDE AND TIE. This is somewhat like the famous races combining walkers and horseback riders. You'll need teams of two and one bike for each team. Plan a course about two miles in length in an uncongested part of town. You'll need some adults to monitor six trees or poles along the route that are tied with a red ribbon. Each team begins at the starting line, one walking, one riding. When the first ribboned tree is reached by the rider, he leaves the bike and starts walking in the direction of the next tree. Soon the walker arrives, picks up the bike and rides on to the next marker where they trade again. Win or lose, it's very good exercise.

# SECTION 2: EXTRACURRICULAR, NOT EXTRA STRESS

Certainly we want the best of everything for our youngsters—but don't give it to them all at one time. Too often, parents plan an after-school schedule for kids that fills in every moment until dinner, and sometimes even after. School, coupled with sports and other organized activities, can exhaust a child and stress a parent. Plan together how to spend the free time—with emphasis on the word "free." For a happy balance, try these ideas.

❑ **333.** GROUPS ARE GOOD. Extracurricular activities bring social, physical, and emotional benefits for most every child. And, they're beneficial for an only child or an overlooked child from a large family. Discuss with your youngster what she hopes to attain by being part of a group. Being on a losing team teaches the importance of good sportsmanship, a desire to try harder, and grace in defeat. Being on a winning team teaches good sportsmanship, team spirit, the reward of diligence, and generosity in victory. Setting up a camping tent teaches ingenuity, self-sufficiency, and the ability to follow directions. Being the treasurer of a group teaches math and honesty. Being the president teaches leadership and humility. Not being an officer teaches how to follow and how be a team player. Earning badges or beads teaches the feeling of achievement and the willingness to investigate a spectrum of subjects. Playing in a recital teaches memorization and poise. Training a horse teaches precision and patience as well as care for an animal. Unless you plan to let your child grow up to be a hermit, she'll need to know how to work effectively with others. A group activity can be a useful microcosm of society that teaches valuable character traits while expanding her knowledge base. So, in choosing activities, encourage one that especially involves interaction with others.

❑ **334.** NO PRESSURE DECISION. You and your youngster know the time needed for homework, leisure, family activities, and sleep. And you certainly know better than coaches and club leaders whose job it is to encourage participation. Each autumn have a family discussion as to which extracurricular activities are really important. Consider the time commitment, the cost (uniforms, instruments, costumes, dues, excursions, and equipment) as well as the benefits (fun, education, physical activity, new skills). Only then, make your decisions.

❑ **335.** A DUO COMMITMENT. Most extracurricular activities require commitment from both parent and child. Consider this before you sign up. Is the parent committed to being supportive: attending events, arranging transportation, providing funds? Is the child committed to a time period such as the entire school year or at least a semester? Since benefits aren't always immediately apparent, establish the concept of giving the activity a fair try (a minimum of three or four months) and then deciding whether to continue. A team may seem exciting when the uniform comes, but rather boring a few months later. Club friendships can take time to flourish. So, before joining up, fully discuss the youngster's commitment required by the organizers of the activity, as well as the commitment required of you as parent.

❑ **336.** HOW MANY ACTIVITIES? Having an organized activity every day is actually harmful for a child. Certainly there are special times when there may be extra practices, but a life of solid structure and relentless routine can stifle creative and spontaneous thinking and play. With your youngster, go over the possible activities for an unstructured day: backyard play, play with friends, play with a pet, reading by the fire, working on a craft. Two or three days a week of organized activities provide a good balance. If both parents work, boys' and girls' clubs offer a safe place for after school play (unstructured time) and organized activities (structured time).

❑ **337.** NOT FOR BABIES. While three-year-old ballerinas and soccer players look cute, wait until age five before starting most group lessons and sports. Don't let a child start too early and get burned out on an activity he might really enjoy later. Also, pushing a child into physical and social situations too soon can be physically and emotionally damaging. Although you will consult with your child, you are still in charge and just because the neighbors have a toddler violinist doesn't mean you have to have one, too! Learn to say "no" when life and activities are just time-fillers. Some activities are grand at age four, others at age fourteen.

❑ **338.** WHO PAYS? For many activities there will be an initial charge for membership or dues plus the cost of equipment, books, craft supplies, or instrument rental. Even if parents can afford to pay all of the cost, let a youngster contribute a small amount, such as ten percent. When a kid has an investment in the activity, she is more apt to work to get the most for the money.

❑ **339.** PRACTICE NOW! That can be one of the most dreaded phrases of childhood. So, when considering lessons or teams, be up front as to the time commitment for practice. Tedious batting practices, hours on the piano bench, or the work involved in earning badges are considerations when choosing an activity. Since you as parent take care of the costs and transportation, the child should be willing to do the needed practice. List the pros and cons of an activity, with practice time definitely a part of the decision. Before a youngster can hit a home run or have a lead in *The Nutcracker*, there are hours of learning involved. Don't let activities become unpleasant nagging sessions. If practice is to be at home, set a minimum time (like 30 minutes) and let a timer be the watchdog.

❏ **340. RAINBOW OF CHOICES.** The decision won't be just between soccer and Scouts. Consider all the options, taking into consideration the activities that close buddies enjoy. Consider banjo lessons, crafts classes, reading classes, gymnastics, magic clubs, swim lessons, computer clubs, foreign language clubs, and rocketry groups, even the unusual such as harp lessons and mountain climbing lessons. Remember, that there is always next year for those activities not chosen this time. And unless you have a child prodigy, you don't need to insist on piano lessons for ten continuous years. Tell your child, "You won't know if you like something until you really try it." But remember, don't force a child into an activity just because that was your own childhood heart's desire.

❏ **341. ARE YOU A FREELOADER?** At-home parents often complain that working parents are freeloaders when it comes to helping with kids' activities. The jobs of chauffeur, coach, chaperone, scout leader, cookie-drive chairperson, costumes maker, and such are difficult to fairly divide. When a child is considering an activity, talk about your possible input. If you work outside the home, talk with the leaders so that they know you are willing to help in some tangible ways such as Saturday activities, providing food, making costumes or scenery on weekends. Don't just beg off entirely. This puts your child in an uncomfortable position, and there are many benefits to your really striving to take part when possible.

❏ **342. CHEERING SECTION.** Don't be among the missing when your daughter hits a home run or your son makes first class in scouting. Be sure the whole family takes part in the cheering section!

❏ **343.** TIME ALONE. Spontaneity and unplanned fun are parts of the fleeting joys of childhood. Educators and psychologists worry that rigid routines are producing passive robots and pressured kids. Give a youngster time to explore on his own in a safe environment. Don't permit your child to become a puppet with others pulling the strings. Be sure your weekly plan makes time for creative aloneness. Don't let your child live with a daily schedule of school, organized activity, dinner, homework, chores, television, and bedtime. Let some of the adventure of the weekend days filter into the weekdays. Lessons learned when alone include how to make do with what is at hand, how to combine several games and toys into a greater game, how to repair what is broken, how to be content without outside stimulation. Diligence, patience, and creativity are exercised in time alone, and you may hear those wonderful words "I did it myself!"

❏ **344.** GOOFING OFF. A youngster's free time diminishes with every passing year. Time to "goof off" is soon gone. Encourage totally zany activities and safe adventures at your house. Not everything has to be a grand learning experience. At the end of the week, ask kids what was the craziest thing that happened during the week. You may be surprised at some of the responses.

# FIVE
## GOING PLACES

# SECTION 1: THANK GOODNESS IT'S FRIDAY

At last the weekend has arrived bringing free time for the family. Still, there is so much to do! Of course there are errands to run and home projects to tackle, but the real focus of the weekend is family. (Make quick work of work by reading chapter 11—"Can Chores Be Fun?") Because your home is probably your biggest investment, give it good use by planning some events right there. And, you'll also want to take the time to enjoy family-oriented excursions. Here are ideas for both.

❑ **345. NOT FROM ABOVE.** Each Monday (sometimes the gloomiest day of the week), talk about the excursion possibilities for the next weekend. Don't just announce (as if you are king) what the family will do. Listen to suggestions—even take a vote if needed. Keep a list of places to visit and add to it regularly. And ask other families how they spend their weekend togetherness times.

❑ **346. FRIEND-FOR-A-DAY.** Acquaintances can become friends when they spend time together. Plan ahead with your youngster for him to have a Saturday with just one friend. Start that day right after chore time. Talk about possible things to do: cycling, making a tree house, knapsack lunch, an art or craft project, taking photos, game time, dinner with the family, listening to music, and stopping for ice-cream cones when taking the friend home.

❑ **347. OVERDONE OVERNIGHTS.** The frequency of "overnights" is giving them overexposure. They should be a *special* treat and parents and kids should work out a plan for them in advance (even though it may not be exactly followed). Depending on ages, from one to six friends can be invited. Begin the event with a make-your-own-pizza supper, followed by a vigorous outdoor activity such as volleyball. Then it's time for a chosen-in-advance video and dessert. Roll out the sleeping bags and turn on the music for conversation and pillow fights. In the morning, kids do a total cleanup while parents make stacks of pancakes. Then, don't let the event drag on—send the sleepyheads home.

❑ **348.** THE WAKE-UP PARTY. This variation on a slumber party starts at 7:00 in the morning when guests arrive in their pj's, carrying their pillows. Trays with pancakes, sausage, and juice are ready to take to the bedroom, plus a gooey coffee cake for midmorning. Activities include hair style and manicure changes, a pj fashion show, and pillow decorating. Using white pillowcases and indelible marking pens, each guest decorates a case, then everyone writes messages on the others' pillowcases.

❑ **349.** SUNRISE EXCURSION. Even though it may be tradition to sleep late on Saturday, go on a sunrise excursion. Plan to be on a hilltop facing east at dawn and take binoculars and breakfast with you. Get your lawn chairs in place so that you see the first glow before the curve of the sun explodes on the horizon. Have a guessing game as to how many minutes it will take for the full circle of the sun to appear. Serve a sunrise breakfast of round foods in yellow and orange colors: slices of oranges, bagels with cream cheese, granola cookies, plus lemonade to drink. On the ride home, let kids draw pictures of the sunrise or see how many words they can think of that rhyme with the word "sun."

❑ **350.** AMATEUR ARCHITECTS. Check out a book from the library about different styles of architecture. On neighborhood walks, teach kids to look for the different styles: ranch, Georgian, colonial, southwest, and so forth, indicating the special features of each. Note the different kinds of roofs—both the style (gable, mansard, hip) and the material used. Then look up houses/homes in the encyclopedia to see examples of residences in various parts of the world.

❑ **351.** HOUSE SNOOPING. Unless there is a "No Trespassing" sign posted most owners don't object to neighbors walking through a house under construction. If the owners are on hand, welcome them to the neighborhood and ask permission to look around. With youngsters (not toddlers) and after warnings about open stairways and nails, visit a newly framed house. Determine the floor plan for the house and how it would suit your family. See the views from the various rooms. Decide which bedrooms are for kids and which are for parents.

❑ **352.** YEAR-ROUND CHRISTMAS. Many shopping plazas feature year-round Christmas stores. Visit one as a family and pick out just one new decoration for the coming holiday. Older youngsters and adults can find good ideas for handmade ornaments and might then get an early start on their projects.

❑ **353.** TO THE TOY STORE. What more exciting place for a child than the toy store. But it doesn't have to be a "Buy this for me!" occasion. So that you aren't panicked when birthday party invitations come, keep on hand one or two gifts. Let your child pick out toys she herself would like—that way you know the gifts will be winners. Also, in advance of a birthday or Christmas, have your youngster show you toys and crafts she would like. This way you can note brand names and prices for your own information or passing on to a relative or friend.

❑ **354.** SIMILARITIES, DIFFERENCES. Visit a church different from your own. (Youngsters may go to Sunday school, parents to church.) Stay for the fellowship time afterward. On the way home, see how many similarities there are between this church and the one you attend (prayers, hymns, Bible stories). Then see how many physical differences there are (architecture inside and out, vestments of those officiating, traditions such as kneeling). As you visit other churches, note the wide variety in the services but especially the things you have in common.

❑ **355.** WISE SHOPPERS. Involve kids in reading product labels at the market. Show them how to find calories as well as fat, sugar, and salt content. When choosing a snack, let them compare products and serving sizes to determine what a normal amount might be. When home, let youngsters package their snacks in serving-sized plastic bags so that the entire amount isn't eaten at one sitting.

❑ **356.** MUNCHING MESSENGERS. Let gradeschoolers help speed your grocery trip. Give them two or three items to find and bring back to you for approval. Eventually you will be able to divide your list in half. Another day, ask each assistant shopper to find one new item that would be tasty to try (if it fits the budget). As a reward for good help, buy a bag of munchies for your messengers to enjoy on the way home.

❑ **357.** GOING VISITING. Going visiting was a welcome diversion in decades past, one worthy of revival. Let kids take part in planning a social visit. First, select someone who would enjoy a one hour get-together. Next, make the call and say that you'll be bringing refreshments. Let kids make cookies or a cake and punch. Then, talk about what one does during such a visit, other than eating. What can a youngster share in conversation? Is there something he can bring along to show? Would he like to take a photo? Also describe the end of the visit—thanking the person and saying good-bye.

❑ **358.** WAITING ROOM WAITS. Most waiting rooms have truly ancient and boring magazines for kids. In your car, keep a portfolio of paper games (like follow-the-dots), stickers, paper and crayons, crossword puzzles, small books, and other interesting activities so that waiting time isn't a total waste. These can also be used in the car when waiting at the park for the ball game to end or waiting at the train station for the commuter.

❑ **359.** EXCURSION CHAIRPERSON. Most newspapers have a special section devoted to weekend activities: concerts, movies, special events. Each week, one youngster can peruse the section and come up with a good suggestion. (If it turns out to be a dud, don't grumble, there's always next week.) The chairperson plans when to leave, the route, car seating arrangement, food to take along, and amusements for travel time.

❑ **360. CULTURE? NO WAY!** Don't be afraid of introducing kids to museums and concerts. At least once a month, select an enriching excursion. (See chapter 6 for ideas.) Advance preparation (listening to a symphony recording, reading about famous painters) will make all the difference in enjoying the event.

❑ **361. EVENTS THAT COST.** When you have to pay for tickets (to the ball game, circus, ice show), make the selection far enough ahead so that you can read up in advance. Check the team statistics, learn the players names and positions, read the review of the circus and talk about all the varied acts. Ask, "If you could be in the circus, which act would you choose?" Look up ice skating in the encyclopedia and read the descriptions of all the special moves. If the ice show has a specific story, go to the library and read a book about the plot.

❑ **362. ANCIENT BASKETS.** Gather long grasses from a prairie or other untended roadside area. While they are still pliable, show a child how to weave them into a mat or basket. Keep this handwork on the dining table and watch how it dries and changes in color. Use the mat as a coaster and use the basket (with a jar inside) to hold wildflowers.

❑ **363. YUCKY SNAKES.** While you may not want reptiles as pets, youngsters need to know which ones to steer clear of and which ones aren't harmful. Visit a pet store and look at more than just the puppies and fish. Often the store owner will be willing to remove a snake from its habitat and show how it can be held and stroked. Since snakes are the most feared of all reptiles, this demonstration diffuses some anxiety. Get to know the snakes indigenous to your area (the library will have a good picture book) and discuss the proper action should one turn up in your yard or on the trail.

❏ **364.** HOT AIR.   Hot air balloon companies offer fabulous and expensive rides into the sky. But, it also can be fun to just observe the takeoffs and landings. Look in the yellow pages for hot air balloon companies. Call and find out where and when they will be taking off (usually early morning or late afternoon). Go and observe the noisy excitement. Kids may want to start saving for such a trip.

❏ **365.** FARMER-IN-THE-DELL.   Most areas have an open-to-the-public farm, a place for hands-on petting or the picking of fruit or pumpkins. Go to see the animals, then pick apples or cherries, and when back home, enjoy a family project of making a pie or two. The eating is extra special when you've made it yourself!

❏ **366.** RINK-WATCHING.   Even the youngest kids enjoy a visit to a roller skating or ice skating rink. When merely rink-watching, pick out one person to especially watch—see when he slips up or where she makes a good move. Or, observe an ice hockey team in practice. When kids are old enough to try their own skills, make skating a special treat. At the same time, you may rediscover your own skating skill.

❏ **367.** VEGGIE FARM.   Ask the manager of a vegetable store to tell you where you can see locally grown vegetables. Call ahead for permission to visit to see how many different veggies are grown at one farm. Find out who in your family has eaten the most different vegetables. Buy seeds and grow some vegetables that your kids like. Let them do the planting, weeding, harvesting, and preparing. Lettuce, tomatoes, carrots, corn, and radishes are favorites, but also plant a vegetable not as familiar to your family.

❏ **368.** FABULOUS FIFTY CENTS.   Visit a garage sale or thrift shop. Give each youngster fifty cents and turn him loose to locate a useful or fun bargain. Display the items at dinner that night, and then put the fabulous finds into use.

❑ **369.** LLAMA NOT LAMA.   While a lama is a priest in Lamaism (a form of Buddhism), the llama (pronounced the same) is a South American animal related to the camel but without a hump. It is kept as a beast of burden and valued for its soft woolly hair. Llama farms often welcome visitors, and youngsters enjoy seeing these unique animals that are also kept as pets. You can find a llama farm in the yellow pages of the phone book. Call first before visiting.

❑ **370.** OSTRICHES AND EGGS.   While you're tracking down unusual animals, consider a visit to an ostrich farm, a newer and profitable business. These nonflying birds, originally from Africa, can run really fast. Be sure to see the eggs and young birds and find out how they are marketed. On the way home, talk about the saying that ostriches hide their heads in the sand and thus think they are invisible. That's why a person who doesn't face facts is said to be an ostrich.

❑ **371.** A IS FOR ASIA AND ABACUS.   Many cities have stores and markets featuring Asian products. Visit one and admire the beautiful porcelain items. View the unusual foods and find something you've never seen before. Often there is a department with toys and clothing, too. But one thing not to miss is the abacus. This ancient Chinese device, also used in early Greece and Rome, can be used to add, subtract, multiply, divide, and calculate square roots and cube roots. Consisting of rows of beads in a frame, it has been adapted to teach arithmetic to blind children. Ask for a demonstration and consider buying one just in case your adding machine or calculator malfunctions! It also makes an interesting conversation piece when left on a living room table.

❑ **372.** SWITCHING YARD.   At many railway yards, you'll find a fascinating area called a switching yard. Call in advance and you'll be welcome to see how freight is handled, tracked, and how the freight cars are sorted and made into trains. Read the variety of names on the freight cars. See how many different uses they have (hauling grain, oil, animals, and so forth).

❏ **373. SMALL AIRPORT.** Take a picnic for eating on the lawn of small airport. Watch the variety of planes parked, taking off, and landing. Go in the building and see all you can see—some small airports have an observation area where you can clearly see the planes and even hear the control tower talking with pilots.

❏ **374. THE LISTENING HIKE.** All family hikes don't need to be through the woods or up the mountain. Plan one for a relatively flat area with some open fields. Sit under a tree for lunch. Then, suggest a listening time: everyone stretches out and shuts eyes. Identify sounds such as birds, planes, crickets, dogs, cars, streams. Make up a story about some of the sounds: "Once upon a time, there was a hummingbird who wanted to be a jet plane. . . ." Let each one suggest a sentence or two as the story develops.

❏ **375. MOO TO YOU.** Many dairies welcome visitors. See how cows are fed, washed, and milked. Find out how milk gets from the dairy to the grocery store without spoiling. See how many different products the dairy produces. If there is a sales room, take home a dairy product you may not have tried before.

❏ **376. CARE BEAR SURPRISE.** When hiking with the family, younger kids sometimes become grumpy and tired. To keep them excited about the destination, explain that care bears live in the clouds and keep their eyes on the hikers. And, they reward them with a small candy bar or little toy when they reach the top of the hill. Of course, the surprise has to be at the hilltop but you can manage this by letting one parent go ahead, supposedly to scout out the area, leave the surprise, and then help look for it when all arrive.

❑ **377.** WANNA BEE?   Look up beekeeping in the yellow pages and call to see if you can visit a bee farm. Learn how honey is made and how bees toil from sunrise to sunset (hence the term "busy as a bee"). You will see the bees' pollen baskets and learn how some bees have the jobs of caring for young bees while others clean the cells of the comb. There are over 300 honey varieties so try a new one for eating on toast, in hot milk, or mixed with chocolate sauce.

❑ **378.** ON THE ROAD AGAIN.   On the outskirts of most towns is a truck stop. Go there for lunch one day—the grub will probably be hearty and good since eating well is a highlight of a trucker's day. See the facilities for resting and showering. Look at the big rigs and see how many have self-contained sleeping units. Do you see any women drivers? A trucker may actually talk to you and tell you about the load being hauled.

# SECTION 2: EATING OUT WITH STYLE

❑ **379.** GRACIOUS EATING WITH ONE COMPLAINT. Since eating out is more expensive than eating at home, and it should be viewed as a treat for the entire family, don't rush through the meal and don't permit kids to spoil it with whining and arguing. In advance, tell them that going to a restaurant is special and requires their best manners. Also announce that they only get one complaint ("He kicked me" or "I don't like this food") and after that it will be ten minutes earlier to bed for each complaint. That usually reminds kids to solve problems amicably.

❑ **380.** NO WASTE.   When going to a restaurant, insist that youngsters select some nutritious elements in the meal. With a hamburger, suggest a salad, rather than fries. Do not ask the question "What do you want?"

rather phrase it "What will you eat?" It's money-saving and food-saving to order kid-sized portions, divide an order, or take home leftovers to eat later.

❑ **381. CULINARY CONVERSATION.** Use these questions that focus on food. What is the specialty of this restaurant? What items on the menu sound tasty yet are nutritious? Is there an entree that no one in the family has ever tried? Looking at the right hand column, what is the most expensive dish on the menu? If we could make this food at home, which item would you choose? Who is the most uniquely dressed person in the restaurant? What is she eating? (Remind kids not to stare.) What do you think her profession is? What do you think our bill will be?

❑ **382. GOURMET VOCABULARY.** See who knows the meaning of strange words on the menu. You can also take along this list of terms for a quiet guessing game while waiting for the food: braised, consomme, bearnaise sauce, prawns, torte, fromage, poisson, linguini, crepe, roulade, knackwurst, mit schlag, bisque, borscht, chateau briand, chutney, Creole, escargot, goulash, mousse, paté, sukiyaki, sushi, sweetbread, tripe, wiener schnitzel, Yorkshire pudding. When back home, you may want to look up the ones that no one knew.

❑ **383. WHAT'S THE TIP?** An easy way to show kids how to figure the correct tip to leave (about 15 percent unless fabulous service) is to double the tax. For example, if the bill is $40 and the tax in your area is 8 percent, you'll see a tax of $3.20 on your bill. Double $3.20 is $6.40, so leaving $6.50 is usually acceptable. This is good math practice for kids.

❑ **384. NOT ALWAYS DINNER.** When you plan to eat out over the weekend, it doesn't have to be dinner. Consider having a hearty breakfast eaten at a restaurant that features things kids like (such as a pancake house). Go to a buffet-style restaurant for lunch. Look at how people pile their plates high with food. See if you can observe wasted food. Have popcorn at a six o'clock movie and then go out for a light supper afterward.

❑ **385.** FOOD SPIES.   If you buy food at a fast-food stop, young children might enjoy eating in the car near the take-out window. They can watch the cars as they pass through and guess what the driver has ordered and see if he immediately starts to eat it. Or, eat inside and see if everything is eaten with fingers and if there are more adults than kids eating. Or, visit a grade school during lunchtime and wander past the rows of tables, observing what's being eaten. At the grocery store, look for folks who eat as they shop.

❑ **386.** FARMERS' MARKET.   Instead of buying lunch, stroll through a farmers' market where the many free samples offered will probably satisfy hunger. Let kids buy something interesting to take home for dinner.

# SECTION 3: TRIPPING ALONG

❑ **387.** GO WITH A PURPOSE.   Travel can be more than just getting away from a busy life and relaxing. See that your family trips combine some education with the fun. For example, if you are going to Yellowstone Park, read up on geysers before leaving. While en route to Philadelphia, have the family read together the Bill of Rights and the Preamble to the Constitution. Before enjoying Disneyland, learn about the cartoon business—yesterday and today. If going fishing, visit a bait shop and ask the salesperson to explain lures and the types of fish they attract. Share the purpose with kids by saying, for example, "We're driving to New Orleans and on the way we're going to listen to the style of music called the blues."

❑ **388.** CONVERSATIONAL CAPS.   Before leaving home, buy a plain white cap or hat for each family member. Take along sturdy thread and needle, and a tube of glue. As you travel, you'll find patches, pins, small figures, decals, and other items that can be affixed. The caps will be conversation pieces along the way and mementos of the trip.

❑ **389.** **LEAVE THE DRIVING TO SOMEONE ELSE.** Families are finding alternatives to expensive travel modes. Buses offer these advantages: the entire family can enjoy gazing out the large windows, the opportunity to walk around in the bus and at rest stops, no traffic jams or getting lost, onboard bathrooms, large comfy seats, bring-along snacks whenever you want them, and sometimes interesting people to talk with. Start with a day trip to a family-oriented destination. You may like bus travel so much that you decide to make a circle tour of the country at a bargain price.

❑ **390.** **MAP IT OUT.** When traveling by car, don't permit map ignorance in your family. On a map showing your town and also your destination, mark the route. Let youngsters take turns being your skilled navigator. A good navigator always knows the mileage to the next town (math), possible educational stops en route (history), highest mountains nearby (geography), and town populations (reading). The navigator also chooses the next rest or meal stop (intelligent analysis).

❑ **391.** **AMUSEMENT CENTER.** Buy an inexpensive shoe bag and attach it to the back of the seat (in front of the kids). Let them choose some items for the many pockets, but you should put in some surprises. Tailor it to the ages of the children and the length of the trip. It's an orderly place for paper and crayons, finger puppets, small cars, doll and doll clothes, the comic section of the Sunday paper, granola bars, sunglasses, a bottle of water, a map, postcards and pen, small puzzles, and games.

❑ **392.** **WHIP OUT THE PROJECT.** A teacher often gives an assignment to write a report about a family trip. This can be a bore to do when back home from the vacation. So, make plans to get the report finished while on the way. Take along the necessary paper, pen, and laptop desk, and let the entire family give input for the report. It can also be used as a permanent travel journal.

❑ **393.** GET SMART WHILE SITTING.  Whether on plane, train, bus, or in the car, there are bound to be some dull stretches with nothing going on. One of the best brain teasers is the book *Brain Quest for the Car* by Gold (New York: Workman Publishing, 1995). It is ideal for gradeschoolers and older kids and their parents. It contains over 1000 interesting questions and answers about Americana, plus score pad and pencil. These are not trivial, but worthwhile facts.

❑ **394.** SEDENTARY SCAVENGER HUNT.  Before leaving on your trip, work together on a computer to make a list of things you'll see along the way. List types of buildings (factories, barns, skyscrapers), makes of vehicles, products advertised on signs, states on license plates, types of animals, names of department stores and food franchises, and scenic objects such as lakes, picket fences, and snow-capped mountains. Make several copies for each person so you can play several times. The object is to be the first to find and check off each item on the list. You'll hear "Cow on the right" and "Jeep in front of us." No, the driver may NOT play!

❑ **395.** INDELIBLE MEMORIES.  Provide a T-shirt for each family member and also a piece of heavy cardboard that fits inside (to use as a portable desk). Take along a set of indelible markers. During the trip—in the car, at the picnic table, before bed—each person draws something connected with a good event that day. It could be a train ride, a deer, a snowy mountaintop, a banana split, a clown. Gradually the shirt will become a hand-created memento of good times.

❑ **396.** NOTABLE NOTEBOOK.  In advance of the trip, help each youngster make a special game notebook. You'll need a three-ring notebook with vinyl page protectors, some zip-lock type plastic bags, dry-erase markers, and a small cloth. First search through magazines, coloring books, and activity books for interesting pages to color, bingo games, follow-the-dot pictures, mazes, and workbook pages. Put each of these in a page protector so that the game can be played, then wiped clean, and played again. At the front of the book, insert through the rings a bag with the markers and cloth so that these essentials stay with the notebook. Put in some blank pages for writing letters or taking notes and for other pencil and paper games.

❏ **397.** **THE STORY AROUND YOU.** While riding in the car, tell a story round-robin style. (Each person adds a sentence in each round.) However, the sentence must include something the storyteller can see. First person: "I was sitting in the car when one of my shoes suddenly spoke to me!" Second person: "I was so surprised, I almost drove into a road sign." Next person: "But, I was saved by a cow I saw dancing by the fence." And so the story goes, round and round.

❏ **398.** **ADJECTIVE STORY.** Make one copy of this story before leaving on a trip. Without revealing the story line to the family, ask each person to suggest an adjective (descriptive word) that you fill in, in the order given. Then read aloud for lots of laughs. Adapt this story to your family and your own trip.

**The True Story About Our _____ Trip**

On a _____ day, the _____ (your name) family set out for _____ (destination). In the car were _____ (name), _____ (name), and their_____ parents. Mother drove the _____ car and the others sat around reading _____ books and eating _____ food. Finally they got to their _____ destination. Here they got out of the car. _____ (child's name) said it was a _____ sight. _____ (child's name) thought it was a _____ day. The parents said it was worth all the _____ money that the _____ vacation cost. They all agreed that it was truly a _____ trip.

❑ **399.** DON'T RUSH. Travel doesn't have to be a scramble from place to place. Each day choose a place to sit down and talk. At the Grand Canyon, imagine how explorer John Powell felt in the 1800s as his boat sped down the gorge. In a town, talk about what looks new and what looks old and notice the ages and races and activities of the townsfolk. At a beach, imagine what it would be like to be washed upon the shore after a shipwreck. At the zoo, imagine and describe a conversation between two animals. At an amusement park, decide what new kind of ride you'd like invented.

❑ **400.** TRAVEL CONNECTIONS. Everyone in the family can play this car game consisting of words connected with travel. It starts with the word "car." The next person must come up with a travel word beginning with the last letter in "car." So she might say "restaurant." The next would say "train" and the next might say "nachos." Now when someone uses a word that doesn't seem to have a travel connection, the game stops while he explains: "I plan to eat nachos the next time we stop." And so the game continues with some far-fetched and funny connections.

❑ **401.** TRAVEL COLLAGE. While a scrapbook or photo album can be a good memento of a trip, a travel collage can bring back memories and serve as wall art at the same time. When traveling, save picture brochures, maps, photos, ticket stubs, samples of unusual soil or sand, postcards, travel stickers or decals, and so forth. Back home, buy an inexpensive frame at least 18 x 24 inches in size. On cardboard, paste a map as the background and artistically arrange and glue on top of it all the other mementos of the trip.

❑ **402.** VANITY PLATES. Often while traveling you'll see license plates that have a message in them. See who can find the most unique. And, while looking at plates, keep a list of states shown on them. Count how many states you find on your trip. You can also add up the numbers on the plates of the car just ahead of you. See who can find the biggest total on one plate.

❑ **403.** HOME VACATION.   Plan a vacation near home, saving the cost of travel to a faraway place and thus the cost of overnight accommodations. Make a list of interesting places within a hundred mile radius of your house. Let kids vote on which destinations they might like. Then plan together the complete vacation day: on the road an hour before breakfast, midmorning arrival at the destination for activities and lunch, late afternoon departure with dinner on the way home. Let kids take turns planning a home vacation and choosing one friend to take along.

# SIX

# IS YOUR KID CULTURED?

SECTION 1: CULTURE WITH A CAPITAL "M" FOR MANNERS

SECTION 2: ART FROM THE HEART

SECTION 3: ALL THE WORLD'S A STAGE . . .

SECTION 4: MEET YOU AT THE MOVIES

SECTION 5: TAKE NOTE OF MUSIC

SECTION 6: DANCING—WITH TWO LEFT FEET

SECTION 7: A WAY WITH WORDS

# SECTION 1: CULTURE WITH A CAPITAL "M" FOR MANNERS

While manners are now greatly relaxed compared to a few decades ago, there are still some basics every youngster should know that go well beyond "please" and "thank you." Teaching these principles at home will help make good manners automatic when kids are out on their own. And, don't forget to praise the well-mannered child, showing that you value responsible and poised behavior.

❑ **404.** AT THE TABLE. Don't let mealtimes become nagging times. On Monday, choose one aspect of good table manners, explain it, encourage it, and tell the family to be alert to it all week long. The next Monday, talk about how everyone did, and introduce a new idea. See how many of these basic table manners your kids know: starting to eat when all are seated or served (or a parent picks up his fork), keeping elbows off the table, eating with the mouth closed, not talking with food in the mouth, using utensils correctly and knowing which to use, passing common dishes around—not across—the table and asking permission to take some on the way, passing salt and pepper together, coping with a bone or other inedible objects, covering a cough or sneeze, placing utensils at the "four o'clock" angle on the plate when finished, and asking to be excused. Occasionally have a bad manners meal when family members try all the bad manners imaginable. This will be fun, but it will make bad manners so memorable that good manners will become more important.

❑ **405.** NEW FOODS. When children are young, have them try new foods. They can ask for a very small portion when eating out. At home, they can have a "royalty serving" (about two tablespoonsful), which should be eaten. Explain that it is bad manners to make derogatory comments about the taste or appearance of food.

❏ **406.** INTERRUPTIONS. Doorbells and phones ringing can be very disruptive during a meal. Each week assign one youngster to handle these. Unless an emergency, callers should be asked if they can call back or a message should be taken so the call can be returned. Letting the answering machine take the call is another option. If it's kids who are telephoning or ringing the doorbell, encourage your youngsters to tell their friends that the family eats between 6:30 and 7 (or whatever the time) and that they aren't available then.

❏ **407.** FAMILY FRACTIONS. Just how many french fries or how much salad should one take from the serving dish? It's a matter of fractions. For example, if there are four people in your family, the first person may take up to one-fourth, the second person may take one-third of what is left, the third person can take one-half of the remainder, and the last person can have all that is left. Show youngsters how to figure the appropriate amount and they'll never embarrass themselves or cause an argument by taking too much.

❏ **408.** INTRODUCTIONS. Although it's a current fad to call everyone by first names only, insist that your youngster know and use the last names of friends when introducing them to you. As soon as nonfamily members enter your house or car, they should be introduced to a parent. Younger people are introduced to older people: "Chris Smith, I'd like you to meet my dad, Mr. Cooper."

❏ **409.** TWO IMPORTANT WORDS. Teach kids that it's almost impossible to overuse the words "thank you." On some occasions, a thank-you on the spot is sufficient, such as when a youngster stops in at a friend's home and the parent gives him a soft drink. A phone call of thanks is acceptable after a casual meal. However, a party, a planned dinner, or a gift still require a written thank-you.

❏ **410.** NO RESPONSE. Countless gift-givers complain

about kids not responding to gifts received. At age three or so, start the habit of thank-you notes for gifts. Until the child can write, it can be a drawing with the parents lettering "Thank you Aunt Amy" on the paper. But, when a child learns to write, the thank-yous are their own work—perhaps you'll address the envelopes. Teens are expected to write promptly—good practice for when they're on their own.

❏ **411.**  **NO THANKS, NO GIFTS.**  When a parent got tired of nagging her grade school son to write thank-you notes for birthday presents from friends and relatives, she came up with this effective solution. She collected the gifts and was about to put them in a box on a high shelf when her son asked what she was doing. She calmly replied, "These aren't really yours until you've said 'thanks' for them." The son wrote his thank-you notes that very day. Another parent says that he and his son place the opened birthday gifts in the center of the table so he can look at them (but not touch them) until the task is completed.

❏ **412.**  **YOU LOOK PRETTY.**  When kids get compliments, their response is often embarrassment and head-hanging. Encourage kids not to belittle themselves or express shyness, rather, show them how to accept compliments graciously. Help them to respond by practicing these lines: "It's new. Thank you for telling me." "I worked hard on it, so I'm glad you like it." "What a nice thing to say!"

❏ **413.**  **MANNERS AT FRIENDS' HOMES.**  You hope your child is a good guest, and he will be if you talk together about how a guest should act. Ask what he expects of a pal playing at your house—then he'll understand what he should do at his friend's house: never snoop in private places, never touch precious objects, wipe feet when coming inside, ask permission to use the phone, never ask to stay for a meal, help to put away toys and games when finished playing, and say good-bye and thank you when leaving.

❑ **414.** CONTRADICTING AND INTERRUPTING. In family conversations, we're usually so casual that several people are talking at once, or arguing a point. This makes it hard to remember to be more polite in public. Kids should be taught not to monopolize conversation but to give others the opportunity to speak. And, unless it is extremely vital, they should not contradict.

❑ **415.** ENTERTAIN BACK. When your youngster begins to get party invitations and is invited to go on excursions or trips with other families, explain the obligation of "entertaining back." Of course, if your child finds that he doesn't enjoy the company of that person, it can stop there. But, if he wants to continue the friendship, he should remember to return the favor. Continually being entertained by others and accepting invitations without reciprocation is very rude and should be discouraged. There's no need to entertain back in the same manner—a fancy meal at another's house can be paid back with popcorn and a movie.

❑ **416.** SAYING "NO" POLITELY. You are training your youngster to refuse alcohol, cigarettes, drugs and other controlled substances. And, you are teaching her to refuse to take part in cheating, or in shoplifting and other petty crimes. But, also teach her what to do when a group is misbehaving: speeding, trashing, or abusing others. Remind kids to always have at least a quarter on hand so they can call for help, to separate themselves from the mayhem, or to ask you to come and pick them up.

❑ **417.** LET'S DANCE. Some kids seem to have natural rhythm and good moves. Others border on the clumsy side. Start when children are young to teach them to dance. If you don't know current dance steps, ask others to teach them, or get them lessons. There are many occasions in life when knowing how to dance is important, and when a child has this skill, she is much more socially comfortable.

❑ **418.** MANNERS ARE NOT SEX-RELATED. Being male or

female does not excuse youngsters from being kind and caring. Practice these with your youngster: seating someone who may require it, holding a door open for others, offering an arm or a hand to someone, and helping others to get into today's smaller cars.

❑ **419.** CONVERSATIONAL MANNERS. Teach young children to take an interest in others by asking questions—that's the start of good conversation. Show the difference between showing interest and prying. Before a child has dinner with another family, talk about some topics he might share (as well as some things not to be mentioned).

❑ **420.** DON'T REWARD RUDENESS. Impolite habits and unacceptable language are often learned from older siblings or peers who encourage this behavior because they think it is mature or funny. When your child is boorish, don't laugh, but also don't explode since that rewards rudeness with extra attention. Rather, talk to the child (and the older offender if you know who that is) and say that such conduct is offensive, and can be punishable if it continues.

❑ **421.** FORMAL FAMILY DINNER. Every few months, practice all the best manners imaginable by having a formal dinner. Set the table with good china and linens and appropriate silverware. Let family members dress up for the occasion. Serve something special such as turkey, salmon, or beef with all the trimmings. Have sparkling cider for toasts. Eat by candlelight as family members practice their conversational techniques along with good table manners.

# SECTION 2: ART FROM THE HEART

Feel insecure at an art museum? Does modern sculpture look like lumps of clay? Read on for ideas to interest your youngsters in the art world.

# VISIT AN ART MUSEUM

❏ **422. BEFORE GOING TO A MUSEUM.** When youngsters are four or older, it's time to visit a museum. Call in advance to find out about free days, availability of strollers, use of cameras, and places to eat. Take a maximum of three or four kids. First, visit your library and borrow some art books, but don't ponder each page. Let kids look through them at their own pace. Then, announce the date for the excursion, put it on the calendar, and refer to it as a great privilege.

❏ **423. ON THE WAY TO THE MUSEUM.** Talk about colors and what colors are each child's favorite. Ask what artists draw with: crayons? pencils? oil paints? Ask who can remember something from a picture in the art book: a boat? a flower? a child? Explain the four museum rules: no running, no shouting, no touching the art work, and have fun.

❏ **424. BEFORE ENTERING THE MUSEUM.** Sit on the steps for a snack. Explain that the paintings are very precious so there will be guards to protect them and also to help people. As you enter the museum, look at the architecture, say hello to the person on duty at the door. Then, to save backtracking, visit the restrooms now.

❏ **425. SELECTING "MY PAINTING."** As a quick first stop (you'll come back later), visit the museum gift shop to look at the postcards of paintings that are on display in the museum. [Ask in which rooms these paintings are displayed.] Let each youngster and parent choose a postcard (her "personal painting") and purchase it. Using string or ribbon that you've brought along, make a small hole in one corner and let little children hang the card around their necks; others can keep it handy in a pocket.

❏ **426. VIEWING PICTURES.** Don't sign up for a tour—that's too regimented for this first visit. And remember, you don't need to see every room in the museum. Leave some for another time. Choose rooms that seem most interesting or least occupied. Move at a leisurely pace and don't give a running commentary—just look and listen to kids' comments. Remind each one to be on the lookout for his postcard picture. Then, after some viewing, ask a child to find a picture with his favorite color. Have them look to see if happy pictures have bright colors and mysterious pictures dark colors. Don't skip the modern art. Ask what the artist might have felt when he painted the picture. Does the painting's title give a clue?

❑ **427.** WHO PAINTED THESE PICTURES? Show where most artists sign their works and read a few of their names. Show how the artist's name and other information about the painting is often posted next to the picture. See if it gives any further information about the artist, ownership, date painted, and if for sale, the price. Look for paintings by Rembrandt, Picasso, El Greco, Monet, Renoir, Wyeth, Cassatt, and Seurat.

❑ **428.** WHAT'S THE PICTURE ABOUT? If you're with school-aged kids, sit down on a bench in one of the rooms and give each child a paper and pencil. See how many different subjects they can list: a storm, a family eating, a child watering flowers, Jesus, landscapes, rich people, buildings, battles. Compare the lists.

❑ **429.** AM I IN A PICTURE? Look for people and animal paintings. Are there paintings of children? old folks? soldiers? angels? dogs? sheep? cows? moms and dads? Encourage each youngster to find a picture he thinks he could fit into or would like to be a part of—as a warrior, queen, horseback rider, and so forth. Let everyone point out places that look interesting for play, living, working, or visiting.

❑ **430.** "IF I WERE A MILLIONAIRE" LUNCH BREAK. After about an hour of viewing, take a restroom and lunch break. Talk about a picture that each youngster would like to take home if he could afford the (most likely expensive) price. Why does he like the picture—because it is beautiful? big? funny? sad? Do others like the same picture? Is it the picture on his postcard?

❑ **431.** AFTER LUNCH LOOKING. Before heading for home, help kids to find their postcard pictures (the information desk can help). Return to favorite paintings and make note of the painting's title and the artist's name. If permitted, photograph each youngster with his favorite painting. If photography is not permitted, do take a photo of the group outside so that this excursion can go in the family memory book.

❑ **432.** GIFT SHOP INVESTIGATION. Return to the museum shop and investigate books, games, and other artistic gifts. Listen for kid comments that may give you ideas for birthday and holiday gift-giving. Consider the purchase of an item that would be useful in your youngster's art education.

❑ **433.** KEEPING THE MUSEUM VISIT ALIVE. Back home, put the postcard pictures on the family bulletin board or let children send them to grandparents, telling about the excursion. Talk about favorite paintings and what made them special. Encourage an art project at home but don't suggest what to draw, rather just see what your youngster creates. Display the finished pictures. Now that the museum is no longer intimidating, plan a followup trip. As children grow older, discussion on technique, historical art, religious art, patrons, the Masters, and so forth can be part of the experience. A tour led by a docent will also be valuable.

## ART IN THE HOME

❑ **434.** BOOKS TO BORROW OR BUY. Put an art book on a table or pedestal that everyone passes. Open it to one page, and turn a page each day. Some books you will want to look at together or read include *The History of Art for Young People,* by H. W. Janson and Anthony F. Janson (New York: Abrams, 1987), *The National Gallery of Art* by John Walker (New York: Abrams, 1984), and *Children Are Artists* by Daniel M. Mendelowitz (Stanford Univ. Press: Stanford, Calif., 1963)—an old but wonderful book.

❑ **435.** WALL OF ART. Rather than having kid-art on the refrigerator, stacked on the counter, or being sneaked into the rubbish, create a wall of art in a hallway. With youngsters, go to a frame shop and ask to see their least expensive, slightly damaged, or poster frames. Let each child choose one. Back home, help them frame their best artwork and then hang all the frames in a group with some at adult eye level and others at kid eye evel.

❑ **436.** HOME ART GALLERY. Hang sturdy string or a clothesline at eye level across a child's bedroom or the family room. Let him clip to it his latest art projects. When the line is full, let family members pretend they are at a museum and comment on their favorites.

❑ **437.** TELL ME ABOUT IT. Parents want fingers on hands, chimneys on houses, and hair that isn't green. This kind of intrusion or "improving" of kids' art can be discouraging. Rather than asking "What is it?" say "Tell me about it." Suggest youngsters show and explain their latest art work to the entire family at supper, or to friends who come by.

❑ **438.** KITCHEN EASEL. As soon as kids are old enough to color or paint, invest in a simple easel. Put it in the kitchen (where spills are easily cleaned up), provide the artist with an apron or big T-shirt as a cover-up, and let the child paint as you prepare dinner. This allows you to supervise and encourage, and subtly brings you and your youngster together on a regular basis.

❑ **439.** OUTDOOR ART FAIR. Make good art a part of your home atmosphere. Visit a fair at a school or park.

Look at the pictures and prints. If reasonably priced, let a youngster select one for her own room or give her a painting or art object as a gift.

❑ **440.** BREAD PEOPLE. Cut the crusts off bread slices—several slices per child. Show youngsters how to knead the glob until it feels like clay (older, coarser bread may need a few drops of water added). Now it is ready to be molded much like clay. It makes a good activity to do on a tray while traveling in the car. Afterward, it can be put outside for the birds.

❑ **441.** WHAT'S INSIDE? When youngsters are old enough to handle a knife for soap carving, have them envision the object that is hidden inside the soap (famous sculptors do this before they begin chipping the marble). Then, show them how to cut away the soap to reveal the object inside. (Tie up soap scraps in netting for use in the tub.) Display the finished product and when the artist is tired of it, it can be used at bath time.

❑ **442.** PAPIER-MÂCHÉ. This is the French word for pulped paper that can be made at home and used for modeling. Supervise the cutting of several newspapers (regular newsprint, not colored or glossy) into one-inch wide strips. In a large bowl or pail, cover the paper with water and let soak overnight. The next day divide the mass—a portion for each child. Knead the soaked mass and squeeze out the excess water (using a strainer or sieve works well). Then mix in ordinary paste. Now it is ready to be molded into small objects and dried. Or, it can be used to make a mask, doll's head, animal, or a relief map. As it hardens, it becomes durable and can be easily painted.

❑ **443.** ROLLING PIN ART. This requires an old rolling pin that you tightly cover with string, wound around (close or far apart) or glued in a design. Glue the ends of the string in place and let dry. Cover the work surface with newspaper and then plain poster paper. In an aluminum tray that is large enough for dipping the rolling pin, pour thick poster paint. The youngster makes a print by rolling the dipped rolling pin on the paper. If you have two rolling pins and two trays of paint, you can roll a second design across the first when the first is dry. The paper makes nice place mats, wrapping paper, or wall decorations.

❏ **444.** COLORFUL COLLAGE. Abstract or representational art work can be made using the collage method. (The term comes from the French word meaning to paste or glue.) It teaches the use of color, proportion, and materials. Torn paper collage is a good way to begin. Colored paper, tissue paper, wallpaper, magazines and even newspaper can be combined for a pleasing effect. Cardboard or canvas board is the base for pasting down the various elements. This art form lets the artist try the placement of the elements before gluing them into place. As proficiency increases, objects such as buttons or leaves can be added. Collage is a good all-family art project.

❏ **445.** SAND PICTURES. Show kids how to mix sand with powdered tempera paint (one-quarter cup sand mixed well with two teaspoons of dry paint). Put the colors in shakers or spice containers with most of the holes covered with tape to limit the flow of the sand. Affix a picture hook to the back of a sturdy paper plate. With a pencil, kids can sketch on it a simple picture or design. Next, they start with the background color by spreading glue on the desired area, then shaking on the sand mixture. Excess sand is then shaken onto a paper towel and returned to the shaker. Follow the same procedure with the next colors until the picture is finished. It dries quickly and can be hung almost immediately.

❏ **446.** RAINY DAY ART. On a drizzly day, get the family together for this simple art project that has great results. Everyone is given paper to use on a tray or cookie sheet. Using washable markers or colored chalk, each makes a picture or design. As soon as there is a misty rain, set the trays outside for just a few minutes. The colors will bleed together to form an interesting painting. Bring the paintings inside and dry them on newspaper before hanging.

❏ **447.** TUBE BRACELETS. Show kids how to make the popular eye-catching bracelets worn by both gals and guys. At a pet or aquarium store, buy a package of standard airline tubing and a package of connectors. Let kids decide the bracelet length—usually about seven inches. Attach a connector at one end and then fill the tube with glitter, sand, sequins, tiny nuts and bolts, even paper and fabric scraps. Use a toothpick to poke the items in the tube, leaving about a half inch at the end. Then firmly push this end into the connector. It's the style to wear several and they can even be used to hold a house key by pushing the tubing through the hole in the key.

❏ **448.** POTATO BEADS. Girls will really enjoy making these necklaces out of real potatoes. A parent should peel and cut a large raw white potato into three-fourth inch chunks. Kids then poke each chunk through the center onto a kabob skewer, being sure the chunks don't touch. Set them on a cooling rack to air dry, turning them every three days for a total of two weeks. Now the chunks are hard as rocks and can be painted with acrylic paint to look like turquoise. Let them thoroughly dry before highlighting with dabs of black paint wiped off with a paper towel. The black will stick in the crevices for a natural turquoise look. The "beads" can then be strung with needle and fishing line.

❏ **449.** MACARONI JEWELRY. Girls can make necklaces and bracelets, boys like to make head bands and belts. All you need are lengths of yarn, dry macaroni, and Cheerios. To make threading easy, put glue on one end of the yarn and let it dry. While Cheerios come in colors, you can make colored macaroni this way: Mix a half cup of rubbing alcohol with a little yellow food coloring and immerse noodles, then dry on newspaper covered with wax paper. To make green, add blue food coloring to the mixture and repeat the process. You can also start with red food coloring for red noodles, then add blue for purple noodles. Alternate cereal and noodles for interesting designs.

❏ **450.** LUNCH BOX ART. Let a child turn her lunch box into a game. Using acrylic paint on a plain plastic lunch box, paint on the grid for a tick-tack-toe game. Inside the box, place two colors of paper clips (to represent the X's and O's) in a film canister. Friends will enjoy lunching and playing together.

❏ **451.** FELT BOARDS. This creative toy can be played with at home or in the car, and it makes a fine homemade gift from a child to a friend. Check your fabric scrap bag for pieces of felt, or go to a craft or fabric shop and buy remnants or small pieces in about eight colors. Have at least one-half yard each in green and blue. Using a sturdy dress box as a base, create a background of blue sky and green grass inside the box. Glue these in place. Then let kids cut out many objects and shapes: house, tree, dog, sun, parent, child, wagon, and so forth. Also cut circles and rectangles that can be used to make up figures, being sure that there are some small pieces for eyes and mouth. These felt cutouts will stick to the background and let kids make pictures and stories. The lid of the box keeps all the pieces inside when play is over.

❏ **452.** ART AT SCHOOL. Many schools have cut back on teaching art or may just permit drawing as a diversion without any professional input. Call or visit your school to inquire about the art program. Art appreciation is just as important as art "doing" so encourage and help the teacher plan field trips to museums (art, sculpture, photography) and the display of good art at the school. Art teaches history, design, zoology, anatomy, architecture, botany, costuming, perspective, and more. At school meetings, voice your opinion on the importance of art instruction.

# SECTION 3: ALL THE WORLD'S A STAGE . . .

❑ **453.** LIVE THEATER. Television, movies, and picture books cannot match the magic of live theater—seeing Peter Pan fly across the stage or Beauty dancing with the Beast. A school play, youth theater, or summer theater may not be as grand as Broadway, but still, take children to plays several times each year. Live theater requires a youngster's commitment of mind and body as she follows the words and the action and is drawn into the plot. The characters are real people she cares about. It is as different as seeing a live circus or looking at a picture book about animals.

❑ **454.** SHADOW PLAYS. Hang a sheet in a doorway and place a floodlight about eight feet behind it. Let kids play between the sheet and the light, acting out nursery rhymes and scenes from familiar books. See if the audience can guess who the actors are portraying.

❑ **455.** THE PLAY'S THE THING. Rig a curtain near one side of a room and create a stage. Let kids begin by recreating favorite stories—allowing them to play the lead parts and a parent playing all the other parts. Fairy tales and cartoon movies are a good place to start. As youngsters take an interest in plays, they can create costumes and simple scenery. And if they get really good, they can charge a dime for spectators! Libraries have books of simple plays for all ages, but some of the best plays are made-up spur-of-the-moment ones. Encourage this kind of creativity by suggesting a situation or plot line.

❑ **456.** HAND PUPPET THEATER. Take a very large box, remove both ends, and cover one end with a long piece of fabric, attached only at the top. Place the box on a table with the open end toward the audience, the curtained end to the back. Puppeteers bring their arms up under the fabric, which shields the kids from the audience, and they speak the words for the hand puppets. Suggest familiar stories such as *The Three Bears* or *Pinocchio*. As they get more proficient, youngsters can each manage two hand puppets and make up some stories on their own.

❑ **457.** MARIONETTE THEATER. String puppets are more expensive than hand puppets but offer a wider range of movement. There are kits for making string puppets but they can also be purchased ready-made. The homemade stage can be a sturdy box with the top side and the audience side open. Help youngsters write a short play that can be acted out by the puppets. Invite neighborhood kids to view the show.

❑ **458.** AUTO THEATER. When on a long drive, create a play inside the car. First, state a premise suitable to the ages of the children: a princess needs to find food for her hungry people, or a rock band suspects trouble at a school concert. Then get volunteers for parts: princess, farmer, magician, band leader, troublemaker, class president. Without rehearsal, start the dialogue (it helps if a parent begins). Let actors speak when they choose, interrupt one another, give sound effects, and see how the plot turns and twists.

❑ **459.** THEATER AT SCHOOL. Although school productions can be corny and even boring, they do serve a good purpose. Parents should promote theater at school and all the family should attend the plays and pageants from preschool through college years. School theater encourages poise and participation as well as the skills of memorization and public speaking. It also introduces to young audiences the skills of sitting, watching, listening, learning, and appreciating.

❑ **460.** FAMILY PLAY READING. The library has excellent plays that you can borrow. When children read well, borrow a play, assign roles among family and friends, and have your own play-reading evening. While it is enjoyable to just read plays—from Euripides to Shakespeare to Neil Simon—this activity can be expanded by purchasing mystery play kits at a game store and having a party. These kits include ideas for the characters, certain lines of the script, clues, and even suggested refreshments for the intermission.

❏ **461.** THEATER LINGO. Explain to youngsters the difference between producer and director, and the meaning of these theater terms: plotting, prompters, blocking, flying scenery, On and Off Broadway, summer stock, tragedy versus comedy, Greek theater, Kabuki, Theater of the Absurd, and Theater-in-the-Round. Discuss the roles of famous actors such as Tallulah Bankhead, Helen Hayes, Sir Alec Guiness, Orson Welles, Sarah Bernhardt, Marlon Brando, and Katharine Hepburn. See who in the family can name a play written by these famous playwrights: Anton Chekhov, George M. Cohan, Sir Noel Coward, Gilbert and Sullivan, Lillian Hellman, Victor Hugo, W. Somerset Maugham, Arthur Miller, Harold Pinter, Thornton Wilder, and William Shakespeare. You'll find that this is a good education for you, too.

❏ **462.** TONGUE TWISTERS. Speaking in front of family and friends and not being shy or embarrassed is a good first step toward being able to speak in public. Parents and kids can take part in a weekly tongue twister event—perhaps at supper on Mondays—and see who really excels by the end of the week. Start with "Peter Piper," "She Sells Seashells," and "Theophilus Thistle." Be quick to laugh at your own mistakes.

# SECTION 4: MEET YOU AT THE MOVIES

❏ **463.** KID MOVIES. Probably the first movie your child attends will be a movie made just for kids. Prepare your youngster by seeing that he is rested, fed, and has a cushion to sit on. If it is a classic, summarize the plot in a simple way. Reaffirm that it is a movie, not real life, and that if it is scary, he can shut his eyes. Take along a blanket in case he wants to curl up and sleep. After the movie, talk about what was funny, exciting, or interesting.

❑ **464.** AGE APPROPRIATE. Don't be pressured into letting your youngster attend movies that you don't approve of. If there's nothing appropriate to see, rent a video and pretend you're at the theater. Line up the chairs, darken the room, serve popcorn and sodas, and enjoy the show. Nowadays movies come out fairly quickly on video and you can save a lot of money by just being patient. As with a regular movie theater experience, talk about plot, characters, violence, stereotypes, and so forth when the movie is over.

❑ **465.** ART FILMS. By the time kids are preteens, introduce them to some of the fine classical films—those that may not be at the multiplex theater but rather at a small theater that shows art films. Pick ones with authors and actors who are respected. Encourage the reading of other books by the same authors.

❑ **466.** ACADEMY AWARDS. Create an interest in more than just the best films and actors. When the nomination list comes out, talk about all the various categories that will be honored. See as many of the films that you feel are appropriate for your youngsters. Then have a party on awards night—a simple dinner with friends of all ages who enjoy movies. Let the participants vote in all the categories and see who is the best at assessing greatness, then present awards of your own.

❑ **467.** BE A REVIEWER. Don't take a friend's word about what films to see. Read newspaper reviews for additional ideas. Some publications have a weekly listing of all movies with ratings plus comments on aspects of the movie that parents should be aware of (violence, sex, profanity). Make a thoughtful family decision rather than just choosing the movie with the biggest first-week viewership. When you and your kids have seen a movie you especially enjoyed, encourage others to go.

❑ **468.** LIGHTS, CAMERA, ACTION. Video cameras let everyone be part of a movie—writer, director, cinematographer, actor. Show kids how to use the camera and then encourage them to make a mini-production. You may have a future Spielberg under your roof!

# SECTION 5: TAKE NOTE OF MUSIC

❑ **469.** BABIES LOVE MUSIC. Before kids know the difference between rock and Rachmaninoff, surround them with music. Play joyful music first thing in the morning. Play marches during play time. Play soothing music at naptime and bedtime. Sing to children and teach them to sing. When riding in the car, play music tapes they enjoy. And turn on the radio to a music station as background for conversation or snoozes. Easy-to-operate toddler cassette players make useful gifts.

❑ **470.** HOME INSTRUMENTS. Long before you consider buying a piano, let youngsters play with small instruments. Create a special bin so that all the instruments are readily available: cymbals, sticks, triangle, drum, harmonica, castanets, bells, and tambourines are a few that you can inexpensively buy. After showing how each are played, let kids accompany recorded music that has a good beat. Suggest they march to the music. Finally, encourage kids to make up songs to sing as they accompany themselves.

❑ **471.** INSTRUMENTS TO MAKE. Let kids make their own instruments and then record their music. Here are five they can make with a little help from you. *(1) SHAKERS.*

Pour one-quarter cup of dry beans into an empty container the size of a pint water bottle. Screw the cap on tightly and shake. *(2) RHYTHM STIX.* Cut the spoon end off of old wood utensils. Tie on a bright tassel for the end of each stick. Then show a child how to make rhythm by hitting the stix on a turned-over pie plate. *(3) BODY BELLS.* You can buy "jingle" bells cheaply at a craft store. String them on a pipe cleaner for wrist and ankle bells, attach them to a ribbon for waist bells. *(4) DRUMS.* Collect empty soup or vegetable cans, wash, remove labels, and let kids spray paint them. (Be sure there are no sharp edges.) Cut shelf paper or paper bags into circles and attach over the open end of the can with rubber bands. Use the eraser end of unsharpened pencils to beat out a rhythm. *(5) BOUNCING BUTTONS.* Help kids sew buttons to the tips of the five fingers of a glove. Show how to tap the finger buttons on the thumb button for a bouncy click.

❑ **472.** BOTTLE SCALE. Obtain eight identical bottles and place them in a row. Fill each one with water, using a small amount in the first, then more and more with the greatest amount in the eighth one. To make a music scale, start with the first bottle by blowing over it. Then, tune the second one a tone higher by adding or deleting water. Continue until you have do, re, mi, fa, sol, la, ti, and do.

❑ **473.** MUSIC LESSONS. Encouraged by a parent or the desire to play in the school band, a youngster may opt for lessons on a musical instrument. Within reason, let her choose her instrument, and consider renting it at first. The commitment should be for at least six months; after that time she can quit or choose another instrument. No matter what she chooses, she'll learn to read music. This exposure to music should be pleasant, not forced, but parents should be insistent on a specified amount of practice time. The entire family should attend programs and recitals.

❑ **474.** MUSIC WITH AN ATTITUDE. By the time kids are in school, they begin to form opinions about music styles. Be open to listening to various kinds of music as long as the words are not offensive. Have music with supper each night, taking turns playing favorite music. And since you listen politely to their music, kids will do the same for the music you choose. See that you have in your home collection at least one recording in each of many categories: symphonic, ballet, opera, musical comedy, choral music, dance music, rock, ballads, soul, country and western, reggae, and so forth.

❑ **475.** **BANNED AT YOUR HOUSE.** Let your kids know that they may not spend their money on music that has destructive values. In her book *Raising PG Kids in an X-Rated Society* (Nashville: Abingdon Press, 1988), Tipper Gore says: "We should be deeply concerned about the obvious cumulative effect of this cult of violence that has captured the public's imagination and pervaded our society. Few parents realize how much the angry brand of music that is part of it has presented suicide, glorified rape, and condoned murder. The message is more than repulsive—it's deadly." Let your youngsters know that you are just as concerned about the music they listen to as the television or movies they see.

❑ **476.** **A SYMPHONY FULL OF INSTRUMENTS.** Schools often have trips to hear a local symphony. Beforehand, find pictures of instruments in an encyclopedia and read a little about each. Encourage your youngster to listen for particular instruments: a harp, the tympani, glockenspiel, French horn, or double bass. Also introduce him to the protocol of reading the program notes, listening without conversation, and applauding at the end (not between movements).

❑ **477.** **LISTEN FIRST.** There are many symphonic pieces that will interest kids: the *1812 Overture,* which features cannons; *Grand Canyon Suite,* which makes grand musical pictures; *Peter and the Wolf,* which tells a story; and *Pictures at an Exhibition.* Other ones with special appeal are *The Sorcerer's Apprentice, Afternoon of a Fawn,* the *Alpine Symphony,* and *Also Sprach Zarathustra* (the theme used for *2001: A Space Odyssey*). You can borrow these from the library.

❏ **478.** WHO WROTE THIS STUFF? A cultured person is acquainted with the names of classical composers. From this brief list, let each youngster choose "her composer." Look up the name in the encyclopedia to find facts. Find among your own recordings (or borrow one) a composition by the composer and listen to it together. Some names are: Johann Sebastian Bach, Ludwig von Beethoven, George Bizet, Frederic Chopin, Claude Debussy, George Handel, Wolfgang Amadeus Mozart, Gioacchino Rossini, Jan Sibelius, Richard Strauss, Peter Ilich Tchaikovsky, Giuseppe Verdi, and Ralph Vaughan Williams.

❏ **479.** THE VOICE AS AN INSTRUMENT. See who in the family can sing the highest and the lowest notes. Explain the voice ranges (soprano, mezzo-soprano, contralto or alto, tenor, baritone, and bass). Encourage singing in the shower with high notes like chirping birds, and low tones like frogs. Using a dictionary, see who can define one of these vocal music terms: *a cappella,* aria, recitative, duet, *appoggiatura,* and *basso buffo.*

❏ **480.** FIRST MUSICAL. Classic musicals are always being revived on Broadway and in theaters across the country. Summertime is a great time to attend a musical comedy production. To help understand the words, listen to a cassette of the songs before attending. Musical comedies make good listening in the car, and you may hear some of the family singing right along. Encourage your school's music department to put on a popular musical and be sure to support it.

❏ **481.** FIRST OPERA. The majesty and pageantry of an opera production far outshines the opera plot. However, before taking a youngster to an opera, definitely read the plot and discuss the historical context. Tell what language it will be sung in. You may find that there is superscript (the words in English shown above the stage) and this is some help. Opera stars are often showcased on television, so look for these programs as an introduction to the opera world.

❑ **482.** MUSICAL TERMS IN DAILY LIFE. Painlessly introduce musical terms by incorporating them into family conversation. For instance, instead of saying "Come quickly," say *"allegro."* For slowly, use *"largo." "Con brio"* means with great liveliness. For "Speak loudly" (or softly), say *"forte (or sotto) voce."* To pick up toys, say *"vivace,"* which means with lively speed. When a child is about to take too large a helping of ice cream, say *"non troppo,"* meaning "not too much."

❑ **483.** DINNER MUSIC. It may not sound quite as lovely as the roving violinist in a fancy restaurant, but you can have your own dinner music at the table when eating is finished. Give out bells, kazoos, drums, spoons, and glasses so that each person has an instrument. Choose recorded or radio music with a lively beat. Let one person be the conductor and indicate when an instrument should be played and how fast or loud. This idea is also fun for an all-adult dinner party.

❑ **484.** SAW MUSIC. A single-handled carpenter's handsaw is now looked upon as a serious instrument. The saw has been played at elegant weddings and with symphony orchestras. This old-time music maker is one that you can introduce to a gradeschool youngster. With the saw handle between your knees, use one hand to flex the long blade (cutting side down) and the other hand to run a violin bow across it. With practice you can get various tones, even a scale. The music can be ear-assaulting or hauntingly beautiful.

❑ **485.** PATRIOTIC SONGS. While most youngsters know the national anthem, "The Star-Spangled Banner," use car time to teach other patriotic songs. Find them in song books and create your own song sheets. Learn these songs: "America," "America, the Beautiful," "God Bless America," "I'm a Yankee Doodle Dandy," "The Navy Hymn," and the songs or hymns of other military units. Tell kids that the word patriotism comes from the Greek word *patris,* meaning fatherland.

❑ **486.** FAVORITE HYMNS. Many hymns are common to all faiths. You will find these in hymnals, and many encyclopedias have the words that you can copy: "Abide with Me" by Henry Lyte and William Monk, "A Mighty Fortress Is Our God" by Martin Luther, "Blest Be the Tie that Binds" by John Fawcette, "Faith of Our Fathers" by Frederick Faber and James Walton, "Glorious Things of Thee Are Spoken" by John Newton (who also wrote "Amazing Grace") and Joseph Haydn, "Nearer My God to Thee" by Sarah Flower and Lowell Mason, "Onward, Christian Soldiers" by L. Sabine Baring-Gould and Sir Arthur Sullivan, "Rock of Ages" by Augustus Toplady and Thomas Hastings, and "The Battle Hymn of the Republic" by Julia Ward Howe. Many of these hymns have interesting stories with them and knowing the background will make them memorable.

❑ **487.** "MUSIC HATH CHARMS." That saying is overlooked by many schools who have weak or nonexistent music instruction. While bands and choral groups are popular, one of the most important school classes should be music appreciation. Don't let this education slip through the cracks—talk to the principal and superintendent at your youngster's school, write letters, attend meetings, and encourage the PTA to allot some of its funds to underwrite such a class.

# SECTION 6: DANCING—WITH TWO LEFT FEET

❑ **488.** TODDLER TWO-STEP. As soon as a child can walk, show him how to move to music. He'll be happy to mimic you. Then take him in your arms and dance. Play dance music during his activities. When it's time to pick up toys, play fast music to encourage speed.

❏ **489.** FIRST LESSONS. While tiny ballerinas are adorable, don't start dance lessons too young and before muscles are ready to be stretched. About age five, consider dance lessons such as ballet or tap for both boys and girls. It's good training in being graceful and poised.

❏ **490.** THE DREADED COTILLION. Many youngsters learn from friends how to dance. But in order to really make your youngster a confident dancer, you may want to consider enrolling him in a cotillion—an organized dance class for boys and girls. These teach current dances plus how to waltz, fast-step, tango, and so forth. At the same time, they afford opportunities to learn the etiquette of dancing and to make friends. When the kids return home from each lesson, let them share what they learned with others in the family.

❏ **491.** FIRST BALLET. Since many kids think attending a ballet performance is going to be boring, start with something intriguing. A good first ballet is *The Nutcracker,* which is performed many places during the Christmas holidays. In some areas, local ballet students perform with the professional company. The ballet is usually shown on television, and seeing it there doesn't dim the excitement of the actual production. Children as young as three will find it fascinating to watch the live production—provided they've had a nap before attending.

❏ **492.** MORE THAN BALLET. Check your newspaper for dance programs at theaters and colleges that feature modern, jazz, or tap dancing. Choose one that has interest to your kids and go early enough to read the program. Exposing them to various kinds of dancing may intrigue them into wanting lessons.

❏ **493.** DANCING IN THE DARK. Parents often don't get time to dance together. Before a child's bedtime, turn the lights low and put on some of your favorite dance music. Let your youngster watch you dance together, then a parent can dance with a child, and finally, all three dance together.

# SECTION 7: A WAY WITH WORDS

Speaking distinctly and correctly is one of the leading signs of a cultured person. Learning should start early and continue through the teen years when bad habits tend to creep in. Two good ways to promote correct speech are to speak accurately yourself and to encourage reading.

❑ **494.** NIX THE BABY TALK. Let the baby do baby talk, but parents should just smile at the cuteness and speak correctly. However, don't discourage early speech by correcting children. Certain mispronunciations often linger until first grade—don't emphasize them, they'll probably go away. Encourage young children to speak by listening to what they say and then asking questions that require more than a yes/no answer.

❑ **495.** DOES YOUR CHILD KNOW THE BASIC VOCABULARY? Although "mommy" and "daddy" are usually the first words, beyond those is a basic vocabulary that if learned could make home a more peaceful and efficient place. These twenty-four words/phrases should not only be taught, but clearly understood: yes, no, maybe, please, thank you, now, later, today, tomorrow, come, sit, stop, help, ask, tell, share, give, follow, quiet, pick up, left, right, hello, good-bye. Kids who understand these few words are a joy to their teachers, too!

❑ **496.** SIX FAULTS YOU CAN CORRECT. Borrow a simple grammar book at the library and tackle these problems for your kids and yourself. *(1) Troublesome pronoun.* If you incorrectly say "Give the paper to Dad or I" (instead of me), you can expect your child to say "He and me want cookies" (instead of he and I). Go over the simple rules of pronouns as nouns or objects. *(2) Vile verbs.* Knowing the proper use of lie-lay, teach-learn, bring-take, says-said and others will increase kids' confidence in both writing and speaking. *(3) Non sequiturs or run-ons.* In Latin, non sequitur means "It does not follow." Children often think so rapidly that words spill out randomly, such as "I fell off my bike and when is supper?" Permitting this in speech will carry over into writing. *(4) Happy agreement.* The pronouns have to match. For example, "Each one took their cookie" (each one is singular and thus "their" should be "his" or "her"). Or, "Everyone must mind their manners," but since the pronoun "everyone" is singular, the possessive pronoun must be singular— as in the first example. *(5) Adverbs and adjectives—not the same.* Of course adjectives modify nouns and adverbs modify verbs telling how, where, when or to what degree. Thus it is correct to say, "That is a good story. She told it well!" "He walked slowly." "It was a slow day." *(6) Sound alikes.* Principle/principal, capital/capitol, counsel/council, who/whom/whose, and its and it's. Grab your dictionary and with your youngster look these up. Here's a start: "It's" is always the contraction of "It is." "Its" is always the possessive of "it" even though, unlike other possessives, it has no apostrophe.

❑ **497.** OFTEN MISPRONOUNCED WORDS. Start with "becuz" and "gotta" and "wanna." Sloppy speech in early years is hard to cure. Say "nuclear" instead of "nucular," and don't sound the "L" in calm, balm, Psalm, palm. And, remember that "both" means "the two" so never say "the both" (as in "the both of them were hungry), which would mean "the the two."

❑ **498.** STREET SLANG. Profanity, trash talk, and slang are words usually used to show anger or frustration, or to hurt. Often the words are meaningless on their own. Such inappropriate terms, originally used to shock or get attention, are unfortunately now so common they've lost even that value. Kids pick up these words from peers, but if a parent also uses them, the parent should unlearn them. An educated person doesn't need them, and parents should take a strong stand against their use. Help a child find real words—better words to express feelings.

❑ **499.** PHRASES THAT HURT. Talk about hurtful words: fatso, four-eyes, stupido, and so forth. Name-calling, as well as sarcasm, insisting on having the last word, muttering insults, and being officious ("Get out!" "Bring it!" "Shut up!") are all signs of a person's losing control. Show kids how to handle the frustrations that bring on these phrases and thus gain control. Play-act alternate ways of speaking when upset and calm ways of responding if these words are directed at you.

## WORD FUN

❑ **500.** BURIED WORDS. A monster is going to bury all the words in the world except five. Everyone lists the words she wants to save, followed by a reason why that word is important. Then share the lists and see if any words appear on more than one list.

❑ **501.** SOMERSAULTING WORDS. Don't hesitate using colorful language with kids—practice at mealtimes and on car rides. Choose words that have unique sounds: whoosh, bumptious, smithereens, marshmallows, cantaloupe, gypsies, caterpillars, abracadabra, murmur, giraffes, curmudgeon, dillydally. Then, when kids know the meanings of the words, let them make up funny sentences such as "The curmudgeon hit the cantaloupe and smashed it to smithereens." "Caterpillars murmur for marshmallows."

❑ **502.** RAMBLING STORY. Someone writes a sentence to start the story and then passes the paper to the second person who adds another sentence. The paper is then folded down so only the second sentence shows. Others continue to add sentences, only seeing the preceding one. It makes a great story when read aloud.

❑ **503.** A BIG DEAL. Reading leads to good speaking. When your child is responsible enough to have her own library card, make it a special occasion. Talk about it in the days ahead. Make the trip one for just parent and child. Let her sign up for the card, borrow some books, and then go out to buy a special wallet or purse in which to keep it.

❑ **504.** CHARACTER SWITCH. Switch characters between books. For example, if you've read to a child the story of Pocahontas and the story of Cinderella, reread the story but put the other character into the title role. Does Cinderella lose a moccasin? Does Pocahontas stand up to her wicked stepsisters? The switch brings lots of conversation and laughter.

❑ **505.** READ AND POINT. Start word/picture associations when reading to young children. When you read the sentence "The dog came running" have your youngster point to the dog. Point to the "d" in dog and emphasize it as you say it. You're not teaching reading, but just the connection of the oral word with the written word and with the picture.

❑ **506.** ANALYTICAL READING. When a youngster has finished reading a book and has enjoyed it, talk about what made it special. Was it the exciting main character? the twisting plot? the description of the mysterious setting? the odd way a character spoke? Start when kids are young to analyze the importance of words in writing, as well as in everyday conversation, a politician's speech-making, school debates, and essay-type examinations.

❑ **507.** TOP TWENTY GRADE SCHOOL CLASSICS. Although *1001 Things to Do with Your Kids* listed many books youngsters should read, here's a list of what many consider the top twenty. See how many your kids have read.

*The Adventures of Tom Sawyer*  Samuel Clemens
*Aesop's Fables*  Aesop

| | |
|---|---|
| *Alice's Adventures in Wonderland* | Lewis Carroll |
| *Andersen's Fairy Tales* | Hans Christian Andersen |
| *Anne Frank: The Diary of a Young Girl* | Anne Frank |
| *Anne of Green Gables* | Lucy Montgomery |
| *The Arabian Nights' Entertainments* | Andrew Lang, editor |
| *A Christmas Carol* | Charles Dickens |
| *Don Quixote of La Mancha* | Miguel de Cervantes Saavedra |
| *Gulliver's Travels* | Jonathan Swift |
| *Heidi* | Johanna Spyri |
| *Just So Stories* | Rudyard Kipling |
| *Little House in the Big Woods* | Laura Wilder |
| *The Little Prince* | Antoine de Saint-Exupery |
| *The Phantom Tollbooth* | Norton Juster |
| *Pinocchio: The Adventures of a Little Wooden Boy* | Carlo Collodi |
| *Tales from Shakespeare* | Charles and Mary Lamb |
| *Treasure Island* | Robert Louis Stevenson |
| *The Wind in the Willows* | Kenneth Grahame |
| *Wizard of Oz* | L. F. Baum |

❑ **508. TOP TWENTY HIGH SCHOOL CLASSICS.** How many of these great books has your teen read?

| | |
|---|---|
| *The Age of Innocence* | Edith Wharton |
| *All Quiet on the Western Front* | Erich Maria Remarque |
| *The Ambassadors* | Henry James |
| *Babbitt* | Sinclair Lewis |
| *The Bridge of San Luis Rey* | Thornton Wilder |
| *Emma* | Jane Austen |
| *Ethan Frome* | Edith Wharton |
| *The First Circle* | Aleksandr Solzhenitsyn |
| *For Whom the Bell Tolls* | Ernest Hemingway |
| *The Forsyte Saga* | John Galsworthy |
| *The Great Gatsby* | F. Scott Fitzgerald |
| *Human Comedy* | William Saroyan |
| *Les Miserables* | Victor Hugo |
| *Look Homeward, Angel* | Thomas Wolfe |

| | |
|---|---|
| *Moby Dick* | Herman Melville |
| *My Antonia* | Willa Cather |
| *1984* | George Orwell |
| *A Passage to India* | E. M. Forster |
| *Sons and Lovers* | D. H. Lawrence |
| *Vanity Fair* | William Thackeray |

❑ **509.** **BUILD A LIBRARY.** Some books are worth keeping forever, even though they've been read many times. Start a library shelf for each child. Add to it by buying good books at a garage sale or getting hand-me-downs from friends. As kids get older, box up some of their favorites to keep for their own children.

❑ **510.** **CHAPTER BOOKS.** While it is easy to whip through a quantity of kiddie books, when a child enters kindergarten, consider starting on books with chapters. This has many benefits for kids up to about age eight (when they often prefer to read on their own). First, it is a continuing story from night to night—something eagerly looked forward to as the plot develops. Second, just one chapter book usually has as much reading value as a few dozen kiddie books, so you save money, and bookshelf space, too. Third, you're reading good classical literature (such as Laura Ingalls Wilder's *Little House* series or *Little Britches* by Ralph Moody). Chapter books often tell of good times in the past and are historically interesting as well as entertaining.

❑ **511.** **THE BOOK BUNCH.** In a neighborhood of grade school kids, parents can take turns driving the weekly library trip with several young readers. The library often has a week night or Saturday story hour, kid-friendly computers, and a thick-carpeted room for lounging and reading. One parent can set up the schedule for the "Book Bunch," which means that a parent only drives once a month, allowing the other parents special time with their other kids or spouse.

❏ **512.** POETRY POSSIBILITIES. In poetry, each word is carefully selected to create the mind-picture as well as the rhythm or rhyme. Include poetry reading as part of your youngster's education in words. A good basic book to borrow or buy is *The Oxford Book of American Light Verse*, edited by William Hamon (New York: Oxford Univ. Press, 1979). You'll find the full poem of "Take Me Out to the Ball Game" by Jack Norworth, songs by Oscar Hammerstein and Cole Porter, "The Village Blacksmith" by Henry Wadsworth Longfellow, as well as "A Visit from Saint Nicholas" by Clement Moore.

❏ **513.** SILLY STORY. Ask kids to suggest adjectives (descriptive words) that you will write as a list of about twenty—words like silly, crummy, sloppy, yummy, darling. Next, take a simple story that a child can read (*Red Riding Hood* or *Goldilocks and the Three Bears*) and ask the youngster to pause before each noun (a person, place, or thing). At that point, you'll read the first word on your list. So, the story becomes: "One day (silly) Red Riding Hood put on her (crummy) coat and took a (sloppy) basket of (yummy) food to (darling) Grandma."

❏ **514.** THE BOOKWORM. Encourage reading year-round by helping each child make a bookworm. The worm is composed of links of construction paper with a large piece at the beginning showing the worm's smiling face. When the first book is finished, the youngster writes the book name on a link and attaches it to the head. Then as more books are read and links are made, the worm gets longer and longer. Soon it will be so long that it can be hung from a curtain rod, strung across the breakfast nook, or cascaded down the stair railing. With several children there can be several worms. Young children will get a link for each book, gradeschoolers who read chapter books will get one for each chapter or twenty pages.

❏ **515.** PHOTO-JOURNALIST. Look through your latest snapshots and choose ten to be laid out on a table. Give family members paper and pencil and invite them to study the pictures and then write a fictional story about them. You'll be surprised how creative and unique each story is.

❑ **516.** **DEAR AUTHOR.** When a youngster has particularly enjoyed a book, encourage her to write a letter to the author, in care of the publisher shown in the front of the book. She should tell specifically why the book appealed to her. Most authors will respond, and a letter from a "real" author will be treasured.

# SEVEN
# LET'S GET TOGETHER

SECTION 1: BUILDING MEMORIES TOGETHER

SECTION 2: PARTY TIME!

SECTION 3: GETTING TOGETHER WITH GRANDPARENTS

# SECTION 1:
# BUILDING MEMORIES TOGETHER

It doesn't take money to build family memories. It's often the little things that count—little things that are fun and loving—and will probably be passed down to the next generation.

❑ **517.** MY HOW YOU'VE GROWN! Once a year, on a memorable date such as New Year's Day, measure the height of each family member. You'll need a painted one-by-four piece of lumber that is seven feet in length. Start by writing on it the length in inches when a baby is born. Then, measure each year and put the date by the height. Parents should be measured, too. Keep your height gauge in the family room, nailed to a door frame so it can be easily removed if you move.

❑ **518.** THE FAMILY BANNER. With input from all family members, design your own family flag that can fly outside your door or on a backyard pole. You'll need a piece of sturdy fabric and indelible fabric markers to draw objects or faces, or to make a design. Kids like the flag flown for a birthday or when friends are invited over. It can also be taken to the park or beach to identify your family's area.

❑ **519.** TIME CAPSULE. Plan a family party to prepare and bury a family time capsule to be dug up in ten years. Ask relatives and good friends to bring personal items, newspapers, and photos to share. In advance, help kids dig a hole and obtain a sturdy metal or plastic container. Each person tells about his item for the capsule as someone takes a video to record the event. Finally the capsule is wrapped in plastic and buried. Be sure to mark the location with a rock or stake. And remember to have a party ten years later to dig it up!

❑ **520.** YOU'VE COME A LONG WAY BABY! Each year, make part of a quilt for a youngster's sixteenth birthday celebration. It will consist of large squares of fabric, four panels across and four down. Make just one panel each year, decorating it with something symbolic of that year. The first year might be a teddy bear, the second year a swing, and so forth. Just before the birthday, add the sixteenth panel, the filling, and backing. It makes a memorable gift that a youngster can hang on a wall, cuddle up with, or save for his own child.

❏ **521.** LITTLE SURPRISES. Many families build memories around traditions that seem fairly insignificant. One family has a special tray that food is served on when a child isn't feeling well and must eat in bed. Another warms a big bath towel for the birthday person's use. A son occasionally puts a flower on his mom's computer. Another family is known for April Fool's Day pranks. Another has a once-a-year totally-backward-meal-day—steak for breakfast and pancakes for supper. And for a family living in a warm and humid climate, a happy tradition is putting clothing in the freezer overnight for a refreshing start of the day!

❏ **522.** HAND PRINTS IN CEMENT. When you move into a new home or are remodeling a house, there may be wet cement. (If not, get a bag of ready-mix.) Before the cement dries, let each family member put his hand print in the cement (the dog can make a paw print). Then write the name under each print and date your masterpiece. As years pass, it's fun to see how hands grow!

❏ **523.** FIFTH SUNDAY. Make a holiday (no work, all fun) on the four days a year that are fifth Sundays. Mark the date on the calendar well in advance and plan to do something unique—something no one in the family has done before. If you need suggestions, the weekend editions of the newspaper or a travel book from the auto club will give you ideas for local events and destinations you may never have heard of.

❏ **524.** SAME PLACE, DIFFERENT TIME. Each year, take

a family portrait (ask a friend to take the photo) in the same place. Choose the front door, the fireplace, by a tree, or by the family car. Be sure that family members are in the same place in each photo to permit easy comparison as the years pass.

❑ **525.** NAME THE HOUSE. Each home has some distinctive feature that can be used in giving the house a name. Have a contest to select a name for your house (Mountain View, Pink Palace, Remodeler's Dream, Hunter's Hideaway, Smith's Retreat). Consider putting a sign on the house with the name, or using the name on computer-made stationery.

❑ **526.** MY BUDDIES. What fun to look back at photos of childhood chums! When your youngsters—toddlers to teens—are together with their friends, take plenty of candid shots, but also have kids pose so you can get a good picture of each face.

❑ **527.** TWO FOR ONE. When getting family photos developed, take the double print option. Let each youngster keep her own photo album while the parent keeps the family album. Divide the photos—one set for the family album, the others among the kids. Together relive the events while you fill the albums. Don't forget to put a date and place on each page and identify nonfamily members.

❑ **528.** MY HOUSE, MY ROOM. In the autumn, just before school starts, let kids try on their new school clothes. Then, take a picture of them in their bedroom and another on their bike in front of the house. It will be interesting to see how the house, the room, and the child changes each year.

❑ **529.** MEMORABLE TREAT. Enlist the help of grandparents who may have enjoyed a taffy pull in their youth. One family makes it a yearly summer tradition, now enjoyed by the fourth generation. Here's their recipe:

## TAFFY

1½ cups sugar
¾ cup light corn syrup
⅔ cup water
½ teaspoon salt
1 teaspoon vegetable
   glycerine (found at a health food store)

2 tablespoons butter
2 teaspoons lemon juice
4 drops of yellow food
   coloring

In a large pan, combine the first five ingredients and mix well. Then cook and stir, removing it from the heat when a candy thermometer reads 250 degrees. Now, stir in the butter and coloring and pour onto a greased flat pan. So that the edges don't harden, occasionally use a metal spatula to fold over the sides until the mixture is cool enough to touch. Then brush on the lemon juice. Now it's time to butter hands and gently stretch the taffy until it is elastic. At this point you can actually pull it into a rope. When the pulling fun is over, cut the rope into small pieces for munching.

❑ **530.** MEALTIME MEMORIES. When the family eats together regularly, meals can be one of the prime memory building times. Monthly (or on a regular basis), inquire about what mealtime events were the most fun. It may be the meal where the kids planned the food, or the night when awards were given for doing chores that month, or when everyone came in costume. Or, it may have been "Bad Manners Night" when everyone tried to break the rules of mealtime etiquette without being noticed. Perhaps it was when the final chapter of an exciting book was read. (You'll find more on this topic in *1001 Things to Do with Your Kids*, ideas #68 through #81.)

❑ **531.** HUNTING TRADITIONS. Don't let the Easter egg hunt be your only hunt. Make happy memories by creating various occasions for a hunt: at a birthday, always hide one gift and let the receiver find it by searching for it as others give "hot," "warm," "cold," or "freezing" comments; at Halloween have an in-the-house hunt for candy as an alternative to the door-to-door method; at Christmas when there is an unwrappable gift such as a bicycle, create clues that lead to the gift. For sandbox fun, bury biodegradable packing popcorn and give a prize for the first child finding twenty-five of them.

❑ **532.** **BABYHOOD PRESERVED.** Set aside one of your baby's special little outfits plus a soft toy or small rattle. Make a copy of the birth certificate and select one or more baby photos. When the child is about five, work with her to make a memory box. At a frame shop, buy a deep frame that will accommodate and protect the items (some even come with Velcro to affix the elements to the backing). Make a pleasing arrangement with the certificate or announcement in the back, photos, clothing, and so forth on top. Use glue or Velcro to hold it to the backing, then finish the framing. When the youngster moves to her own home, let her take her memento frame as a reminder of her babyhood.

❑ **533.** **MORNING GREETING.** Start the tradition of a unique greeting and encourage the phrase to be the first words exchanged each morning. It can be "good morning" in another language such as *"bonjour"* (French), or "Up and at 'em" said with a high five.

❑ **534.** **JOKATHON.** Family reunions can be very nostalgic. Add humor to large gatherings of relatives by having a joke contest. Let folks know in advance that there will be prizes for the funniest story. Help your children practice their joke-telling skills so they can compete.

❑ **535.** **BIRTHDAY BREAKFAST IN BED.** Even if it's a school day, have everyone gather in the bedroom of the celebrant for cereal and a cupcake with a candle on it. The cake can come at dinnertime, but this tradition starts the day right.

❑ **536.** IF THEY WRITE A BOOK ABOUT YOU . . . Who knows which family members will become famous! Help future biographers by keeping a family diary. It can be as simple as a loose-leaf notebook kept at the dinner table. The first person finished eating can note highlights of the day or week. Just a few lines written regularly provide an interesting resource.

❑ **537.** ELECTION PARTICIPATION. Let kids have memories of your regular participation in local and national elections. Include them by sharing the sample ballot, reading some of the propositions together, and deciding on how "the family" should vote. And, let a youngster go to the polls with you so he can see how the system works. Make election day a special day by having dinner in front of the TV and watching the early returns.

❑ **538.** CHRISTMAS MANGER. A wonderful Christmas memory is the assembling of the family crèche, little by little, on the Sundays before Christmas. Start the first week of December by reading the story of Mary and Joseph and let kids place those figures in the scene. The next week read about the shepherds, and let the kids add them. Next, read about the kings, and put them in place. On Christmas Eve, read about the birth in the manger and place the animals and baby Jesus.

# SECTION 2: PARTY TIME!

Be original and help your youngster plan a really interesting birthday party right at home, rather than at some restaurant or expensive amusement center. If you love parties, you'll want to read my book *The Family Party Book* (Nashville: Abingdon Press, 1996), which will give you hundreds of ideas for parties, games, prizes, and foods—for children, teens, and adults, as well as for reunions. The party themes described below are given in detail in the book. Here are highlights from that book as well as some new ideas.

❑ **539.** THEMES FOR PRESCHOOLERS. This age loves make-believe so plan a party with your child that has some magic to it and lets a child use her imagination. Possibilities are: Pirate Party, Dress-Up Tea Party, Mother Goose Party, Teddy Bear Picnic, Snowball Party, Artist Party, Princess Party, Animal Party, Circus Party, Fairy Tale Party, Train Party, Ballerina Party, and Wizard of Oz Party.

❑ **540.** THEMES FOR GRADESCHOOL PARTIES. These more active parties will be winners: Safari Party, Olympics Party, Clown College, Make a TV Show (video) Party, Old MacDonald's Party, Western Party, Penguin Pool Party, Hobo Party, Mall Party, Castle and Kings Party, Dinosaur Day, Space Mission, Cowboy Round Up, and Let's Go Fishing Party.

❑ **541.** THEMES FOR TEEN PARTIES. These themes provide opportunities for conversation, music, and dancing: Karaoke Party, Time Capsule Party, Pancake Party, Wild and Wet Party, Sweet Sixteen Party, Schools Out Party, Backward Progressive Dinner, Baked Potato Supper, Full Moon Dance, Pentathlon Party (described below), and South Sea Island Party.

❑ **542.** TWO GENERATION PARTY. It's a pentathlon— five different games in one night. Divide the guests into teams of two and make a scoreboard to keep up-to-date on winners. First place gets ten points, second is seven points, third is four points, and the other teams get one point for participating. Some games will require both on the team to play, some just one playing and one as coach. Each game is played for twenty minutes, then a break for sports snacks and sodas, then rotate to the next game. Choose five games from this list: Jenga or pickup sticks, Velcro ball, Scrabble, golf putting into a circle of string, dominoes, darts, Monopoly, hearts, Ping-Pong, or checkers.

❑ **543.** HOLIDAY PARTIES KIDS LOVE. Plan holiday celebrations with your youngsters and include other families. Some occasions and parties are: New Year's Day—Resolution and Football Party; Valentine's Day—Candy-making Party; St. Patrick's Day—Irish Supper Party; April Fool's Day—Pranks Party; Easter—Neighborhood Egg Hunt; Mother's Day and Father's Day—Surprise Parties; Independence Day—Old-Fashioned Picnic and Games Party; Halloween—Hayride and Square Dance Party; Thanksgiving—Potluck Party; and Christmas—Caroling Party.

❑ **544.** A BACKWARD PARTY. Send invitations that are written backward (it's easy if you write it out first and then copy each word from the end to the start). Ask guests to come with their clothes on backward. Serve the birthday cake first, then open packages, then have the other food, and end up with games done in a backward way (run an obstacle course or relay race backward, or play the Ballooney Sandwich game described below). End the party with each guest backing out the door.

❑ **545.** WELCOME TO THE NEIGHBORHOOD. Get to know new neighbors at a weekend barbecue/potluck party. On cardboard, make a large drawing of the neighborhood, showing where everyone lives. Provide name tags that also list hobbies or careers. Let your youngsters plan outdoor relays for everyone and some for kids only.

❑ **546.** GRADESCHOOL GRADUATION PARTY. Guests come dressed as kindergartners in ruffly dresses or short pants, hair bows or slicked down hair, and carrying lollipops. Play little kids games such as "Mother, May I" or "Simon Says." If possible, contact school friends before the party and videotape each of them telling a unique but true story about one of the graduates. Play the video at the end of the party.

❑ **547.** HIGH SCHOOL AND COLLEGE GRADUATION PARTIES. The theme can be "Welcome to the Real World." Invite friends and relatives for a sit-down meal of steak and beans—symbolic of the feast-or-famine days ahead. From old slides and photos, prepare a video production called "This Is Your Crazy Life." Gifts should be useful in the real world the grad is entering: cookbook, alarm clock, bus pass, tie, appointment book, downtown area map, quick energy bars, a broom, and so forth.

❑ **548.** SPARE GIFT. Don't get flustered if your youngster gets a sudden invitation to a birthday party. Keep a unisex gift on hand, such as a game. Always let your youngster, if over age five, do the wrapping and card writing, and if under five, do it together.

❑ **549.** PARTY GIFT FAVORITES. A recent survey showed these toys as the top ten favorites of younger children: kitchens and kitchen dishes and foods, small racing cars, a working watch, hop ball, small Barbie-type doll or action figure with clothes and equipment, sleeping bag, set of wild animals, telephone, Etch-a-Sketch, and easel with paper and paints. When visiting a toy store, look at these items and ask your kids how they rank on their own wish lists.

❑ **550.** A UNIQUE GIFT. A memorable gift for child or adult is an American flag. You'll find them in a wide range of prices at a flag store (listed in the yellow pages under "flags"). You can also buy a flag of a person's native country. Include a pole and wall bracket, along with a booklet on flag protocol. As you wrap the gift, talk with your child about flag history, and look it up in the encyclopedia if you don't have all the answers.

## GAMES

❑ **551.** CAPTAIN HOOK. Mark out the boundaries of a large rectangular play area and choose one player to be Captain Hook. He stands in the middle of the play area with other players inside the boundaries. On the word "Go," Hook chases any player and attempts to tag him with one hand. A tagged player hooks (holds) onto Captain

Hook's hand and they continue to tag other players using only their free hands. As tagged players are added to the two ends of the line, all must be sure to hold hands at all times. Players may not run through the line of hooked-together players or outside the boundaries. The last player to be tagged becomes Captain Hook for the next game.

❑ **552.** SONG STUMPERS. While having refreshments, encourage kids to call out the name of a song and see who can be the first to sing the opening line. This is fun when several generations are playing together.

❑ **553.** WEIRD WORDS. Give each guest a small card on which is written an unusual word (keyed to the age of the group) such as clumsy, dribbled, crimson, stingy, bionic, bagpipes, superfluous, dilapidated, statuesque, medicinal, bothersome, ticklish. The object is to work the word into the conversation without it being noticed. After about thirty minutes, have each person reveal their weird word and when (or if) they used it.

❑ **554.** TELL THE TRUTH. With a group of twelve or more, each person writes down something that no one else knows about him. These papers are put in a bowl and then each person selects one. Going around the circle, the person reads the statement and gets one guess as to who has written it. For example, a guest says "Molly, are you the person who climbed in the fountain by the court house?" If it's not Molly, the game moves to the next person who reads the statement he has and tries to guess who wrote it. Sometimes you'll go around the circle several times but as the field of possibilities shrinks, guesses are finally correct.

❑ **555.** PENNY HUNT. In the yard, scatter one hundred pennies. Give a bag to each child and see who can find the most in five minutes. Count up the pennies and if it does not total one hundred, send the hunters out once more. They get to keep what they find.

❑ **556.** TUNNEL RACES. At a fabric store, buy a twelve-foot length of stretchy black tube material (usually seamless jersey), an investment that will last for years. Play relay races through it, or make teams of a parent and child going opposite directions and having to pass each other inside the tunnel. It helps if an adult holds each end of the tube.

❑ **557.** BALLOONEY SANDWICH. Make a start and a finish line and blow up a number of large balloons. Pair off into teams of two (one adult and one child or two kids). The pairs make a ballooney sandwich by standing back-to-back with a balloon between them. They must keep the balloon off the floor, not using their hands or holding hands, as they shuffle from start to finish. Dropping or popping a balloon means they start over.

❑ **558.** BE A STAR. Hand prints in cement are a big attraction in Hollywood as they will be at your party. Have as many large cardboard boxes as guests. Cut the box sides down to about the three inch point. Line up the boxes on the patio or grass. Get bags of ready-mix quick setting cement and prepare according to the instructions. Put it in the boxes (about two inches deep) so that it is still wet when the party begins. As guests arrive, have a spotlight on the boxes and ask the "stars" to make a hand print and sign their name for posterity. These boxes of cement will set up sufficiently so that the guests can take them home at the end of the party.

❑ **559.** HUMAN CONVEYOR BELT. At least eight youngsters lie down on carpet or grass, close together side-by-side and face up. At the command "Go," they turn together to the left, then roll face down, then continue the same direction until face up, all the time remaining tight to the person next to them. Practice this until they can do it without separating from the youngsters next to them. Now load the conveyor belt with human cargo. One child lies down at one end across the other bodies. As the kids now begin to roll, the "cargo" moves along the belt until deposited at the other end. Let everyone have a chance to be the "cargo."

❑ **560.** STRING MAZE. This is fun for kids only or kids and adults. In advance, lay one string from the doorway of a room, under and around furniture to a hidden place. Tie a candy bar or prize to the end of the string. Do the same thing again, starting at the doorway and going a different direction but crossing the first string. Continue with new strings until you have one for each player. Then the group gathers at the door where each is given a string and told that she may not let go of it under any circumstances. However, she must carefully wind up the string and find the prize at the end. There will be lots of climbing under and over strings, a lot of laughing, and a few arguments over who is making a hopeless knot.

❑ **561.** "I WENT TO THE MALL." Ten guests sit in a circle and each is given a slip of paper with one word or phrase written on it. These are the words to be handed out in this order: fan, rocker, scissors, sewing machine, tight shoe, itchy new shirt, horse, sunglasses, perfume, and cuckoo clock. The first person begins by saying, "I went to the mall and I bought a fan" and he starts fanning himself. All the others must also fan themselves. The second person says, "I went to the mall and bought a fan and a rocking chair." She starts rocking **AND** fanning as do all the others. So it goes around the circle, each one adding their purchase and indicating their motion: fan with the left hand, rock the entire body, cut with the right hand, sew using the left foot, tap the floor with the right foot, squirm shoulders because of the itchy shirt, move up and down like a horse, blink because of the sun, sniff perfume, and say "cuckoo-cuckoo." It sounds silly, looks silly, but it is possible!

❑ **562.** THE COACH'S NIGHTMARE. Prepare for a simple basketball game in a gym, backyard, or driveway with a basketball hoop. Announce that there will be two teams—girls versus guys. The girls will be dressed normally. However, provide the guys with their basketball outfits: women's long dresses, high heels, and boxing gloves (or have each one tie one hand behind his back). Get the clothes at a thrift shop. The game will be a nightmare, but a funny one.

❑ **563.** EGGPLANT EXTRAVAGANZA. This relay race, which can be played indoors or out, will need a start and finish line, two poles or yardsticks, and two similar eggplants. Divide the group into two teams. The object is to start at the line and use the yardstick to push the eggplant to the finish line where the next team member takes over. It sounds easy, but participants soon find that when it comes to rolling, an eggplant has a mind of its own.

## PARTY FOOD

❑ **564.** FEEDING YOUNG KIDS. Keep young children involved in preparing the party food. A bakery (or your home bread machine) can make bread in bright colors, resulting in intriguing sandwiches. Another hearty dish is a pig in a blanket—a hot dog wound in refrigerated crescent dough (with a little catsup and cheese inside) and baked. Skewered fruit chunks can be assembled by kids. Forget plates and serve food in baskets. Sprinkles are a favorite and can be used on ice cream, cake, and even hot dogs.

❑ **565.** EATS FOR GRADESCHOOLERS. Let kids assemble their own submarine sandwiches. For dessert, make clown cones by scooping a ball of ice cream and adding coconut hair, candy eyes, cherry nose, and an orange segment mouth. Freeze the ice cream until very hard, and top with a pointed cone just before serving. Make a cake look like a train by cutting a sheet cake into rectangular sections, frosting these, piping on windows and doors, and decorating with candies and licorice for the smokestack and other details. For a safari party, find canteens and backpacks at an army surplus store and use them to hold buffalo burgers and jungle juice.

❑ **566.** HEARTY FOODS FOR TEENS. Pancakes with many toppings (fruits, nuts, syrups, ice cream, yogurt, chocolate chips, marshmallow creme, whipped cream) provide opportunities for fun. Make-your-own pizzas can work in a similar way. Provide an interesting nonalcoholic punch bowl with this make-ahead recipe: For each gallon of apple juice, add one quart of milk, one-fourth teaspoon nutmeg, a half teaspoon of cinnamon, and two teaspoons of vanilla. For serving, pour it in a punch bowl and (again for each gallon) stir in a twelve ounce container of whipped topping. They'll love it!

❑ **567.** CAKES WITH CHARACTER. Have older children prepare, bake, and frost a cake. Then, let them start the tradition of placing a nut in it (even if you buy a cake, tuck one pecan between the layers). The person who finds the pecan gets a little prize. Other traditional items to hide and find in cakes are a ring (the finder is the next to be married), a penny (the finder will receive unexpected money soon), and a yellow button (the finder might get kissed under the next full moon). For cakes (except birthday cakes), make them look beautiful by decorating them with edible (nonpoisonous) flowers that you have rinsed and dried. Let kids use geranium leaves with nasturtiums, daisies, or snapdragons. Or, make a candy-decorated cake with small pieces of candy in the filling and others arranged on top.

# SECTION 3: GETTING TOGETHER WITH GRANDPARENTS

Don't let get-togethers with relatives consist only of big meals with adult conversation. Provide opportunities for youngsters to interact with grandparents and others. You'll find many ideas in my book *The Ten Commandments for Grandparents* (Nashville: Abingdon Press, 1991).

❑ **568.** ONE-ON-ONE. Encourage a grandparent to have an activity with just one youngster at a time. It can be an overnight, a trip to the ball game, a shopping excursion, or picking and arranging flowers. When two are together there are wonderful opportunities for both fun and bonding.

❑ **569.** FAMILY HISTORY. Provide time for your youngster to work on a family tree with a grandparent. Make it a family photo tree, showing each name and if possible, a picture. (You may have to write and ask relatives for their photos.) Or, work together to record a family audio history or make a photo album from pictures that have been long stored in a shoe box. Let grandparents take kids to see the grandparents' old neighborhood—the house they lived in, where they went to school, where they worked—and have lunch in a restaurant where they used to eat.

❑ **570.** PHONE VISITS. Let a youngster make the weekly phone call to a relative. But first, make a list together of things to share—from school and play, or from parent's work, and activities. It gives the relative a different perspective from your usual call.

❑ **571.** GOSSIP AND TRUTH. Kids hear stories about relatives—some true, some not. Find something especially good about each relative and tell your youngster. When you plan to be with relatives, encourage kids to ask them about their youth, work, family, and traditions. Even though some relatives may have more "sterling" character traits than others, let your youngsters make up their own minds about relatives.

❑ **572.** TRADITIONS. Ask your preteen what "firsts" are important: first earrings, first long dress, first car, or a first communion or bar mitzvah. Then, talk with a grandparent about being a part of the tradition. Some will want to buy that long dress, contribute 50 percent of the cost of the used car purchase, or take part in the religious event. It's an important link between the generations.

❑ **573.** ROUND-ROBIN. When youngsters are old enough to write good letters, show them how to start a round-robin letter among cousins and other relatives. Four to six is an ideal number. (Each participant will write a letter and perhaps include a photo, then send it off to the next who will add her letter and send it on.) Help make a list that includes the order the letter is to go, and the address of each participant. See how long it takes for the letters to come back.

❑ **574.** REUNIONS.   Great memories for kids come from family reunions. Gradeschool and high school youngsters can help plan the get-together, whether it's one dinner or a long weekend. Let one youngster set up a mailing list on the computer. Another can plan kids' games and adult/kid relay races. Everyone coming brings a dish for the meal. For everything you need to know about big reunions see *The Family Party Book* (Nashville: Abingdon Press, 1996).

❑ **575.** STORYTELLING.   Encourage grandparents to tell family history stories to kids—they can be even more exciting than fiction! A globe or old photos can be used as props. Stories of life in another country, life during a war, or life without television can be quite fascinating. Kids also enjoy stories told about olden times. Let the grandparent name the stories: "The Legend of the Lost Brother" or "Why Sparky the Dog Got His Picture Taken." These stories can also be told on audio cassettes and sent by grandparents to faraway grandchildren.

❑ **576.** BEDTIME STORIES.   A grandparent who is a good storyteller can record tales for toddlers to listen to as they fall asleep. One grandmother has alternated familiar kiddie songs with stories and poems. While not ready for prime time, she is a star to her grandchild.

❑ **577.** TALENT SHARING.   Initiate a conversation among you, your children, and your parents to see what talents of interest to kids can be shared by the grandparents. Here are some: how to drive a car, enjoying the outdoors, cooking and baking, auto repair, photography, sewing and knitting, painting, workshop projects, computer, sports, music and dance lessons, and religious training. You may be willing and thankful to let the grandparents completely take over one or more of these activities.

❑ **578.** A VERY SPECIAL TRIP. One of the nicest and most memorable connections between grandparent and child is a special trip, often in honor of a youngster's twelfth birthday. Ask your parents if they would enjoy doing this for each child, and if so, have them prepare a list of possible trips for the child to choose from. (The choices could be a sailboat trip, a weekend at Disneyland, a visit to the Grand Canyon, a trip to Hawaii, or even the grand tour of Europe.) Help the youngster make the choice well in advance so there is plenty of time for anticipation. Prior to the trip, spend ample time talking together about sight-seeing, foods, clothes, manners, souvenirs, and the keeping of a journal.

❑ **579.** GRANDMA'S CAMP. Busy parents are happy to support this idea. Overnight at Grandma's Camp takes on a special flair since it takes place under the stars. (But if the weather changes, it can still be in sleeping bags in the living room.) Food is cooked outside, served in a mess kit, and breakfast is always blueberry pancakes.

❑ **580.** GRANDPA'S SECRET GARDEN. One grandchild is taken in on the conspiracy to plant a mysterious garden with Grandpa. Together they buy seeds, prepare the soil, plant, cultivate, weed, and eventually harvest. No one else knows what has been planted until it blooms or produces.

## I LIKE . . . YOU LIKE

Exchanges of gifts between grandparents and kids can be boring—or memorable. (Grandparents who don't really take the time and make the effort to know youngsters just send a check. In turn, kids often give grandparents whatever their folks buy.) Change this impersonal approach by helping kids find out the things their grandparents enjoy (gardening magazines, tools, candy and nuts, card games, a football team, sweaters) and then shop with them for a gift that ties in. Help grandparents learn the interests of their grandchildren (books, trucks, video games, cycling, birds, doll houses, sewing, CDs, sports team caps) so that they can choose gifts with appeal.

❑ **581.** GRANDPARENTS DAY. Of course there can be gifts and a dinner for this holiday that is the second Sunday in September. But when grandparents are not nearby, kids can prepare a very special memory. Each grandchild fills out a paper headed "Ten Extraordinary, Marvelous, Wonderful, Fabulous Things About My Grandparents." Illustrate the list with drawings and mail to arrive on time. The grandparents will read and reread them, maybe even frame them—and certainly feel loved.

❑ **582.** THE PINK GRANDMA. Let young children do their own gift shopping as much as possible. Be handy for guidance, but respect a child's choices and help him stick within his budget by shopping at a 99 Cent Store. One young boy wanted only pink gifts since he knew that was Grandma's favorite color. His mother turned him loose with his five dollars and this is what he bought: a pink fly swatter, a pink dust pan, pink nail polish, a pink guardian angel pin, and his favorite choice, which he named "the most beautiful gift," a glistening pinkish/copper colored scrubbing pad. Grandma especially enjoys cleaning with it!

❑ **583.** FINGER FOOD FUN. Surprise grandparents by having a meal without silverware. Everything served is to be eaten with fingers. Let kids help plan the foods that can include: chicken, pizza, kebabs, spareribs, fried shrimp, fried potatoes, carrot sticks, corn on the cob, apple slices, melon balls, cookies, brownies, and ice-cream cones.

❑ **584.** GRANDMA SAYS . . . that you can tell much about a person by looking at their hands. That's why she gives each grandchild, at about age four, three grooming tools: a small nail brush for scrubbing the undersides of nails, an emery board for smoothing rough nails, and a nail whitener pencil. She demonstrates the use of each and knows that because they have their very own, they will get used more often—especially when she's coming to inspect. With your kids, look at one another's hands and see if they would pass inspection.

❑ **585.** FABULOUS FRAMES. Let kids make picture frames for gifts to grandparents. And, of course, kids will put their own pictures inside these frames made of cardboard. At a stationery supply store, get the sturdiest cardboard available. Using the photo as a size guide, a parent cuts two pieces of cardboard two inches larger all around than the photo. Then cut an opening in one piece a half inch smaller than the photo. Now the youngster is ready to decorate this second piece with paint, ribbons, pennies, shells, buttons, or puzzle pieces glued to the frame. Next, tape the photo in place on the backside and add the second piece of cardboard as a backing. A small easel can be made of the excess cardboard.

❑ **586.** FOR SOMEONE WHO HAS EVERYTHING. One gift that kids can give is the gift of love and appreciation. Help kids write an alphabet-of-love card for a relative. Following each letter of the alphabet, put a word that decribes the recipient. For example: A—affectionate. B—boisterous. C—clever. D—daring. And for X and Z consider X-tra special and Zany. Using a dictionary may help!

# EIGHT
# THERE'S A BIG WORLD OUT THERE

SECTION 1: GROWING UP GRACEFULLY

SECTION 2: MANAGING MONEY

SECTION 3: A SHRINKING WORLD

SECTION 4: THE FUTURE IN YOUR HANDS

SECTION 5: GETTING ALONG WITH OTHERS

SECTION 6: LIFE WITH AND WITHOUT TELEVISION

# SECTION 1:
# GROWING UP GRACEFULLY

Parents need not fear the preteen and teen years if they prepare for them with their children. And the important word here is WITH. Don't wait until the teen years to discuss the four D's: dating, driving, drinking, and drugs.

## DATING AND SEX

❑ **587.** DATING REQUIREMENTS. Before a youngster starts to date, talk together about your "need to know" concerning certain facts. These are: the full name and phone number of the date, the means of transportation, the destination or destinations, and the time he or she will be home. Be insistent that no youngster goes out the door without sharing this information.

❑ **588.** ASKING FOR A DATE. When asking for a date, a youngster should ask well in advance and give specific information as to the event. And, kids should learn how to graciously turn down a date or calmly accept a "no." Sometimes a youngster will ask a friend to call on his behalf, however, if a youngster isn't mature enough to make the call himself, he isn't old enough to date! A little role playing at home will help kids to get over their shyness and will help the one responding to the question.

❑ **589.** WHEN MAY I DATE? In your family rules, which you have in written form, specify the age for solo dating (sixteen is quite common). You won't be pestered at age eleven if the rule has been known all along. Your rules might state: At about thirteen, it's acceptable for a boy to come over to study; at thirteen it's okay to attend chaperoned preteen parties, which are not really dates; by fifteen there can be double dating—with you or another parent driving.

❑ **590.** WHO MAY I DATE? Set basic standards before dating begins. Don't permit your youngster to date kids you do not know anything about. School dropouts, out-of-town visitors, one with a gang affiliation should be ruled out. Also, let your kids know that they are to date youngsters about their own age—a two-year difference being the max.

❑ **591.** POPULARITY AND PRESSURE. These are just two topics of interest to preteens. *Girltalk—All the Stuff Your Sister Never Told You* by Carol Weston (New York: Harper Perennial, 1992) has a casual style that will bring parents and daughters up-to-date information on relationships with each other and with boys, etiquette tips, meeting new people, and all the other topics that can be worrisome. It's a good book to read together—a little at a time each evening.

❑ **592.** IT TAKES GUTS. Give your youngsters support in saying no to silly, stupid, or illegal behavior or fads such as randomly picking up a stranger, cutting classes, shoplifting, using alcohol or drugs, tattooing and body-piercing, drag racing, or doing graffiti or vandalism. Some of these activities are considered fun on dates. While it takes courage to go against the crowd, saying "no" actually garners respect. Teach your kids lines such as "I'm too busy for that," or "No thanks, I'll pass," or "Sorry, catch you later."

❑ **593.** IT'S WRONG! So much education on the subject of sex is based on a parent's view of what is right and what is wrong. While a teen's obedience to these standards is essential, knowing the **reasons behind** the obedience are important when there is great peer pressure. Parents should start early to go beyond "It's wrong!" and provide facts to support your own values. When you provide kids with this ammunition, they may in turn share it with peers.

❑ **594.** STRAIGHT SCOOP. To share accurate information, a parent often needs the backup of some straight-forward facts. For parents of teens who want to replace myth and misinformation concerning puberty, sex, contraception, sexually transmitted diseases and more, the book *How Sex Works* by Elizabeth Fenwick and Richard Walker (New York: Dorling Kindersley Inc., 1994) offers a good opportunity for discussion together. Parents might want to read the book before the teen does. It includes actual questions from teens with answers from the professionals.

❑ **595.** PARENTS' RIGHTS. Rather than letting clinics subvert family relationships by secretly counseling kids on morally important matters, it is up to parents to actively participate in this counseling. In a society where most schools will not give a child an aspirin without parental consent, parents should have the minimal right to be notified (not asked for permission but notified, even if after the fact) when a minor daughter is receiving a drug related to sexual activity or having an abortion. It is not only a right, but a duty to be your youngster's mentor.

❑ **596.** THE THIRD CHOICE. Teach your youngsters that there are not just two choices: contraception or pregnancy. The third choice is abstinence. Parents should not complacently accept the inevitability of today's rate of teenage sexual activity. Read Kristine Napier's book *The Power of Abstinence* (New York: Avon, 1995). Then initiate a discussion on the subject.

❑ **597.** WHY NOT PREMARITAL SEX? Explain to kids that early sex experiences have bad results: one-third of all abortions are done for teens; babies born to teen moms are more likely to be brain damaged or retarded; venereal disease is epidemic and can cause sterility or death; and there are more attempted suicides among pregnant teens than girls of other ages. Also discuss the fact that a girl labeled "easy" has a difficult time shaking that reputation and regaining respect. Locker room talk isn't a myth nor is the burden of living with guilt. This is brutal information, but it's part of your parental job to share it and then talk about it together.

❑ **598.** AIDS. Your goal isn't just to help your youngster avoid HIV infection, it's to help him make smart decisions. Start a conversation by taking a cue from the media that gives plenty of information. If you feel a youngster is (or is going to be) sexually active, you must be **very explicit** concerning the dangers ahead. Go beyond what is taught in school by ordering, reading, and discussing the free booklet *Aids Prevention Guide* from the National AIDS Clearinghouse, P. O. Box 6003, Rockville, MD 20849-6003. It's written specifically for parents.

## DRIVING

❑ **599.** NOT AUTOMATIC. The car may be automatic, but permission to drive isn't. While the law states an age when kids may drive, the level of maturity varies in teens. Let driving be a privilege granted only to responsible kids. Let them know in advance what you expect in the way of grades, integrity, and responsibility.

❑ **600.** MORE THAN DRIVER'S ED. Don't count on kids learning it all in school. See for yourself by sitting right next to your youngster and observing driving habits during the period she has her learner's permit. Give her many opportunities to drive so that you both have confidence when she starts to drive alone.

❑ **601.** DRIVING TABOOS. Start with gradeschoolers to inform kids about bad driving practices such as driving without a license, cutting off another driver, drag racing, picking up strangers, speeding, and drunk driving. Also point out tailgating, failing to use the lane change indicator and check in the mirror, speeding through intersections on the yellow light, and even leaving keys in the ignition and failing to lock the car. When out together in the family car, point out these bad habits in other drivers.

❑ **602.** FIRST OFFENSES. You'll make your point about safe driving practices if you come down hard on the first offense—taking the car without permission, getting a ticket, or other infractions. It won't harm a youngster to do without the car for a month—he'll think twice about his actions the next time. Although it is grim information, tell kids that an accident can change the life of another family, of himself, and your family.

❑ **603.** REWARDS. Start slowly when allowing a youngster to drive on her own. When she has exhibited good driving practices for about six months, she can then drive others. Compliment her when she's been responsible and increase the number of times she can borrow the car.

❑ **604.** A CAR OF MY OWN. At about age thirteen, let a youngster know that only when he has his license and proved his abilities as a good driver will you consider the purchase of a car for him. However, he can start a car fund for the future. Talk about the cost of buying a vehicle, insurance, and maintenance. Set up a plan where the parent (or grandparent) will pay half if the youngster earns the other half of the cost with a part-time job. You may want to provide opportunities for earning extra money at home during this time.

## TOBACCO, ALCOHOL, AND DRUGS

❑ **605.** A GIRL WITH A CIGAR? An increasing number of girls are taking up smoking, even cigar smoking. Despite devastating health damage, smoking is an expensive habit that makes for smelly breath and clothing. Tell them the truth: the majority of boys prefer girls who don't smoke. If you smoke, make it clear to your kids that you don't approve of anyone smoking and you wish you could stop. Make it clear that it is easier to just not start than to quit. One smoking grandfather feels so strongly about this that he pays for a year of college for any grandchild who does not smoke.

❑ **606.** POT PRESSURE. Kids often believe the myth that marijuana is harmless, but three decades of research have disproved that. Inform your kids that today's grass is ten times stronger than that smoked a generation ago. While a few youngsters might not show a reaction, others get drowsy or act drunk, have impaired judgment, reduced attention span, vision problems, reduced learning ability (due to brain cell impairment), and severe loss of motivation. And, the drug stays in the system, decreasing resistance to infections and damaging lungs far more than cigarettes. The need for drugs is a sign that the youngster is not willing to face up to challenges in a mature way. It's a cry for your help.

❑ **607.** COCAINE, PCP, LSD, AND HEROIN. Get the facts and share them with your kids—**don't be timid.** Start by describing these four temptations. Cocaine (coke) is a powerful and expensive stimulant that can last for days, then cause intense depression, resulting in a craving for a new high. PCP (angel dust) is cheap and deadly, causing hallucinations, mood disorders, paranoia, hostility, brain damage—the symptoms sometimes recurring years after use. LSD is an unpredictable drug that can cause severe psychotic symptoms (some users believe they can fly and jump out windows), "bad trips," and mental damage that can last forever. Heroin, an expensive hard-to-kick drug, requires a "fix" several times a day. Addicts suffer from chills and nausea as well as liver damage and hallucinations. Withdrawal is painful and often not effective. Because addicts often share unsterilized needles, AIDS is spreading through the heroin-addicted population. The methadone program that supplies a synthetic narcotic free of charge has had some success. In order to support these habits, many users turn to stealing that further complicates their lives.

❑ **608.** JUST ONE LITTLE DRINK. With alcoholism affecting kids as young as ten, start your education early. Explain the dangers. Auto accidents caused by drunk driving are the leading cause of teenage deaths. Alcohol use is a crutch for those who think it relaxes them, gives them confidence, or helps them forget troubles or fall asleep. It is actually a depressant and even those who drink in moderation gradually require more frequent and stronger drinks to get a lift. Few people can say that they drink less and less as the years pass.

❑ **609.** KEEPING CLOSE. The best way to protect kids from drug use is by maintaining good and open communication, remaining actively involved with them and their friends, giving them opportunities to increase self-esteem, and expressing high expectations for their achievement in school and career. However, once drug involvement has begun, it is important to seek professional help immediately through school counselors and other professionals.

## SECTION 2: MANAGING MONEY

A recent Harris poll found that 88 percent of high school students said they had "learned everything they know about money from their parents." Whether parents have been good or bad examples in the past, they can now learn financial skills and instruct kids how to avoid financial pitfalls.

❑ **610.** THE SAVING RATIO. Starting when children are young, encourage them to save 10 percent of their income—income being allowance and gift money. Take them to the bank and go through the procedure of opening an account. You may want to start the account with a gift of $100 since there are often benefits of having an account in three figures. Nowadays, you may not be dealing with a kindly investment officer, but rather with an impersonal ATM. Show kids how these machines work. When statements come, and at earnings time, be sure to show kids what their money earns. Help them determine both long-term and short-term goals. Delaying gratification and saving for something is great financial training.

❑ **611.** MATCHING FUNDS. Parents (and grandparents) can make matching fund deals with youngsters. Perhaps the teen is considering the purchase of a first car, a 4-H animal, or ski equipment. In order to encourage saving, offer to "go halves" (pay for the second half of the investment) if the youngster saves for the first. But remember to treat all your young savers to the same special deals.

❑ **612.** BAD EXAMPLES. Keep a watch out for investment scam stories in newspapers and on TV. Teaching your child to be wary of the promise of amazing returns is the foundation for savvy investing. Show how a credit card account charges interest and how instant gratification can cause big trouble. And, if you have made injudicious investments, "fess up" since this bad example will be especially meaningful.

❑ **613.** NO SECRETS. By the time kids can add and subtract, take them into your confidence concerning your budget and investments, but explain that this information is to remain within the immediate family. When you decide on an investment (a home, car, bond, and so forth), go over the finances and show exactly where the money comes from, where it goes, and what the long-term result will be. Sometimes this shared analysis will help *you* to see the nonmerits of the investment.

❑ **614.** BUDGETS AND ALLOWANCES. Having money and learning how to budget it should be taught when youngsters first receive an allowance. Talk about how it must last (one week for young children, two weeks to a month for older ones). Remember that an allowance is given for being part of the family. Work together to make a list of what the allowance should cover and total up this amount. The list can include school lunches, bus fares, school supplies, entertainment (such as CDs and movies), church contributions, special purchases (wants that are more expensive than parents are willing to buy), and money for gifts to be given that month. For other spending needs, provide the opportunity for kids to earn money.

❑ **615.** THE CLOTHING BUDGET. Entirely separate from the allowance is a youngster's clothing budget. In the late summer, before school begins, sit down with each child and look over all the clothes and shoes. Get rid of things that are worn out or do not fit. Make a list of bottoms that need tops and vice versa, as well as under and outer apparel. Make a guesstimate of the total cost and then deduct one-fifth (to increase your effort to make good buys). This figure is a six month budget, and if there are "must have" fad items, provide opportunities for the youngster to earn the money, or put the item on her wish list for a birthday or holiday.

❑ **616.** CREDIT FREE. Early in a child's life, establish as a general rule that one saves first, and buys second. Credit cards can be a handy and useful tool but only when the account is paid off monthly. Show your child a charge account statement, look at the interest charged on an unpaid balance, and figure what it would cost to not pay the bill. Share facts on the dangers of abusing credit cards—and set a good example yourself.

❑ **617.** TALK ABOUT RISKS. Although a bank savings account pays a small amount of interest, the purchase of a stock might bring attractive returns—or big losses. Explain the concept of a mutual fund and look at the component companies. What does your youngster think of Levi Strauss or Nike as an investment? Teach kids to be alert to the daily Dow Jones Industrial Average announced on television, and what, if anything, it means to the family.

❑ **618.** PRETEND PURCHASE. As a learning experiment, let a youngster pick a stock that is attractive to her and make a pretend purchase of 100 shares. Show her how to keep a log of its ups and downs, splits, and dividends. Then after one year, compute the profit or loss.

❑ **619.** TICKER TAPE VISIT. Teens can learn from a visit to a stock broker's office. (Just watching the ticker tape is fascinating.) Or, if you're nearby, visit a stock exchange.

❑ **620.** GET SMART. Depending on age, your child will enjoy one of these two items: a video for gradeschoolers called *Piggy Banks to Money Markets* (Los Angeles: Price Stern Sloan, 1993) and *Learn to Earn* by Peter Lynch and John Rothchild (New York: Simon and Schuster, 1995, a book for older kids. Watch, read, and learn together.

❑ **621.** A REAL INVESTMENT. If you are inclined to buy a stock yourself, sell your youngster one share of the stock. Choose a company that has appeal to kids. As they get older, young people may appreciate a safe and conservative investment gift as a college graduation or wedding remembrance.

❑ **622.** THE MIRACLE OF COMPOUND INTEREST. With pencil and paper, show youngsters how compounding interest can make a difference. As an example, say that you put 100 dollars in an account where you earn 5 percent interest. At the end of the year, show that you have earned $5.00 without doing anything but leaving it in the bank. At the end of the second year, what would you have? You'd have $5.25 more, making a total of $110.25. Now, how long must you leave the money in the account to double it? This shows kids the importance of shopping around to get the best interest rate and then letting the money work for them.

❑ **623.** THE MONEY JAR. For many of us, going out to eat is a treat. To make it more affordable, use the money jar method. On a counter in the kitchen or family room, place a large glass jar with the lid taped in place. Have a slit in the jar top that will accommodate coins. Excess change, money from recycling, fines for using profanity, and other donations all go in the jar. Counting it is fun for kids and it makes the going-out event more appreciated.

❑ **624.** CAR WASH ENTREPRENEURS. Earning money takes a twist with this multiactivity project. With grade and high school kids (your own and their friends), choose a date well in advance for a car wash. Advertise it with flyers and posters created by the youngsters. While some kids do the cars, others occupy the car owners with twenty-five cent lemonade, a bake sale, and mini flea market. Afterward, discuss the money earned, divide it up, and see if it was worth it.

❑ **625.** HOLIDAY HELPERS. Many folks welcome extra help during the busy holiday season and enterprising youngsters can easily earn extra cash. Help your youngster create an attractive flyer offering services such as package wrapping and mailing, snow shoveling, Christmas tree purchasing. During the year, there are opportunities beyond babysitting and lawn cutting: dog washing and walking, putting up screens, replacing batteries in smoke detectors, house cleaning, or making minor repairs. Show how a youngster can key her services to seniors as well as busy young families.

❑ **626.** ZILLIONS. Teaching kids to be wise consumers is a project of Consumers Union in their magazine *Zillions*. Because children between ages eight and twelve have more than $17 billion at their disposal, they need to be knowledgeable in the face of media hype and peer pressure. There are interesting stories and facts on bikes, sports equipment, snack food, "hot" clothes, in-line skates, boredom busters, and many other topics related to spending. Ask for a copy at a newsstand or library and you may decide to subscribe.

❑ **627.** PENNY PEBBLES. Sometimes homes are surrounded with landscaping that includes two different colors of pebbles. One grandmother found that some of the red gravel had got mixed with the green gravel. Since neither she nor her husband liked this bend-over work, they hired their young grandchildren to put the colored gravel pieces back where they belong. For this task they paid a penny per pebble. Since their grandkids enjoyed the project, the grandparents now keep a list of other tasks such as polishing silver, dusting baseboards, cleaning kitchen drawers, cleaning hanging light fixtures, and running sprinklers.

❑ **628.** SATURDAY VISIT. Let your child visit your workplace for half of a day so she can see how you earn a living. Let her be useful by making copies, filing, cleaning out a drawer, and so forth. On the way to the office, talk about how you got this job. On the way back, talk about your plans for future work. Ask your youngster what she thought were the interesting or boring parts of what you both were doing.

❑ **629.** KIDS READ *THE WALL STREET JOURNAL?* Why not—it's a great learning experience. Start gradeschoolers reading the page one column "What's News?" and, as they get older, read and share other short stories of interest. Help them understand terms found in articles: supply side, gross national product, balance of trade, Dow Jones Average, NASDAQ, Federal Reserve, and so forth.

# SECTION 3: A SHRINKING WORLD

History, geography, politics all touch us as well as the world around us. Prepare kids for the world of tomorrow by talking together about these important subjects.

❑ **630.** IF I WERE PRESIDENT. Someone about the age of your child will grow up to be president of the United States. Initiate a discussion and ask, "What do you think that youngster is doing now? If you were going to be president, what subjects should you study? If you became president, what would you try to accomplish?" Don't be judgmental: you can learn from a child's imaginative answers.

❑ **631.** WHERE IN THE WORLD ARE YOU? Obtain a globe (better than a world map) at a garage sale or buy one of the inexpensive cloth ones that fit over an inflatable ball. It doesn't matter if it isn't totally up-to-date—that gives you an opportunity to talk about recent changes. Play this game: One person looks at the globe and picks out a place name while the others aren't looking. She announces the name "Zanzibar"—or whatever—and all youngsters start searching for it. After one minute, parents are permitted to look, too. The first to find the place is the next to choose, but eventually make sure everyone has a turn.

❑ **632.** CHANGE THE LOCATION. While reading or telling stories to children, change the locale to something unusual. For example, the story of the three bears could take place in Russia; the *Cat in the Hat* might be in South Africa; or *Heidi* could live in Mexico. Wherever you choose, let the child find that place on a map or globe and, as the story develops, you can change the story further to suit the geography of that area.

❑ **633.** WALL CHART. Since many youngsters have a poor knowledge of historical chronology buy *The Wall Chart of World History* by Edward Hull (New York: Dorset Press, 1988). This fold-out book contains a wealth of information in pictures and words, and the fourteen connecting panels trace history in a time line from the biblical times to the current times. It's a good springboard for conversation, questions, research, and school projects since it shows what was going on concurrently throughout the world at any time.

❑ **634.** DATE CONTEST. Have a family contest to see who remembers the importance of the following twenty dates:

| | |
|---|---|
| 230,000,000 B.C. | Age of dinosaurs begins |
| A.D. 0 | Approximate date of birth of Jesus |
| 476 | Approximate date Rome falls, which ends ancient history and begins medieval history. |

| | |
|---|---|
| 1000 | Approximate date Leif Eriksson explores North America |
| 1215 | Magna Carta signed |
| 1271 | Marco Polo travels to Orient |
| 1300–1600 | Renaissance |
| 1440 | Gutenberg invents movable type for printing |
| 1492 | Columbus lands in America |
| 1564 | Shakespeare writes during reign of Elizabeth I |
| 1620 | Plymouth Colony established in America |
| 1776 | U. S. Declaration of Independence |
| 1815 | Napoleon Bonaparte defeated at Waterloo |
| 1860s | Lincoln is president, U.S. Civil War |
| 1903 | Wright brothers' first airplane flight |
| 1914–17 | World War I |
| 1939–45 | World War II |
| 1944 | First digital computer |
| 1946 | Television era begins |
| 1969 | Man walks on the moon |

❏ **635.** FOLLOW ONE TOPIC. Talk about national and world issues that are historical in nature and will affect the future: orphans in China, Middle East peace, pollution, the two-parent workforce and day care, drugs, apartheid, terrorism, and so forth. Let each youngster choose one topic to follow in the news. After about six weeks, see what new facts each one has to share.

❏ **636.** FLAT MAP. Show kids what a small world it is. Attach a flat world map to a wall and use pins to locate your hometown, where you've vacationed, where relatives live, where you go on business, where there are conflicts in the world, where relatives have fought in wars, and where certain food products are raised.

❏ **637.** PEN PAL. When a child writes well enough to communicate—usually by age eight or nine—ask if he'd enjoy a pen pal. You'll be able to locate one through your school, place of worship, your overseas contacts, or a pen pal club. Such connections make "foreign" seem friendly.

❏ **638.** STAMP COLLECTING. Stamps give glimpses of the world since they show landscapes, historical sights, flags, and famous people of many nations. Visit the post office to see stamps and a collector's shop to see many more. If kids are interested, obtain a beginner's stamp book. While you can buy beautiful stamps of many countries, start with a small selection, and if this becomes a child's collectible, purchase more philatelic supplies.

❏ **639.** POSTER DECOR. Visit a travel agency with your youngster and ask if there are any excess posters you can have. Let her use them to decorate the family room or her bedroom. Talk about the scenes and identify the countries. Decide which country the family would like to visit.

❏ **640.** THE GEOGRAPHY OF A TRIP. When taking a major trip with the family, don't just concentrate on historical sights and local foods. Prior to the trip, spend a little time each week learning about the size and terrain of the area, the climate, business and industry, political history, dialects or language, and interesting products to buy.

❏ **641.** NOT A PARTY. Rather than emphasizing party affiliation, talk with kids about political priorities—what you and they believe government should do. How are these goals realized (or not) in your country and in other countries? Can your family take part in local politics and problem solving, or write letters to state and federal officials? Encourage full participation in government, starting with being registered to vote.

# SECTION 4: THE FUTURE IN YOUR HANDS

Tune in with your kids to the world of science, discovery, and the concerns for the environment. Borrow this book from the library and you may want to own it: *Science As It Happens* by Jean Durgin Harlan and Carolyn Good Quattrocchi (New York: Henry Holt, 1994). It's a wonderful collection of family activities for children ages four through eight.

❑ **642.** SCIENCE IN THE KITCHEN. Encourage an inquisitive spirit with simple experiments in the kitchen. These include mixing food coloring to make new colors, seeing how yeast makes bread rise, watching how clear gelatin solidifies a liquid, heating a small amount of water with salt in it and letting it evaporate to form salt crystals, making paste from water and flour.

❑ **643.** EARTH DAY. Each April, the world celebrates Earth Day—an opportunity for families to show appreciation for the environment. Start by clipping newspaper articles and noting local observances. Of the many options, choose one as your family's cause, whether it is reclaiming a park, combating graffiti, or planting trees, and set aside time to work on it this week.

❑ **644.** CONSERVATION AT HOME. Let kids organize home recycling (cans, glass, plastic, paper) and also the recycling of possessions no longer in use. Go for a trash walk (with gloves and bags), cleaning up your neighborhood. Look critically at your own property and beautify it. Support legislation that protects the environment. Even scrutinize your water and energy bills and see what steps the family can take to conserve.

❑ **645.** SCIENCE IN THE WORKSHOP. Show a child how to string empty thread spools to make simple pulleys for hoisting small toys. Create an inclined plane from pieces of wood, then roll cars down it to see how steep the plane can be tilted before the car tumbles off. Demonstrate how a spirit level shows a flat surface or a vertical one, and how the two form a right angle.

❑ **646.** LIFE BOOK.   Help a youngster appreciate the variety of plant life—trees and flowers—by making a life book. Go on walks and carefully collect, identify, and then press various specimens. See how many trees and flowers grow right in your own neighborhood. Let the child encase the dried specimens in plastic or glue them on paper to make a book that can be easily added to.

❑ **647.** STAR QUESTIONS.   Encourage interest in the heavens by looking at the stars on a clear night. Ask kids: "Do you think there is life on other planets? What is the brightest star? The largest star cluster? Is there a star that blinks?" (You may have to look up these answers.) For a second session, have a star map so you can identify the Big Dipper (Ursa Major, the Great Bear), the Little Dipper (Ursa Minor, the Little Bear), Polaris (the North Star), Venus (Earth's sister planet), and the Milky Way (our galaxy).

❑ **648.** UNDER THE SEA.   Marine biology is a popular subject and one that immediately interests kids. Visit a public aquarium, then go to the shore to look at tide pools, and eventually enjoy snorkeling and scuba diving for a closer look at marine life. Let your youngster create a realistic fish tank (not just a bowl of goldfish) and learn how to maintain it.

❑ **649.** MOON WALK.   Show kids the progression of the phases of the moon. Before bed, go out and see what phase the moon is in. Make it a tradition to go for a "moon walk" on the first night of each full moon.

❑ **650.** FOR 3-6 AND 7-12.   The National Wildlife Federation now has a magazine for three- to six-year-olds, and it's as creative and fun as its *Ranger Rick* for seven- to twelve-year-olds. It's called *Your Big Backyard* and features games, stories, plenty of pictures plus a monthly poster, all keyed to children from three to six. A twelve-month subscription is just $15, from NWF, P.O. Box 777, Mount Morris, IL 61054-8276.

❏ **651.** **TINY LIBRARY.** Bookstores carry pocket-sized books that identify birds, insects, flowers, and trees. Offer to buy one for a youngster who is interested in one of these fields. Give a small reward for identifying five birds (or flowers, and so forth), then ten, then twenty-five. Show your interest as you learn together.

❏ **652.** BUG SEARCH. There are many little creatures right in your own backyard. Help kids overcome fear of harmless bugs by carefully observing them. Arm kids with a big spoon or hand spade, a shallow box, and a magnifying glass. Look in buggy places such as dark corners, the underside of leaves, sidewalk cracks, and under rocks. See who first finds a bug and can carefully lift it with the spoon into the box for observation and identification. After viewing it through a magnifying glass, put the bug back in its home. Another day, provide kids with a garbage can cover to place in the garden in a cool or shady spot. Leave it for forty-eight hours and then carefully turn it over. Investigate, identify, but don't harm the little creatures who have moved in. You will see worms and other insects just as you can when turning over a rock when on a nature hike.

❏ **653.** BUTTERFLY BABIES. In the spring, show your child the miracle of metamorphosis by preparing a little home for a caterpillar and watching it turn into a butterfly. Read in an encyclopedia about the stages of life, from egg to caterpillar to pupa to chrysalis to butterfly. Cut the top from a half-gallon milk carton and cut windows in each side. Tape fine gauze over the windows and rubber band a gauze square on the top. Provide food (leaves) and moisture (cotton dipped in sugar water.) Now go outside—it won't take you long to find a caterpillar marching along. Carefully move it into the carton, taking along the twig or leaf where you found it. You will see it shed its skin, form a chrysalis, and usually in a few weeks, there will be a butterfly. Watch it hatch. Now it's time to place your butterfly house outside and remove the top so the butterfly can go free.

❏ **654.** **BRING THE OUTDOORS IN.** Don't let indoors be devoid of the wonders of nature. A piece of driftwood combined with pine cones makes an interesting centerpiece. A shell collection can be on a fancy plate in the living room. An interesting rock makes a good paperweight. Field flowers and weeds, daisies and dandelions make attractive bouquets. Each week ask one youngster to bring an interesting nature item inside and place it in the middle of the table so you can admire it and talk about it at dinner.

❏ **655.** **MINI-GREENHOUSE.** Help kids cut the bottoms off gallon-sized plastic milk jugs. At the nursery, let a youngster choose some tomato plants for his garden. Cover with the jugs to enhance the growth and also to protect the plants from unexpected frosts. On warm days, the jugs can be removed for a few hours.

❏ **656.** **PET ROCKS.** Use a fishbowl to display the interesting rocks youngsters collect. At the library, look for a book on rocks and identify the finds. Use big rocks as bookends. And, if a youngster really enjoys rock collecting and displaying, consider a gift of a tumbling machine—the kind that polishes rocks to show off their true beauty.

❏ **657.** **CRICKETS TELL THE TEMPERATURE.** Crickets are known as the songsters of summer, but their chirping can also indicate the current temperature. Test them this easy way. In the evening, go to a quiet grassy place where the family can listen for cricket calls. Explain that crickets chirp for several reasons: to warn others of danger, to protect their territory, and to attract mates. As the weather gets warmer and their metabolism rises, their chirps come more rapidly. Once kids are attune to the chirps of a cricket, have them count the number they hear in a fifteen second peri-od. Then, add forty-two to this figure and you will have a somewhat accurate air temperature. So, if they hear twenty-eight chirps in fifteen seconds, add forty-two to that and see if the temperature is 70 degrees.

❑ **658.** TRACKING. When hiking, divide the group in two, each with an adult. The first group starts out ten min-utes ahead of the second group, the first leaving clues as to where they are going (rocks in the shape of an arrow, a little pile of leaves, a flower on a trail marker). See if the second group can arrive at the same destination. Have some pre-agreed meeting place should your tracking not be particular-ly adept.

❑ **659.** FIELD GLASS TAG. In a forest preserve or tree-filled park, play tag without running. In the center of the designated area, indicate with sticks two places where "It" can stand. All the others hide where they can see one of the two sticks, but where they themselves can scarcely be seen. "It" has binoculars and can move only between the two sticks while looking all around through the binoculars. If "It" sees a person, she calls out that person's name while pointing that direction. If she's guessed right, the person says "Yes," and becomes the new "It." If she's guessed wrong, there is silence and she must start looking again.

❑ **660.** THE RAIN MAKER. How does the rain get into the clouds? Show how with this experiment. The child heaps ice cubes into a small foil pan. The parent heats a small amount of water and then pours it into a large, clear canning jar and places the pan on top. The air right under the pan is cold as it is high in the sky. Let the child shine a flashlight into the glass to see the rising water vapor and a cloud forming under the pan. Peek under the pan to see the droplets condensing on the bottom side. Replace the pan and keep watching together until the droplets become heavier and then fall back into the water like rain falling from a cloud. In almost the same way, water is picked up from the earth and as it cools in the sky it condenses into droplets.

❑ **661.** TIDEPOOLS. Small bodies of sea water provide safe living places for many aquatic animals. Plan a visit to tidepools in your area. Bring along mats or cushions so kids can lie down and look right into the water for small fish, moss, and sand crabs. Stay in one location for many minutes so that shy creatures will come forth.

❑ **662.** GETTING BATTY. Bats need not be fearsome, even though youngsters should be taught not to play with them. Still, when they appear at night, swooping through the air, you can give your family a chance to see them a bit closer. Bats don't see objects, but they do hear objects that break into the cone of sound that they create by their high-pitched squeals. So, when something enters that cone of sound, the sound bounces back to the bat. Try tossing peas into the air in front of or behind a bat. The bat will pursue what it thinks is a moth or other snack. Bats are smart enough, though, to soon realize that you're playing a game and they will quit.

❑ **663.** RAINBOW GARDEN. First talk about rainbow colors and help a child to draw a rainbow on paper. Next, choose a plot of ground where the youngster can make a rainbow flower garden. Prepare the soil, cultivating it into six parallel arches about one foot wide and about six feet long. Visit a garden shop to pick out seeds of six varieties having the same growing conditions. If using young plants, you'll need about six of each. Here are suggestions in rainbow colors: red carnations, orange nasturtiums, yellow marigolds, green fern, blue dwarf delphinium, purple African daisies.

❑ **664.** DOLPHIN LISTENING. Ask: "Are sounds louder in air or water?" Let your youngster listen to scissor blades opening and closing. Then fill a large bowl with water.

Have her press one ear against the bowl as you open and close the scissors in the water. She will find that the water carries sound vibrations better than the air and they will sound much louder. Explain that in this way dolphins hear noises from one another under the water.

❏ **665.** IT'S ALL IN YOUR HEAD.   Have a child listen carefully as he hums a tune. Then ask him to press his ears shut with both hands. Ask him to hum again. He will find that the sound is louder coming through the bony parts of the head than it is coming through the air. Show how to touch the jawbone while humming and feel the sound vibrations.

❏ **666.** SPRING READING.   At the library borrow one of these three books to read and enjoy with your children—including teens. The first two books are by the same author, Sharon Lovejoy, and evoke memories of a much simpler childhood: *Sunflower Houses* (Loveland, Col.: Interweave, 1991) and *Hollyhock Days* (also Interweave, 1994). The third is *Nature Crafts for Kids* by Gwen Diehn and Terry Krautwurst (New York: Sterling, 1995). The latter features fifty unusual projects using nature's materials.

❏ **667.** SWEET TWEET.  Help youngsters learn about local birds with *The Audubon Society Field Guide*—available for various regions (New York: Knopf, 1993) or *The National Audubon Society Interactive CD ROM Guide to North American Birds* (New York: Random House, 1996). The excellent pictures and descriptions will show youngsters how to quickly identify local birds and how to keep a list of birds the family has seen.

❏ **668.** FOLLOW THE SUN.   Help a youngster chart the sun: the time it rises, the time it sets, the path it takes overhead. At a garden shop or garage sale, buy a sun dial and place it in the yard so it can tell kids the correct time.

❏ **669.** FOREVER FLOWERS.   Take a walk with kids and choose small flowers and leaves to decorate a bookmark.

*THERE'S A BIG WORLD OUT THERE —*

Arrange them between paper towels and press under heavy books for about two weeks. Then, help kids cut a piece of heavy white paper to a two-inch by seven-inch size. Using a small paint brush, spread glue over the backside of the pressed flowers. Then arrange them, glue side down, on the paper. Let the glue dry, then cover the entire bookmark with adhesive-backed clear plastic. Punch a hole in one end and tie a colorful piece of yarn through it.

❑ **670.** **WHAT'S INSIDE?** When a toy or appliance breaks and is no longer repairable, let kids take it apart and see what's inside (with the understanding that a broken item is **never** plugged into an electrical outlet). This helps to demystify mechanics and physics. A parent can give input as to the purpose of the inner workings.

❑ **671.** **BIRDS AT YOUR WINDOW.** To bring birds to your window sill, let your youngster make this attractive bird feeder. First, he should take a pine cone and spread it lightly with peanut butter. Next, put it in a paper bag with about a half cup of bird seed. Close the bag and shake it until the bird seed adheres to the peanut butter. Now place it near a window and observe how many different birds come to enjoy it. See who can identify some of the birds.

❑ **672.** **SPIDER WEB ART.** Let kids locate a spider web in the yard and observe whether it is occupied. When no spider has been seen for three days, the web can be collected. First, lightly spray the web with hair spray on both sides. Using a piece of black construction paper, touch the middle of the paper to the center of the web. The hair spray will cause it to stick to the paper. Gently detach or cut the web from where it is anchored on the branch. Again spray the web with hair spray. Now you are ready to observe fantastic workmanship.

CRYSTAL MAKING. A parent heats one cup of hot
a child measures a little more than a half cup of
ur the water into a heat-proof glass container

(such as a small canning jar) and let the child add a half cup of the sugar and then a bit more until no more sugar will dissolve in the hot water. Tie a length of string to a pencil and balance it across the top of the jar with the string hanging straight into the solution. Place the container where it won't be moved but can be observed. Depending on the size of the jar, the water will evaporate in a few days or a week. The sugar will form crystals up the string.

❑ **674.** WORM FARM.   Most kids find worms fascinating and although you can buy a ready-made farm, it's more fun to make your own. Cut the top off a one gallon plastic milk container. In the bottom, put two inches of dirt, then two inches of organic matter (grass clippings, leaves). Then repeat this procedure, being careful not to mix the layers. Moisten the layers until damp but not soaking. Next, move in the earthworms. You can find these in your garden or buy them at a tackle shop. Put them on the top layer and watch them dig in. When you can't see them, cover the top with cardboard and put the container in a dark place such as a closet (no, the worms won't escape). For the next few weeks, watch through the container sides as they multiply. After a month or so, turn them loose in your backyard to aerate the soil.

# SECTION 5: GETTING ALONG WITH OTHERS

The important skills of building friendships, handling relationships, and making decisions are ones that are taught gradually at home throughout the years. Here's how to get started.

❑ **675.** FINDING FRIENDS.   Initiate a conversation with kids about friendship. Ask: "What is a friend? Are your friends just like you? How are they different? Do you have friends of different ages, different ethnic backgrounds?

Why are friends important? Can you trust friends? What is your responsibility when a friend has bad habits? What happens when a friendship ends? Who is your current best friend? Why are you a good friend?" Then talk about places where new friends can be found.

❑ **676.** **THE LANGUAGE OF FRIENDS.** Although friends should be able to be frank, show kids that certain actions and phrases can destroy a relationship. Lazy youngsters who never want to do anything or try something new aren't much fun as friends. Gossipy kids who are always talking behind someone's back and telling you all that's wrong aren't real friends. Spoiled kids who always want their own way and complain that no one pays attention to them make poor friends. Bossy kids who deal in name-calling, sarcasm, getting the last word, and giving orders to others are not fun to be with. Ask kids how they themselves stack up in these categories.

❑ **677.** **NO GRUMPS.** Most everyone has something they could complain about, but people who constantly talk about small problems are depressing to be around. Teach kids to bring up problems with the aim of settling them, not just talking about them. Discuss the signs of a cheerful person and see how many of the signs you and your child exhibit.

❑ **678.** **YOU NOT ME.** Encourage youngsters to become vitally interested in other family members—their school or office work, sports interests, challenges and triumphs, and small things, too. It gives others a good feeling. We get along best when others care about us, celebrating our victories and comforting us when we're down. Play this little game: ask family members to find out something good about another family member during the day—any time up to dinner. Then at dinner, ask each one what they've learned.

❑ **679.** **I PROMISE.** Don't say those words lightly. In dealing with others, both inside and outside the family circle, our word is important. Talk about the words promise, pledge, vow, oath, contract. Ask: "Which of these already exist in the family (for example marriage vows or a contract to purchase the house). What does the Pledge of Allegiance mean?" See if each person can come up with a promise she plans to keep this week.

❑ **680.** **SHARING WITH FRIENDS.** When a young child is coming to play at your house, talk with your child about his own toys. Let him put away any toy he is not willing to share. Or, start the play by dividing toys into two groups, one for each child. Trade later.

❑ **681.** **ACCENTUATE THE POSITIVE.** Praise is great and it's easier to get along with others when we're appreciated. Find something to praise each youngster for each day. Ask kids to look for things they can appreciate in other family members—and **tell** them. When you accentuate the positive ("That was great the way you mowed the lawn"), you can also include a secondary message ("Do remember to lock the garage when you put the mower away") which is acceptable in this context.

❑ **682.** **HOLD THAT TONGUE.** Regrets and feelings of guilt can come from speaking thoughtlessly. Tell youngsters that you will try counting to ten before shouting or criticizing, and that you want them to practice the same control. Then speak softly and persuasively. The way you say something, the tone and volume, and your body language can be more meaningful than the words. Teach kids—and yourself—to make good use of phrases such as: "That was nice." "Can I help?" "I really need you." And use nonjudgmental phrases such as "I think . . ." or "It seems to me. . . ." Think of the words you use with your family as words that help them achieve their dreams.

❑ **683.** **JUST SAY "YES."** People who constantly say "no" or "I don't want to" can be a drag. Prepare a series of questions as a practice: "Will you jump off a building? Will you give me some help tonight? Will you play a game with me? Will you smoke a cigarette? Will you give me half your cookie? Will you give your best friend your homework to copy? Will you take five dollars from Mom's purse? Will you show me how to solve a computer problem?" Talk about the importance of saying "no" to bad ideas but trying very hard to say "yes" to good ones.

❑ **684.** **REVOLT.** Talk with youngsters on how to disagree when they feel strongly about an issue. Show how responsible revolt and the convictions of just one person have brought about many important changes. It takes courage to believe in an unpopular opinion and it takes persistence to bring about change within the confines of the law. Work together to make changes in the home as well as in the community.

❑ **685.** **NEARER THE GOAL?** When your youngster is facing a big decision—to take an advanced placement class, to find an after-school job, to join a club, to take part in a time-consuming sport, to spend all his savings on a vehicle, to apply to a particular college—help him to look at it in relation to his goals: "Does this decision get me nearer to my goals?" If not, suggest he think twice about doing it. This helps a youngster to keep focused on long-term success, not short-term gratification.

# SECTION 6: LIFE WITH AND WITHOUT TELEVISION

By the time a youngster finishes high school, she will have viewed about 15,000 hours of television—mostly with little benefit. Too often, watching TV takes the place of more valuable activities—physical play, reading, talking as a family. This chapter will help you balance television time with togetherness time.

❏ **686.** WHAT NOT TO DO WITH KIDS. Don't let them become inactive and lazy "couch potatoes." Don't let them do homework with the TV on. Don't let TV cut off family conversation and take up the time you can use for joint activities. Don't let the TV program guide rule your house! Take this "Couch Potato Quiz" and have your kids do the same. Answer these questions yes or no:

(1) Do your children do homework in front of TV?
(2) Do you eat with the TV on?
(3) Do you need the mere sound of the TV to feel comfortable and not alone?
(4) Are you depressed if you miss the end of a show—or an entire show?
(5) Do you ignore conversation because the TV talks louder?
(6) Is the TV program guide your favorite reading?
(7) When friends stop in or when you entertain, do you leave on the TV?
(8) Do you sit through a show but afterward realize that you don't really remember much about it?
(9) Have you committed certain commercials to memory?
(10) Does TV viewing increase your apathy about violence and world problems?
(11) When you think about relaxing, does TV viewing come first to your mind?
(12) Do you find yourself falling asleep in front of the TV?

More than three "yes" answers indicate that you're a candidate for couch potato and you may want to rethink your free-time activities.

❏ **687.** THERE'S MORE TO LIFE! Could your family exist without TV? When there was a power failure, one family found that TV was not the core of family togetherness. Someone remembered that their boom box ran on batteries, so, by candlelight they listened to CDs and the news of the storm. They had such an enjoyable time in the dark that they plan to do it again—even without a power failure.

❑ **688.** THE ON/OFF SWITCH. The national average for TV on-time is forty-five hours per week. In some homes the television is on, talking mostly to itself, every hour of the day. Teach kids that television viewing should have a purpose, and to turn it on when a chosen show begins and turn it off afterward. Many families find that an inexpensive portable radio is a handy alternative and much quicker at reporting breaking news. You can enjoy the latest news while cooking, the ball game while doing repairs or garden work, music while reading or doing homework.

❑ **689.** SELL THE TV. Yes, that's a definite possibility. This is a cold turkey approach and families who have done it report that there have been profound changes in their young people (and often in the parents, too): better grades, increased physical fitness, new skills. Ask kids what they would think of selling the television set. Listen carefully to their reasons for keeping it.

❑ **690.** MAKE GOOD RULES. If the above suggestion brings cries of revolt, sit down and work out some rules. Cover how much television may be viewed per day, when to view (after homework and chores), what programs are approved or disapproved (actually make a list and post it), no TV with mealtimes, no cheating when parents aren't home, no week night TV if a grade falls to an unacceptable level (such as C minus). Breaking the rules should result in no TV at all for the next week.

❑ **691.** IF NOT, WHAT? You can't replace something with nothing. When you decide to take control of television viewing, be ready with enticing activities to take its place. Outdoor sports equipment, a new indoor game, the introduction of a hobby or collection, a pet—discuss the possibilities and let your youngster choose what she will enjoy on a regular basis. One teen I know got into shortwave radio communication and no longer has much interest in television.

❑ **692.** PLUGHUGGERS. If you need a strong means of controlling television viewing, consider the V-Chip or devices such as plughuggers, which lock onto a power cord with a key, preventing use of the television (or any other device such as a computer). Nintendo also makes a lock that prevents the insertion of game cartridges. Before spending ten to thirty dollars for such devices, talk with kids about being more responsible—but if you get nowhere, lock it up.

❑ **693.** SEX EDUCATION? Although we teach children that television life is not real life, children accept many of the TV values as real and justifiable. The average youngster hears and sees about 16,000 references to sexual intercourse on TV each year and few are within the context of marriage. The impression is that "everyone does it." This means it is important for a parent to monitor viewing and explain the vast difference between TV and reality. Either **you** will teach sex education or television will do it for you.

❑ **694.** THE VIOLENCE FACTOR. The National Institute of Mental Health reports overwhelming scientific evidence linking television violence to aggressive and violent behavior in children. These kids are more pessimistic, less creative, and use violence as a first, not last, resort. Even toddlers who watch cartoons with mock aggression are abnormally cruel to playmates and pets. Other research has shown a connection between violent television and disobedience and lack of trust (kids start believing the world is a mean and fearsome place). Exposure to violence blunts emotional reactions and makes people less caring. Don't be part of the 75 percent of parents who set no limits on the TV their kids watch. Be alert to the fact that prime time TV averages five acts of violence per hour.

❑ **695.** A NEW TRADITION. Create a television hour (or less) when the family can watch together. Say no to programs with the wrong values, and yes to channels with good programming. Choose just one program to see. Rotate the choice of the program among family members.

❑ **696.** SATURDAY MORNING TV. One of the so-called benefits of television is that parents get to sleep in on Saturday morning as kids look at cartoons of rabbits bashing one another over the head. Cartoons typically subject children to twenty acts of violence per hour. Instead, provide a quality video for each Saturday morning, plus a toy box of "Saturday only" toys that will occupy kids until parents are on hand for the day's activities.

❑ **697.** TV TIES TO VIOLENT PLAY. When children watch TV that features action figures, they soon want to buy those toys. And, if parents permit this, they will soon be mimicking the violent actions seen on TV in their play at home. Start when kids are young to tell them you won't permit toys connected with violence in your home—no guns, no tanks, no terminators, no toys that blow up. It won't be easy and you may have to endure some whining, but explain to your children that you want their play to be positive, not negative.

❑ **698.** COMMERCIAL TALK. Yes, we know that commercials pay for the programming but you're not required to give them your undivided attention. Instead, mute the commercial and ask questions or go over the plot or point of the show. You could also discuss the commercials and the ways they entice viewers to use the product advertised.

❑ **699.** USE THAT VCR. Be the master of your television set by taping shows you want to see and then watching them at a convenient time. Teach youngsters how to run the VCR (or maybe they'll teach you). Then, when you sit down to look at the program, you can fast forward through commercials, thereby cutting about fifteen minutes from an hour show. You can save money by taping good movies and viewing them as a weekend treat or in the summertime when new TV shows are limited.

❑ **700.** THE LIBRARY CONNECTION. If a program's topic is of special interest, find library books on the subject or other writings by the same author. Suggest these for reading before or after the program.

❑ **701.** GET MORE SLEEP. Every night between 11 and 11:30, three million children are still watching late night adult programming! Don't permit TV sets in kids' bedrooms. Encourage eight hours of sleep, and more for younger kids.

❑ **702.** THE CRITICAL EYE. Being picky isn't always bad. If you find yourselves in the middle of a bad program (and you just have to know how it comes out), make the best of it. Let one viewer look for stereotypes of women, races, blue collar workers or business people, and personal beliefs. Let another tally violent or gratuitous sex acts. Also monitor the glamorous use of drugs, alcohol, and tobacco. A parent with a tablet can make note of phrases not to be used in the home. Viewing with a critical eye will help to avoid TV trash another time.

❑ **703.** A CHIP FOR A SHOW. Here's a way to encourage kids to think about what they are viewing rather than just looking at any program that comes on. Every Monday, give each youngster fourteen poker chips (or some other kind of marker that can't be reproduced). Each one is worth thirty minutes of television. Apart from shows you've ruled out, they can "spend" a chip on any program. At the end of the week, buy back unused chips for twenty-five cents each.

❑ **704.** MAKE SPECIALS TRULY SPECIAL. When there is something truly worth time and full attention, build it up in the days beforehand. Serve dinner or snacks as the family watches together. During commercials, talk about how this show is special. Occasionally invite friends to join you.

❑ **705.** INVESTIGATE CHANNELS. Don't stick to just the major networks. There are other worthwhile programs out there. Sometimes just viewing the politicians in their deliberations is illuminating and humorous. Encourage kids to go beyond MTV—way beyond—and discover all that TV has to offer. Be willing to look at a show on a new channel once or twice before ruling it out.

❑ **706.** Q IS FOR QUALITY.  Encourage family members to view the best TV this way: for one week, let each one read the guide and choose what he thinks will be the best quality programs. View these together and talk about them later. This often results in the choice of an educational show over a sitcom—and with hope that may become habit-forming.

# NINE

# VIRTUES

The issues in this chapter are fundamental to a youngster's well-being and maturity. You will find it challenging and enjoyable so don't skip over it.

# SECTION 1: VIRTUES AND THE FIVE Cs

While it may seem like hard work to instill virtuous behavior in children, this teaching is one of the most important things you do WITH your children. It is not taught in a moment; it is taught by example, through stories, through consistent moral living.

There are countless lists of "The Virtues" and you will decide for your family which ones are most important to you. Theologians believe that Paul was among the first biblical writers to list virtues when he wrote in his letter to the Philippians to think about things that are true, honest, just, pure, lovely, and of good report. Other scholars have listed faith, hope, love, loyalty, temperance, courage, prudence, humility, trustworthiness, and responsibility. My list is slightly different, but is inclusive of the same ideas. Now it's up to you to talk about them and teach them.

❏ **707.** THE FIVE Cs. One family decided that these five concepts were what made their family tick: *cooperation, communication, compliments, commitment, and compassion.* They put a list of these on the refrigerator and tried to live them. Soon they noticed that when there was disobedience, disappointment, or disagreement (the three Ds) in the family, one of the five Cs had been broken. Talk about the five Cs and see if you find they are the answer to the three Ds.

# SECTION 2: HONESTY

❏ **708.** HONEST TALK ABOUT HONESTY. Start a discussion on honesty by asking which of the following would be acceptable behavior for the average person? (1) Tax evasion (2) Keeping money found on the street. (3) Falsification of credentials. (4) Bringing home office materials. (5) At a store when given too much change, keeping it since they charge big prices. (6) Using crib sheets at school. (7) Plagiarizing or buying reports for school. (8) Using an older sibling's report as your own. (9) Parents being unfaithful to their vows. (10) Telling little white lies. (11) Telling little white lies so as not to hurt someone's feelings. (12) Telling the truth, but not all of the truth. (13) Shoplifting. (14) Lying about age to buy alcohol or tobacco. (15) Buying and using drugs. (16) Not buying, but using drugs given to you. (17) Exceeding the speed limit. (18) Exceeding the speed limit on a lonely road. (19) Pretending to put money in the church collection plate. (20) Sneaking out of the house.

❑ **709.** MAKE IT EASY. Don't play district attorney by grilling and trying to trap a child. Make an environment where honesty is valued and mistakes are not magnified. When you think a child has done something wrong, explain that punishment is always less when the truth is told immediately.

❑ **710.** GET TO THE CAUSE. If you can determine the cause for the dishonest action, you can probably find the cure. Talk with your youngster to see why he cheated in the game, why he took money from your wallet, why he got drunk when he'd promised he wouldn't drink at all. When you find the cause, talk together about alternate ways to solve the problem or challenge.

❑ **711.** NO PROMISES. Never make a child promise that she will never tell another lie. Rather, encourage her to try very hard not to lie. Show her that she should be honest because it is the right thing to do, not out of fear or because of what others may think. And let her know that although some dishonest actions go undiscovered, those wrongs will be eventually recognized and punished—hence it's smarter (and less embarrassing) to be honest at all times.

❑ **712.** DOUBLE STANDARD. Parents should avoid teaching that dishonesty or shoddy ethics is okay under certain conditions. While you may say "Never tell a lie," do you sneak short twelve-year-olds into movies at half price? Or, do you quickly pocket a five dollar bill you find lying on the sidewalk? Or, do you bring home office supplies for use at home? Play "what if" with your kids (make up stories that give them a choice for doing right or wrong) and let them do the same for you.

❑ **713.** "BUT EVERYONE ELSE DOES IT." Parents hear this argument often and need to respond firmly. Because everyone is doing wrong, doesn't make it right. Explain that just as different families look different, have different jobs, and have different ways of behaving, your family is unique. You have set standards and made rules for what you believe is best for the family, and it is your right to ask that these be followed. Use the statement: "I love you too much to let you do that."

❑ **714.** HONEST TODDLERS. Start when a child is young, as soon as she can recall a shared experience, to let her retell what happened. Praise her if she can tell exactly what happened. Say that this is the truth, that this is honest. If she states something that truly did not happen, gently say that it is not exactly the way it happened. Speak with admiration about telling the truth, but make a big distinction between the truth and imagination or make-believe.

❑ **715.** "I TRUST YOU." When children are young, introduce the word "trust" and use it often. Say: "I trust you to put away the train." "I trust you to take one cookie from the jar." "I trust you to take fifty cents from my wallet." Choose occasions where children will find it easy to be trustworthy, and as they get older, show your confidence by increasing their opportunities for independent honesty.

❑ **716.** "YOU DON'T TRUST ME!" When youngsters say this, it usually stems from the fact that the youngster has deceived the parents earlier. So, trust has to be re-earned. Much of parental distrust comes from their not knowing what kids are doing, due to lack of communication. Tell youngsters to talk about their activities so they won't seem mysterious to the adults. Thus, when a teen honestly volunteers information, parents will become more trustful.

❑ **717. LOYALTY TO ONESELF.** Talk about how one can be true to one's own beliefs about himself. A youngster must have faith in his own abilities and the strength to not compromise his standards. Discuss together what these abilities and standards are and how both youngster and parent can work together to support them. If one is loyal to oneself, he does not give in to peer pressure. Talk about ways to battle negative peer pressure that can erode an honest person.

❑ **718. LOYALTY TO HUMANITY.** Here are some ethical questions for discussion: What is our responsibility for others in the family and the community? How can we be "our brother's keeper" and still take care of ourselves? Does this kind of loyalty take money? What are the attributes of a loyal friend? What can one do when a friend has a problem? How can the loyalty of just one person benefit many?

❑ **719. LOYALTY TO ONE'S NATION.** Encourage kids to be honest about their feelings toward their country rather than dishonestly following the herd. Ask: "What are the benefits of our homeland? What benefits do other countries offer that ours does not? If you could live elsewhere, where would you choose to live—and why? If one is going to live in a country as a loyal citizen, what are the opportunities and responsibilities?"

❑ **720. TAKE AN HONEST STAND.** Discuss with the family current community issues of importance, as well as voting, serving in civic groups, and working for political candidates. During a campaign time, consider working together for a candidate. Or, take a stand on an issue that is important to your family and write a letter to the newspaper.

❏ **721.** INTEGRITY IN GOVERNMENT. Let youngsters see the law and government in action. Arrange a visit to a court in session or a meeting of the city council. Quietly listen during the session and afterward ask kids for their opinions. How is the law upheld? Do those in power seem responsive to the people? Would you like to be in law or government? What would be the advantages and disadvantages? What education would be required or useful? Share newspaper articles about law and government rulings that affect kids.

❏ **722.** HEROES. Talk about people that are admired for their integrity. Include some historic figures such as George Washington, Thomas Jefferson, Patrick Henry, Sitting Bull, Abraham Lincoln, Eve Curie, Teddy Roosevelt, Amelia Earhart, John Glenn, Mother Teresa. Why were they heroic? Were they patriotic? Brave? Angry? Innovative? Ask: "Who in public life today might become tomorrow's hero? Are there as many women heroes as men? Are most heroes famous? How can one be a quiet hero?"

❏ **723.** FEELINGS. Someone has said, "The baggage of unethical living is a big load to carry through life." In a nonjudgmental way, ask kids how they feel when they've been honest and how they feel when they've been dishonest.

## SECTION 3: RESPONSIBILITY

When a youngster is successful at doing something, she feels in charge and her self-esteem soars. Here are some ways you can teach responsibility and improve self-worth, thus helping kids to be diligent and self-governing.

❏ **724.** GOOD, BETTER, BEST. During growing-up years, a youngster has many chances to excel, causing some parents to constantly push kids toward higher and higher achievements. But it is also acceptable in some areas to do a good job (as opposed to a better or best job). Some things don't really make a difference. Talk with a youngster about the skills most important to her and focus on these.

❏ **725.** DISAPPOINTMENTS. Mastery is a slow succession of many small gains, and along the way there may be some setbacks. Teach a youngster to learn from disappointments, then shrug them off and move onward. Use the phrase "Don't let that stop you!" and encourage the phrase "I won't let this stop me!"

❏ **726.** TO DO OR NOT TO DO. Let kids know what you expect them to do and what happens if they don't do it. (See chapter 10 on the subject of rules and punishments.) Do not remind, do not threaten, do not restate the punishment. Just be quiet and let the child make the choice—and accept the consequences. This leads to a self-disciplined young adult, prepared to make good decisions.

❏ **727.** STIMULATING INDEPENDENCE. Step-by-step teach your child to master his environment, to become independent of reminders, to be ready to make decisions. Use these lines to encourage independent action: "You can handle this." "You want me to think you don't know how to do it, but I think you do." "I'll be nearby if you should need help." "How do you think this should be handled?" These lines show a respect for a child's growing intelligence and ability.

❏ **728.** STIMULATING INTERDEPENDENCE. A child doesn't live alone on an island, so cooperative behavior is a parent's aim. Working with others can increase self-esteem. Encourage a youngster to take part by using these lines: "We need your input at the family meeting." "You can come with us if you'd like. We'd enjoy that." "It will go faster and better if you help make the cookies." "You had a problem like this before, so sharing how you solved it can help us all." "We're in this together."

❑ **729.** EARNED, NOT GIVEN. While you can't hand a child self-esteem on a platter, you can provide daily opportunities for him to earn it and for you to recognize it. Set tasks and goals you know he can achieve, then move on to more difficult ones. Always verbalize the successes: "Wonderful, you did it!" "How great to do it by yourself." "It was hard to do, but you hung in there."

❑ **730.** DAILY SUCCESS. Make a child's environment such that he feels successful more times in a day than he feels unsuccessful. Arrange the house, his room, and play areas to make dressing easy, toy pick-up easy, hand washing easy, helping in the kitchen and garage easy. This way he'll try to do more things on his own and add to his success list.

❑ **731.** NO NITWITS. Never make a child feel stupid when she doesn't immediately accomplish a task. If possible, explain the "how to" only once. When you constantly tell a child how to do something, you make her feel inadequate. Rather ask: "You got the first part right, what comes next?" or "Could you think of a better way to do this?" The feeling of respect that comes with success brings an important sense of security to a child.

❑ **732.** PERSISTENCE PAYS. Part of self-government is the ability to be diligent—to refuse to give up. When a child is engaged in an age-appropriate activity—learning to ride a bike, finishing a homework assignment, practicing for a recital—there may be setbacks along the way. This is when a parent needs to encourage, to remind of previous challenges and triumphs, and to build on those successes. Help a child make a list of accomplishments (learning to tell time or getting an A in spelling), add to it, and refer to it when persistence is waning.

❑ **733.** GIVING UP. Many things worth doing are not accomplished on the first try. Tell your youngster how many times he fell when trying to learn to walk—yet he did learn. Share the fact that there are some things that need not be learned at present. Don't let a youngster feel guilty about setting the two-wheeler aside for a month or repeatedly getting a C grade in math. Praise him for trying and show that while he didn't get the usual reward for diligence, there will be a time when he **will** succeed.

❑ **734. SELF-CONTROL.** While we don't teach a youngster to bury emotions, we do teach that there is usually a time and place for exhibiting them. Anger is the most common symbol of loss of control. Demonstrate various ways to assuage angry feelings: breathing deeply and counting to ten, leaving the room, tearing yesterday's newspaper in half, beating a pillow on the bed, throwing a ball against the garage door, taking a shower, going for a walk. When you see anger building, suggest one of these, and then talk about the cause when everyone is calm.

❑ **735. THE "GOOD" CHILD.** So much of parental attention is focused on the child who seems to be marching to a different drummer and not getting it together. How important then to also spend time in praise for the child who finds it easy to be responsible, who has good self-esteem, and learns quickly. At day's end, verbally tally all the good things a child has done, and tell him how much you appreciate his goodness. Don't compare or label kids—love them equally.

❑ **736. RESPONSIBLE PET OWNERSHIP.** Too often, parents get a pet because they think it will "teach" responsibility. Before adding a pet to the family, show youngsters what is involved and how they will be accountable for another living being. Obtain library books on care and feeding, and seriously consider the time commitment and the costs. A youngster who wants a pet should take the responsibility to feed, train, groom, and clean up after it. Emphasize the fact that the commitment to an animal can last for many years.

❑ **737. CHOICES.** Give kids the opportunity to make many choices so that they feel self-governing in many areas: what to wear, what to purchase with savings, whom to play with. For some choices, add the word "or": "You may buy one forty dollar shirt or two twenty dollar shirts." "You can choose to come home on time, or come home late and stay home all next weekend." "You may make three five-minute phone calls or one fifteen-minute one." With your child, make a specific list of things he can choose totally on his own and a list of things reserved for parent/child consultation.

# SECTION 4: OPENNESS

Having good communication with youngsters makes family life much more harmonious. Starting early to talk regularly and honestly together will keep the lines of communication open during all the growing-up years.

❏ **738.** NO-MATTER-WHAT. From toddler years onward, remind kids that you love them "no matter what." You may not always like what they do, but you love them. So, encourage a child to share problems and mistakes. Hearing about them is better than being kept in the dark. You stifle this sharing if you react with thoughtless punishment, shouting, or ridicule. Say this often: "It's okay to tell me, because I love you no-matter-what."

❏ **739.** LISTEN EARLY. Parents often don't find their young child's communication very illuminating, hence they tend not to listen. Thus, when the kids get older, they no longer bother to communicate. Take a vital interest in the explanations and descriptions of a child's activities from babyhood onward. Make it natural to talk with them in an enthusiastic and appreciative way. And don't hesitate to ask "Is there anything I should know?"

❏ **740.** WEEKLY UPDATE. When teens suddenly clam up, parents can be frustrated because they don't know what is going on. You imagine that bad things are happening. Establish a weekly update session—each Sunday at dinner or other convenient time. With a calendar in hand, go over the past week's events and then the upcoming week, noting activities of each family member. Ask kids to elaborate on the events, times, places, and activities, as well as any problems.

❑ **741.** COMMUNICATION KILLERS. Family communication is turned off with lines like: "Shut up." "What a dumb idea." "Quit arguing!" "Not now, I'm too busy." Better lines are: "Let's find a time to talk." "How's that going to work?" "Who should settle the argument—you two or me?" "That sounds like a good idea—I want everyone to hear all about it at dinner."

❑ **742.** FIVE TOPICS. Kids who chatter away endlessly at home, sometimes become silent in public. Practice with them responses to compliments and ordinary questions. Then, when going to a social event, take time beforehand or in the car to help a youngster think of five things he can share: a school project, a sport or hobby, a movie or TV show, something funny that happened, or an excursion. If youngsters can't think of five things that are going on, it's time you enriched their lives!

❑ **743.** PUT IT IN WRITING. While watching TV or at some relaxing time, write short notes on paper of a distinctive color. (At one house they're called pink notes.) These can be as short as "I was proud of you at the game" or "Your hair looked good this morning" or "You're special!" Put them on pillows and in pockets or lunch pails. Encourage kids to write pink notes, too.

❑ **744.** SILENT COMMUNICATION. Occasionally a youngster will clam up and refuse to talk, perhaps going into her room and slamming the door. To diffuse the situation it's time for "under the door messages." Compose a message of love to the child and include the hope that she'll write back. Slip your note under her door, then go to your room, shut the door, and read or do some busy work. If you don't get an answer in fifteen minutes or so, try again.

❑ **745.** A CONFIDENTIAL JOURNAL. Sometimes kids like to communicate with themselves. Take youngsters to a stationery store and show them the blank books that can serve as journals or diaries. Encourage them to write as often as they like, perhaps daily, and put a date on each entry. To get them started, suggest the first entry: "Today we bought this journal that will record all the wonderful things that will happen to me." Tell kids you will never, never read their journal without their consent.

# SECTION 5: OPTIMISM

Expecting good, being cheerful, and having a sense of humor: these comprise a healthy point of view for both parents and kids—and at the same time, they make for a happier home.

❑ **746.** WATCH YOUR EMPHASIS. Parental example is important. If you go ballistic when a glass of milk spills, your child will give small mistakes the wrong perspective and think that these events are important failures and occasions for fearfulness. (Your better reaction would be to teach him how to clean up the mess and place his glass in a safer place.) When every small mistake brings shouting, followed by tears or guilt, a child develops a pessimistic and cautious attitude that overshadows the happy times.

❑ **747.** LINES TO OUTLAW. Don't let your youngsters become accustomed to pessimistic statements, which they may have picked up from you. Outlaw "Nothing ever goes right." Quickly counter with a mention of things that have gone right. The same goes for these: "There's not a thing I can do." "I'm so upset, I'll never be happy again." "The world's a mess." "This is hopeless."

❑ **748.** LINES TO LOVE. Teach optimism by expressing hopefulness as a part of daily conversation. Use these lines and teach your youngster to use them: "That's not so bad." "I had trouble learning that, but I finally got it." "It's not the end of the world—let's try again." "I know you'll do it." "Let's work on it together."

❑ **749.** SOUND OF LAUGHTER. Borrow from the library a book of jokes suitable for children. Tell one at each meal. Encourage kids to tell "clean" funny stories and to laugh— even if the laugh is on themselves. Have a "jokathon"—a contest to see which family member can tell the funniest story. When there is laughter, it's hard to be pessimistic.

❑ **750.** IN THE DUMPS. Here's a comforting proverb to share with a youngster who is struggling with failure: *Rejection, mistakes, and failures are the ideal stepping stones to success.* Then talk about what can be learned from the failure. Keep close to a child who is depressed. Show how pessimism is contagious and not beneficial. Find some small thing to be hopeful about, and build on it until the dumps have gone away.

❑ **751.** THE REWARDS OF PATIENCE. While it is difficult for a loving parent not to fulfill a child's wishes immediately, the virtues of optimism and patience are a contributing factor in the development of a well-adjusted and optimistic child. A Columbia University study reported that children, as young as four years of age, who were able to wait the longest for a reward (toy, trip, candy), were able to handle stress more competently than less patient children. Delayed gratification resulted in youngsters with higher test scores, a more optimistic outlook, and the ability to cope with frustration.

❑ **752.** THERE IS A WAY. Reassure a youngster that there is usually a way to accomplish his dreams. Somewhere, somehow, the good things will come if he has patient hope. And, when something good eventually happens, be sure to remind a youngster that indeed there is a way.

## SECTION 6: FAITH

A parent should set the example of a strong faith. This wholehearted faith in a supreme being is essential in these changing and often chaotic times—but this doesn't always come naturally. A child should be given the opportunity for religious study that will introduce her to the inspiring religious writings of the past. Many of these time-tested precepts are invaluable as the basis of a strong family life.

Children may ask about seeing God. The following ideas may help, and can be adapted to the age of your child. You can actually have these three experiences or talk about them to make a point. Although the word *God* is used in this chapter, you can use whatever term you choose for the Supreme Being.

❑ **753.** AT THE SEASHORE. See the waves whipped by the wind, whipped to a froth, and crashing on the shore. You do not actually see the wind, you see the result of the wind. In the same way, you cannot actually see God, but you can see the results of God's activity in your life—in God's caring love for you. You can see love between parents and children. You can see love when a firefighter saves a child. You can see love when someone does a good deed. When you see love, you see God.

❑ **754.** IN THE WOODS. Listen to the rustle of the leaves on the trees. You cannot see the wind causing this, but you see the result of the wind. In the same way you can hear God's angel messages talking to you in the form of good ideas. Be quiet and listen.

❑ **755.** THE WIND'S TOUCH. When a breeze is blowing, you can feel its touch against your cheek. You cannot see the wind, but you feel the result of the wind. In the same way you can feel God's presence with you when you are alone or afraid. You are never separated from your God who always loves you.

## IDEAS TO PROMOTE FAITH

❑ **756.** MAKE A CHOICE. Perhaps you were raised in one religion and your spouse in another, or perhaps you had absolutely no religious training at all. It is difficult for a child to have faith, comfort in difficult times, and a feeling of purpose without religious training. Visit various places of worship and investigate their childhood education. Listen to the speakers, observe traditions, ask about basic beliefs. Discuss the choices with kids, select one that you are most comfortable with, and attend as a family.

❑ **757.** WHAT'S IT FOR? When a child is a toddler, start to talk about God. Tell him he is a child of God. Show him how to talk with God by praying. As children grow older, help them find an explanation for the universe and its consistency, for life, for death, and for life after death. Such basic reasoning and teaching leads the youngster to see the significance of what he does here, rather than to feel that life has no value or plan.

❑ **758.** SUNDAY IS OUR "DAY OFF." That argument is often heard, but it's not beneficial to a strong family life. A weekend that includes a religious observance is a weekend that has added value. When kids are small, tell them that attendance at Sunday school is a "given." And when you leave church for your picnic or dinner at Grandma's, ask kids what they have learned that will be useful in the coming week. Don't let religion become a one-hour-a-week routine—make it meaningful for the entire week.

❑ **759.** THE RIGHT START. While many families say grace

at dinner, it is also a nice tradition to start the day with prayer. Holding hands around the breakfast table for a moment of silent prayer and then a short audible prayer reminds youngsters of God's place in their lives. You can also read a portion of the Bible each weekday morning as kids eat breakfast. For young children, a children's Bible may be more understandable.

❑ **760.** ONE-A-WEEK. The Bible contains many useful and comforting verses that are easy to memorize. Put a new one on the bathroom mirror each Monday and see how quickly it is learned. Here are a few for starters: Matthew 5:48; 2 Timothy 1:7, 4:7; Proverbs 15:1; Psalm 34:4; Numbers 6:24-26; as well as verses from Psalms 23, 91, and 139, the Commandments in Exodus 20, and the Sermon on the Mount in Matthew 5 and 6.

❑ **761.** BIRTHDAY DEEDS. Starting with preschoolers, establish the tradition of doing a good deed on your *own* birthday. Because much attention is placed on receiving gifts, make the day memorable by doing something for someone else. Tell a youngster the night before her birthday that she should think about her birthday good deed. And, when she blows out the candles on the cake, she can share what she did that was caring to others.

❑ **762.** TRANSLATE THE COMMANDMENTS. While these may seem like irrelevant teachings to kids, the Ten Commandments are applicable to today. See if kids can "translate" them into modern terms. For example, "Thou shalt not steal" might become "Thou shalt not shoplift." "Honour the Sabbath day" becomes "Go willingly to Sunday school." "Thou shalt not kill" could become "Thou shalt not glorify the torture and killing seen on TV." Or, "Thou shalt not even *think* killing thoughts."

❑ **763.** THE TIME LINE. On a family room or bedroom wall, affix a long piece of plain shelf paper. Turn this into the Bible time line, divided into Old Testament and New

Testament. Each time a Bible story is learned, draw the character on the time line and write the name of the story. For example, in the Old Testament there will be notations for Noah, Abraham, Isaac, Deborah, Jacob, David, and so forth. In the New Testament section there will be Mary and Joseph, Jesus, disciples, Mary Magdalene, Paul, and John. If in doubt about the order, a Bible dictionary will give you the dates.

❏ **764.** WHO DID WHAT? See if your youngsters can match these Bible characters with a special thing they did:

| | |
|---|---|
| Moses | Killed Goliath |
| David | Healed people |
| Daniel | Received God's Commandments |
| Jonah | Was an early missionary |
| Noah | Fathered the tribes of Israel |
| Ruth | First recognized Jesus after crucifixion |
| Jesus | Was safe in the lion's den |
| Mary | Was David's grandmother |
| Paul | Got swallowed by a whale |
| Mary Magdalene | Was Jesus' mother |
| Jacob | Built an ark |

❏ **765.** BIBLE AS HISTORY. These following words are part of history and yet are still meaningful today. You may know some and have to look up others, but first see how many your kids are familiar with: baptism, Gentiles, gospel, Holy Spirit, Jerusalem, Torah, psalms, Pharisees, Pentecost, patriarchs, Passover, Messiah, apocalypse, atonement, Babel, communion, and sacraments. If you and your kids know at least a dozen, you're Bible smart.

❏ **766.** OTHER BELIEFS, OTHER BELIEVERS. Tolerance and understanding reduce strife in this world. Do your children know the similarities as well as the differences between Christian and Jew, Protestant and Catholic, Hindu and Moslem, atheist and agnostic? Help them gain a basic understanding of the great religions of the world: Christianity, Judaism, Islam, Confucianism, Taoism, Buddhism, and Hinduism. And they should be conversant with the names of well-known religious figures: John Calvin, Francis of Assisi, Martin Luther, Muhammad, the current pope, Billy Graham, Mary Baker Eddy, Joseph Smith, John Wesley, and others.

❑ **767.** BIBLE CHARADES.  When children begin to be familiar with Bible stories, it can be fun to play Bible charades. It works just like the regular game, except all characters are biblical. No words, no props, just action. For David facing Goliath, pretend to pick up stones, then vigorously throw one. For Lot's wife turned into a pillar of salt, walk forward, then turn backward in horror, and freeze. For Peter walking on the water, walk carefully, then sink to the floor with hand outstretched. For the three kings coming to Jesus' birth, walk majestically, pointing and looking upward. You can easily think of many more.

❑ **768.** BIBLE CONCENTRATION.  Using three-by-five cards, write paired words on the cards, then cut them in half. Some paired words are: Moses/Commandments, Noah/Animals, Eve/Apple, Jonah/Whale, David/Lyre, Daniel/Lion, Jesus/Beatitudes, and Paul/Missionary. Make ten to twenty pairs depending on the age of the child. Then place them in several rows face down. A player turns one over and then tries to choose a match. If they match, he collects both cards and gets another turn. If they don't, he returns the cards to face down and the next player takes a turn. The winner is the one with the most cards.

❑ **769.** FAMILIAR QUOTATIONS.  Like the old-time game of Authors or Go Fish, this game consists of Bible quotations written out on cards and cut in half. Deal out the cards, then take turns asking for the half you don't have. For example, if you have the half quote that says, "Do unto others" you would ask another player, "Can you give me, 'As you would have them do unto you'"? The other player must give it up if he has it. (If he doesn't have it, the player that does will probably ask you for your half when it is his turn.) You can keep asking as long as you are successful, but when you get a "no," the next player takes his turn.

❑ **770.** JOURNEY TO THE PROMISED LAND. Young children like board games where they move a marker from a starting point to a finish while avoiding pitfalls along the way. On cardboard, make a road from Egypt to the Promised Land. Mark the road into many squares and put some pitfalls along the way such as "Red Sea," "no food," "giant people," "breaking the commandments," "lost in wilderness," and "stopped at Jericho." All the markers start as slaves in Egypt and move, at the throw of a die, out of Egypt across the Red Sea through the wilderness and on to the Promised Land. If one lands on a square that is a pitfall, he must go back four squares. A Bible or children's Bible will help you in making this enjoyable game.

❑ **771.** PERSONAL NATIVITY. At Christmas, assembling the manger scene (holy family, shepherds, kings, animals) can be a family activity. However, go shopping with kids and buy an inexpensive manger scene for each. This is their own personal nativity that they can assemble in their own room in their own way.

❑ **772.** EVERYONE'S HOLIDAY. Don't limit your children's experience with religious holidays to just your own tradition. With the help of books or friends of other religions, learn about one new celebration each year. Twelfth Night, Passover, or the Swedish Saint Lucia's Day are just some possibilities. Talk about your new celebration with accuracy, respect, and reverence.

❑ **773.** DRAW A SYMBOL. With paper and pen, show kids how to draw symbols of other religions. Draw the cross or Bethlehem Star of Christianity (five points). Draw Judaism's Star of David (six points). Draw the Star of Islam (also five points). Once kids can see the differences, let them make a design, using all the symbols, as a sign of harmony between religions.

❑ **774.** TRAVEL SIGHTS. When on a trip with young-sters, don't overlook religious lessons. Check ahead to see what unique churches, synagogues, or tabernacles are in cities where you'll visit. Go to at least one on every trip and learn together. Talk afterward about the similarities and dif-ferences with your own religion.

❑ **775.** MISSION POSSIBLE. Just as many companies publish their corporate mission, each individual can make a statement of purpose and then focus on ways to reach those objectives. In his book, *The Sales Bible* (New York: William Morrow, 1994), motivational expert Jeffrey Gito-mer urges each person to write out his own mission. This is heavy stuff, but worth the effort. Kids of grade school age upward can answer these questions on paper: Define your-self—who are you and how are you different from others? Who or what are you dedicated to (family, football, making money, and so forth)? Define your services to others. How can you strive to get better, to grow? What is the example you seek to set? What are the ideals you live by, or seek to live by? You and your family members are writing this out *for yourselves,* not others. Don't be embarrassed to flatter yourself. Write your mission with pride and a spirit of adventure. Make a copy, sign it, and put it where you will see it. Then try to live it every day.

## SECTION 7: HUMILITY

Kids need a parent's example as a person grateful for the help of others, and humble enough to express it. Humility also includes modesty and the ability to apologize—useful qualities in family life.

❑ **776.** NOT BETTER THAN OTHERS. A humble person does not think of himself as superior in every way. Explain to your child that no one likes a snob or a racist. Help him recognize where he excels, but also where he still has work to do. Make it a practice to find something good in everyone with whom he comes in contact and think about how many others contribute to this life.

❑ **777.** AND YOU HELPED. When a youngster or parent is lauded for an achievement, make it a practice to express humility by giving credit to those who helped. See if kids can recall something in their day that succeeded because another person helped.

❑ **778.** IT WAS NOTHING. Don't let kids demean their achievement by false humility. It really was something! Give kids the gracious words to accept the compliment in a humble way and then to tell something about how it was done.

❑ **779.** NOTHING TO BE GRATEFUL FOR? Sometimes parents have to subtly remind kids of all they have to be grateful for. They might say "I'm grateful to have a job." "I'm grateful for this house." "I'm grateful for you kids." Then kids should be encouraged to think of the things they're grateful for. "I'm grateful I can read." "I'm grateful for my old bike." "I'm grateful we don't have broccoli often." Once youngsters learn to think this way, they'll find many important things they can be grateful for.

❑ **780.** THE GLAD GAME. For little children who are occasionally cranky, play the Glad Game. Hold the child in your lap and start "I'm glad I have a lap. I'm glad you know how to sit. I'm glad you're sitting in my lap." This silly beginning should help the child overcome his crankiness and perhaps he'll share some things he's glad about.

❑ **781.** SORRY OR NOT. It takes humility to say you're sorry when you've done something wrong. It's a worthy lesson to teach yourself and your children. But, it takes even greater humility to apologize when others *think* that you've made a mistake when you honestly believe you have not. Help kids to say "I'm sorry you feel that way." "I'm sorry your feelings are hurt." "Even though we disagree, I still love you."

# SECTION 8: LOVE

So you aren't a huggy-kissy person? You can learn to be! So you don't have time to care for anyone but yourself and your immediate family? You can make time! It's important to set an example of love and outreach for your children.

❑ **782.** RANDOM ACTS OF KINDNESS. Mottoes like this are often skin-deep but this one has merit. It means that our kindness doesn't have to have a reason. We don't have to be shoved into it. Explain this concept to children and let them create random acts on their own. You will find that, without reminding, they are kind to a younger sibling, offer to help a neighbor, give part of their allowance to a charity, and offer to work "for free." Be sure you praise these random acts!

❑ **783.** HUGS. Starting with the very young, teach a variety of hugs: arm hugs, knee hugs, head hugs, and (of course) body hugs. A symbol for a hug can be made by clenching a fist (closing your fingers) and then taking the thumb of the same hand and tucking it behind the first finger. It looks a bit like a little person being hugged. Make hugs a part of your family greeting and parting. It is said that hugs are practically perfect since they are low energy with high yield, pesticide free and inflation-proof, nonfattening, nonpolluting, nontaxable and are fully refundable!

❑ **784.** CARD BOX. Sending a greeting card is a sign of loving care. Let youngsters send a photocopied letter to all relatives and close friends, asking them to tell their birth date and year, and if married, their wedding date and year.

Let them compile this into a month-by-month list, show-ing the names, dates, and years. (That way you'll all know when a youngster is five or sweet sixteen, or when adults have a special anniversary.) With list in hand, go shopping at a discount card shop (or make your own cards) and write on the envelope the name of the recipient. Make monthly dividers and place the cards and list in a shoe box. On the last week of every month, get out the box and address the cards. Be sure that each family member signs his own name, and if he chooses, writes a message.

❏ **785.** COUSIN CONNECTION. As soon as youngsters enjoy talking and telling stories, set up a connection with a distant cousin. Provide cassette tapes and let youngsters make a tape in private (the conversation is less inhibited), telling about her latest activities. This can also work between a grandparent and a faraway grandchild.

❏ **786.** CONTINUOUS BONDING. For many years it was thought that a parent only bonded with a child right after birth. (Officially, bonding is a deeply felt affinity for anoth-er that establishes ongoing mutual attachment.) Now research shows that bonding can take place later as well as early in a child's life. Holding a child close and telling her that she's a precious part of your family will help to strengthen the bond with very young children. But, close-together activities such as hiking or doing a craft together while talking about his important place in the family, can strengthen the bond with older kids. So, on a regular basis, keep the family bonds strong with both words and deeds.

❏ **787.** WHAT IS LOVE? It's wanting the best for another. It means liking someone as well as loving them. Love is built on joint experiences, not just physical attraction. Tell your youngster how you and your spouse met and fell in love. Tell them that the teen years are often filled with puppy loves but although these are usually fleeting, they are useful in recognizing the real thing when it comes along.

❑ **788.** SERVING TOGETHER. Start the memorable tradition of regularly helping others. It is easy to do this at a shelter where your family can come and serve meals to the homeless or disadvantaged. Your social service agency or church can put you in touch with such a shelter. Prepare kids in advance for what they will see; remind them to be polite. Afterward, have a frank talk about the experience.

❑ **789.** THE BLESSINGS OF OUTREACH. When a youngster is old enough, help her connect with a group that can use her talents. She can be a mentor or tutor to a younger child, read to a senior citizen, make tray favors for a hospital, volunteer at a recreation center, collect donations for the homeless. On a regular basis, a project of just two hours will bless her with new friends, new talents, new insights, and an increased understanding of the goodness and peace that really exists in this world.

❑ **790.** SIBLING HARMONY. Each of your children is distinct and lovable in unique ways. Emphasize this, especially when there is a new baby. Say "I hope you will help the baby grow up into a nice person like you." "I know he's little, but you have such good ideas, so can you think of a way to include him in your play?" Be sure to give each child special opportunities not afforded the others. Reward harmonious play. Choose toys that require cooperation and cut down on sibling rivalry—toys such as building sets or a playhouse.

❑ **791.** FORGIVENESS. Whenever a child does something wrong—no matter the magnitude—set an example of forgiveness. If it was a big mistake and you must punish the child, end the discussion with "I forgive you." If it was something small, just say "That's okay, I forgive you."

❑ **792.** LOVE NEVER ENDS. Children will grow up and move out, but your love goes right on forever and ever. They will always need your love and support. Plan to be in touch each week, and end each conversation with "Remember, I love you."

# TEN
## RULES TO LIVE BY

SECTION 1: LAW AND ORDER

SECTION 2: RULES FOR A HAPPY HOME

SECTION 3: WHAT HAPPENS WHEN . . .

# SECTION 1: LAW AND ORDER

Much of the chaos in home life is caused by a lack of orderly systems for taking care of routine duties. These ideas will help you and your youngster cut through the boring stuff and get on to the fun.

❑ **793.** MANAGING TIME. Show a youngster that there is indeed time for both homework and play. Together, make a list of estimated times for everything in his day. For example, sleep, nine hours; getting up and going to bed routines, one hour; school and travel, seven hours; home meals and snacks, one and one-half hours; chores, a half hour; after-school play/lessons/sports, two hours; after-dinner family activity, a half hour; homework: one and one-half hours; television, a half hour; before-bed reading, a half hour. This shows that everything *can* be accomplished.

❑ **794.** SKILLS TO TEACH. The home is a happier place when each family member is self-governing in certain basic behaviors and skills. See which of these fourteen skills your youngster has already learned and which ones are still to be mastered: to get up when the alarm goes off; to accomplish the morning routine before breakfast or play; to eat nutritious meals; to remember what must be taken to school or activities; to keep a list (rather than try to remember) of things a parent has requested; to take care of clothes and toys; to understand priorities (what must be done first, what can wait); to care for important papers and money and jewelry; to throw away junk; to write down phone messages and put them in a designated place; to return telephone calls; to be aware of all family events; to accomplish chores without being reminded; and to get homework assignments completed on time.

❑ **795.** THE MOTTO. Here are wise words to teach your kids. When they are old enough to write legibly, have them letter this motto on bright paper for posting in their bedrooms, the playroom, or on the refrigerator door. The motto is: *Don't put it down, put it away!*

❑ **796.** KID OFFICE. Being a student with a full social life requires a business-like environment. When a child starts back to school, see that he has a work area of his own: a desk or table with shelves and drawers handy. Using paint or nail polish, show him how to code his own tools: ruler, tape, stapler, scissors, pencils, pens, markers. Also supply clips and rubber bands, tablets and paper, envelopes, and a small card file so he can make cards for friends' phone numbers and addresses.

❑ **797.** FANCY FILES. Files are no longer a dull manila color. At a stationery store, let a youngster choose her own color of folders. Back home, work together to set them up. Her files could include: instructions and warranties on games and equipment, report cards and special school papers, budget and savings account information, letters received/letters to write, ideas on hobbies and collections, pet information, clubs and other activities, ideas and clippings about places to go, and so forth. While these are few compared to your own files, they provide good practice in keeping papers under control.

❑ **798.** BIG BULLETIN BOARD. A bulletin board in a youngster's room can be both decorative and useful. A calendar on the bulletin board lets him note music lesson dates, due-dates for reports, sports practices and games, parties, and other events. While some of this may be on the family calendar, keeping a record of his own obligations encourages responsibility. Work with a youngster to make a bulletin board that is attractive and shows photos, awards, and memorabilia.

❑ **799.** "KEEP DRAWER." Some things seem too precious to throw away. Provide a little-used drawer (or a box on a closet shelf) as a "keep drawer"—a place for a program from a play, a sports award ribbon, photos, postcards—all those things that could cause clutter or get misplaced. At the end of the year, let a youngster choose what to toss, what to put in the yearly scrapbook, what to put in an attic keepsake box.

❑ **800.** YEARLY SCRAPBOOK. Looking together through scrapbooks of childhood years can be pleasant and bring back good memories. Make an annual scrapbook and each year look over the scrapbook made five years ago. See how appearances have changed, what each youngster accomplished, what events were highlights. Things to put in the family scrapbook include: play and sport programs, awards, newspaper clippings, photos, postcards, special birthday cards—all those things that made family life special.

❑ **801.** BAG DAY. Once a month, or as needed, give each family member a sack and turn them loose in the house to find things that aren't where they belong. (Sometimes it's fun to count up each bagful.) Next, dump the items onto a table and sort them by rooms—things that go in the play-room, the garage, a bedroom, and so forth—and place items for one room in one bag. Then let kids choose which bag they'll take in order to return the items to their proper homes.

❑ **802.** COLLECTORS. Some kids love to pick up stuff others might call junk. If it's not harmful or unsanitary, help the collector find places for these treasures. Bottle caps look good inside a large jar. Feathers can be stapled to an old leather belt and hung on the wall. Rocks can be dis-played in a prospector's pan on a shelf. One mother of a col-lector kid has given him a set of matching jars, all from apple sauce, which sit in a row on a shelf—one for pebbles and beach glass, one for sand, one for spark plugs, one for pennies, one for pogs, one for sports pins.

❑ **803.** MY PLACE, YOUR PLACE. Family members need to feel that each has an area just their own. This can be a desk, half of a bedroom (or an entire bedroom), a bathroom, a den, or even a special chair. Help kids to understand that they don't invade your space and you don't look through theirs without asking permission. For a baby, a playpen gives a sense of independence and security, since considering the baby's size, it's comparable to an adult enjoying a cozy nook. See that all family members have places where they can happily be on their own.

# SECTION 2: RULES FOR A HAPPY HOME

To live together harmoniously and efficiently requires some basic "givens"—rules that everyone understands. These rules should cover safety, play, family living, use of the car, dating— whatever areas might cause problems.

❏ **804.** RAINY DAY ACTIVITY. Work together to make a family rule book. Find pictures in magazines to illustrate the points. Don't leave any behavior to conjecture—be specific: We never play with matches. We don't talk to strangers. We don't take the car keys without asking. Review the rules yearly so that they continue to be age-appropriate.

❏ **805.** PRIVILEGES. In the back of the rule book, answer some of the "When can I . . . ?" questions. You will need to think these through yourself and then consult with your family. Here are some possibilities: At age five you may cross the street alone. At age nine you may go to a movie with friends. At age twelve you may have your ears pierced. At age thirteen you may go out with a group of kids at night. At age fourteen you can wear makeup. At age fifteen you may go on a double date. At age sixteen you may go on a date.

❏ **806.** RESPECT FOR AUTHORITY. Show your child that you love her and will always treat her fairly. In return, she is to respect you and do her best to please you. This desire to do the right thing is a form of preventive discipline.

❑ **807. MY MAIL BOX.** Busy families sometimes fail to relay phone messages and other important information to family members. So that there can be no confusion, let each family member create his own box for mail, phone messages, and reminders. Decorated shoe boxes lined up on a desk or counter make a good home post office.

❑ **808. YELLOW RIBBON.** Just as police use a yellow tape to mark an area that is off-limits, so parents can show young children places they are not to be. Buy a roll of bright yellow ribbon and string it wherever you don't want kids to be at the present: in the kitchen, by the fireplace, near workshop tools, in a closet where gifts are hidden, by your computer area. It can be tied in place or just laid on the floor. Teach kids that they can be near you, but that they mustn't cross the line into the cordoned-off area. Occasionally let kids use the ribbon to make their own private play area.

❑ **809. WITH, NOT AT.** One of the best ways to have responsible kids is to have a dialogue—a conversation *with* them rather than just lecturing *at* them. This dialogue should be more about good behavior than bad. Before a youngster goes to a birthday party, a wedding, or an overnight at a friend's home, anticipate things that might happen and discuss ways to handle these challenges. Let the dialogue come from the youngster, with the parent filling in the missing details.

❑ **810. THE FAMILY MEETING.** A once-a-week forum is a good place to consider both rules and gripes, and can also be informative regarding holidays, trips, and parties. Handle such questions as "How can we all get to breakfast on time?" "Who took the keys and didn't put them back?" "Let's make new bedtime rules now that it's summer." In a democratic atmosphere, kids feel comfortable bringing up requests and even asking for arbitration over disagreements. At these meetings there should be a pact that everyone will remain calm—no raised voices, no hurtful remarks. The setting should be pleasant—perhaps by the fireplace with popcorn and apples to eat.

## SAFETY RULES

❑ **811.** MATCH FASCINATION. For young kids who seem intrigued with matches, sit together at a table with matches and a bowl of water. Show how to light a match, striking it away from the body. Let each youngster light and extinguish at least twenty matches—sufficient to bring on boredom. Then give the rule: Matches are only to be used in the presence of an adult.

❑ **812.** FIRE EXTINGUISHER FACTS. While most every house has a fire extinguisher, few family members know where it is—and more important, how to use it. A recommended location is under the kitchen sink since many fires originate in the kitchen. Let youngsters practice removing the extinguisher from its holder and showing how they would use it.

❑ **813.** SHARP TALK ABOUT KNIVES. Train kids in the proper use of knives. Using a table or butter knife, let preschoolers spread butter on toast. As they get older, graduate them to cutting beans, slicing celery, dicing hard-boiled eggs. Teach older youngsters how to carve a roast. A good gift for a preteen or teen is a Swiss army-type knife.

❑ **814.** GUNS KILL. Many people now keep guns in their homes, and even if you don't, your kids may play at homes that have guns. Question other parents about guns at their houses. Guns need to be locked up (not left in night table drawers where kids can find them) and the key must be well-hidden. Not permitting toy guns for play will lessen the danger of an accident. Talk about guns and establish these two rules: Never touch a gun. If another youngster has a gun, immediately leave the area and report it to a parent or other adult.

❑ **815.** SOMEONE'S AT THE DOOR. Practice with younger children just what you want them to do when the doorbell rings. Are they to open the door? Are they to ask who is there? Are they to get an adult? What if they are alone? Actually play-act the procedure with you outside the front door and the child inside.

❑ **816.** SOMEONE'S ON THE PHONE. Although kids love to answer the phone, it's best to do it yourself until a child is able to take a message. If a child is alone, he should be sure to not reveal that fact. Play-act (actually using the phone and holding down the button) so that the child can practice saying "Mom is busy but will call you back." Pretend to be the caller and ask: "Is your Dad there?" "When will he be home?" "Is anyone with you?"

❑ **817.** STRANGER SITUATIONS. A stranger might approach a child on the street or from a car at the curb. Again, play-act the proper response (actually do this outside with a neighbor in a car). The stranger/neighbor asks the child to come over to the car (the child refuses). The stranger/neighbor offers candy (the child says no and runs off). The stranger/neighbor says that the parent has sent her to pick up the child (the child says no and runs away). The stranger/neighbor tries to grab the child (the child runs away screaming).

❑ **818.** THE OTHER PARENT. Clearly explain to children that when parents divorce, there are laws that must be followed by both parents. (Most "missing" children have been abducted by "the other parent.") Gently tell kids that they are not to go with the other parent before getting your OK and, if that parent is insistent, they are to scream for help or run to another adult. If there is danger of abduction, alert teachers, neighbors, and nearby friends. These measures must be taught, but do so in a serious but matter-of-fact way to lessen the fear.

❑ **819.** MANDATORY SEAT BELTS. While everyone knows they should strap in, passengers become more lax with increasing age. When the family gets in the car, make it a race to see who gets his seat belt fastened first. Call out "First done," "Second done," and so forth. Never make exceptions, which can be tempting when you are going a short distance or have a large group of kids to transport.

❑ **820.** WHERE ARE YOU GOING? When a child of *any age* leaves the house, she should tell exactly where she is going and when she will return. If parents are not home, this information should be written and placed where it will be seen. Your rules should also state that if she leaves the destination to go somewhere else, she must telephone home or your office with that information.

❑ **821.** CURFEWS—A MUST! With kid-input, set reasonable coming-home times. These might be 5:00 from after-school play, 8:00 on a school night, 11:00 on weekends, with exceptions for special occasions. Make the time clear: the curfew is 11 P.M. At 11:01, the youngster is definitely late. At 11:15, you will start calling other parents. At 11:30 you may wish to call the police. Let kids know how serious you are about this matter. (Punishments for breaking curfews are in the next section.)

## RULES FOR PLAY

❑ **822.** DISAGREEMENTS. As much as possible, let kids work out their own disagreements, as long as the argument doesn't become physical. If you intervene, ask participants to sit down and quietly think what has happened. Ask each to tell her side. Then ask if they would like you to settle the matter (they usually don't) or can they settle it and continue play.

❑ **823.** PUPPETS TELL WHAT REALLY HAPPENED. When it is difficult for a child to admit guilt or misbehavior, bring out the puppets—one for the parent, one for the child. The parent puppet starts by asking what is going on.

The child puppet usually tells just some of the facts. The parent puppet asks that the story of what happened be told again. (A second telling usually is more detailed than the first.) The parent puppet can say, "Little puppet, I want you to think really hard and see what else you can remember" or "What would Scott (the child) like you to tell me?" This usually brings out all the facts.

❑ **824.** THE FAIRY QUEEN. When kids playing dress-up or house begin to bicker, join in the game by becoming the fairy queen. If possible, wear a crown, a white scarf, or other elegant item from the dress-up box. With your fairy wand (this can be a yardstick wound with ribbon), make queen-like pronouncements instead of ordinary discipline. For example: "The queen wants everyone to speak kindly." "The queen will divide the toys and announce when they are to be exchanged." "The queen does not want to put anyone in the dungeon." This less-personal discipline very often works.

❑ **825.** SNACK ATTACKS. Sometimes kids get in trouble for eating candy or cookies—especially just before meal-time. Solve the problem by working together to make a snack bin for each youngster. You can use any kind of cov-ered container labeled with the child's name. Put in pack-aged nutritious snacks—some salty, some sweet—that you approve of. Two a day should be the max and you should put in enough to last one week. There are just two rules—you can't eat another person's snacks and you can't snack in the hour before a meal. Then, put the youngsters on their honor, with the knowledge that the snack container only gets filled once a week.

## RULES FOR LIVING TOGETHER

(Also see chapter 6, section 1 on the topic of manners, so essential for living together.)

❑ **826.** LITTLE WORDS FOR LITTLE FOLKS. Teach tod-dlers the spoken words of good manners: please, thank you, I'm sorry, excuse me. If a child asks for something without the word "please," or accepts something without saying "thank you," prompt him the first few times with the words "What do you say?" But quickly drop that line. Just ignore the request without "please" and quietly take back the given item if there is no "thank you."

❏ **827.** BORROWING AND RETURNING. It's good manners to ask before taking another's possessions. And it is very good manners to return the item promptly and in good condition. While it is good to share within a family, don't permit borrowing when the borrower does not show proper care for the item. If borrowing goes on outside the family, create a "borrowed" list for the family bulletin board. Show the date and who borrowed things like garden tools, kitchen supplies, toys, books, and so forth.

❏ **828.** CLOSED DOORS. A closed door is a message. It says: "Knock first." A closed door can also say: "Come back later." All family members over age four are entitled to some private time. This can be in the bathroom or in one's own room. However, parents should be alert to what is going on if the door is closed for long periods of time. And, when kids of opposite sexes are in a room, the door remains open.

❏ **829.** OOPS, I BROKE IT. Teach kids to "fess up" to mistakes. Things do get broken or spilled or lost, so make it a family rule to immediately admit what has happened. Don't accept any lame excuses such as "the cat did it."

❏ **830.** BEDTIME PEST. When a young child is ready for bed, be sure that she's had a bathroom trip, a drink of water, a story, and hugs and kisses. Then, unless you want a bedtime pest, explain to her that there are only three reasons for her to get out of bed and come to you: (1) She is sick and you will tend to her in her room. (2) The house is on fire or there is some other emergency you should know about. (3) She has not had enough punishment today and is asking for more. This system usually cures the pest.

❏ **831.** **BABYSITTER TREATS.** Some kids act up when a sitter is to care for them—they either cry or they are disobedient. Make a night with a babysitter into a special night. Call it "Popcorn Night," "Monopoly Marathon," or "Fudge Sundae Night." And, give the sitter the option of extending the bedtime by fifteen minutes for kids who don't cause trouble. Soon kids will be looking forward to having a sitter and planning what games and activities to do together, rather than just watching TV.

❏ **832.** **THE NAP FAIRY.** Young children who fight naptime (and still believe in the tooth fairy) should be told about the nap fairy who brings a little treat to kids who rest without argument. When sleep comes, the parent can place a small item on the foot of the bed.

❏ **833.** **RHYMED RULES.** For children under seven, family rules can be learned more quickly when they rhyme. Teach these to your youngsters:

*Come when called the first time:* When Mom or Dad calls my name, I come as fast as a speedy jet plane.
*Being excused after a meal:* We eat together for family fun, and ask to be excused when we're all done.   .
*Coming in from play:* I wipe my feet when I come in the door. That helps me keep mud off the floor.
*Manners:* "Please" and "thank you" are easy to say. How many times have you said them today?
*Sharing:* I have so many, many toys, I love to share with girls and boys.
*Helping:* "Can I help?" are words I can say. When work is done there's time to play.
*Responsibility for a pet:* I pat my doggie in a gentle way and remember to feed him every day.
*Strapping in:* In the car there's one way to be: Seated and belted means safety for me.

*Crossing streets:* When crossing a street, a hand I hold. That's the rule till I'm five years old.

*Talking with strangers:* I do not talk with strangers I see. This rule for safety is important to me.

*Fighting over toys:* If I argue about toys and don't act right, the toy is put away, out of my sight.

*Snacks:* When I get hungry and want a treat, I ask permission before I eat.

*Taking turns:* Taking turns is the way to talk. Speak one-at-a-time and please don't squawk!

*Bathroom etiquette:* After using the toilet, the thing to do is wash my hands and dry them, too.

*Hitting:* Hitting hurts and makes me sad. I remember what's right so I won't be bad.

*TV viewing:* Once in a while I see TV. But only if the program is good for me.

*Picking up toys:* When finished playing at the end of the day, I quickly put my toys away.

*Clothing:* My clothes never get thrown on the floor, just in the wash or in my drawer.

*When it's bedtime:* When I am told it's time for bed, I don't argue or shake my head.

*Getting ready for bed:* Before I go to bed each night, There are four things that I do right: Go to the bathroom without a fight, brush my teeth so they'll be bright. Wash my hands with all my might, give a hug and say "good night!"

*Staying in bed:* When I'm tucked into my bed I say my prayers and rest my head. I don't get out of bed and play. I think about the fun today.

# SECTION 3: WHAT HAPPENS WHEN . . .

When family rules are broken, there is often need for punishment. These ideas will help impress on young people that they are responsible for their actions.

❑ **834.** KEEP YOUR PERSPECTIVE. Don't punish for every little infraction. Pick your occasions in order to make a point. Overlook minor wrongs with a laugh or a comment "That's silly." You want to teach youngsters that some things are very important and others less important.

❑ **835.** SPANKING. Although spanking is still one of the most common forms of punishment, decades of research show that it is less effective than other means (explained below) for making sure that the mistake is not repeated. When your youngster can understand, about age three, explain that you will discipline him in various ways, but spanking will not be one of them. (Spanking teaches a child that hitting another person is an appropriate response and he will use it with friends or even with you.) Spanking does not focus on the problem and how to correct it.

❑ **836.** TAKE YOUR CHOICE. When kids act up, tell them firmly that they have a choice to make. "It's your choice to nag me about wanting candy and be punished as soon as we get home or it's your choice to help me in the grocery store." Or, "You can choose to take toys away from Brian and then be punished, or you can choose to play happily." Leaving the decision up to the child is a first step toward self-government.

❑ **837.** WHEN AND THEN. When giving children options, state them when possible as "when . . . then" statements. For example don't say "Barry, you can't go to the park until you have cut the grass." Rather, state: "Barry, when the grass is cut, then you can go to the park." It is important not to stress choices negatively, and to put the more attractive activity second, as in the above example.

❑ **838.** EITHER . . . OR. Leave some decisions up to youngsters by stating it this way: "You may either stay up late tonight or you can stay up late one night this weekend. You decide." This empowers the youngster to make the decision.

❑ **839.** FRIENDLY CHOICES. When you are working out a problem with your child, give the child a choice. As an example, Peter has lost his bike, which is essential to his paper route and to getting to school. Start by asking Peter what should be done. (Peter's usual response will be "I don't know.") Next, offer a solution that requires the child's help: "We'll help you buy a new one and you can help pay for it." When Peter rejects that idea, state that it's a way for him to take responsibility for where he leaves his bike. In a firm and friendly tone, give him a choice of walking to school and pulling a wagon on his paper route, or paying three dollars a week for the bike. (This is a plan you can both live with.) Give the choice once. Expect the youngster to test you. Stand firm, remain friendly.

❑ **840.** BAD BEHAVIOR BY PARENTS. When a parent nags and scolds, the child gets attention and feels the power of keeping parents busy with him. When the parent gets angry and then gives in, the child feels the power of getting his way. When the parent gives vengeful punishment, the child rebels, figuring that he has been hurt so he can hurt back. When a parent gives up correcting a child, the child figures the parent doesn't care about him anymore. Working together, you and your youngster can stop this vicious circle!

❑ **841.** LISTEN AND AGREE. When a child comes to you with a complaint or tale of woe, listen carefully and **agree with his feelings.** Child: "Hank pushed me down on the cement." Parent: "That must have hurt." Child: "I got a D on my paper and the guys think that's funny." Parent: "That must disappoint and hurt you." The child hopes you will have a solution, but you must remember that the problem is his, and he has to find a solution. Certainly you will help but not take the lead. By listening and agreeing with his reaction, you are not condoning what happened, you are creating an atmosphere for discussion and solution.

❑ **842.** WHAT IS PUNISHABLE? Here are some examples. For very young children, you'll need to discipline for: ignoring rules, acting mean to friends, breaking things on purpose, tantrums, and failing to share. For gradeschoolers: breaking rules, forgetting chores, failing to do homework, and continually getting bad grades. For older kids, the same plus: cutting classes, getting a traffic ticket, being disrespectful, and taking part in dangerous and illegal activities. Punishment helps kids to remember the right things to do.

❑ **843.** **WHAT ABOUT APPEARANCE?** What kids wear does not have to become a discipline question. Kids can follow modern trends without being dirty or sloppy. With kid-help, divide a youngster's closet and shelves into sections: clothes suitable for school or casual events, play and work clothes, and clothes to wear for family events, church, and social occasions. Don't be swept along into buying expensive clothes. Don't comment on school clothes unless they are totally tacky, too revealing, or have gang connotations.

❑ **844.** **WHAT ABOUT HER ROOM?** One of the biggest points of contention in the family is the status of a youngster's room. The words "Clean up your room" echo around the world. Set a minimum standard of cleanliness (no food items or clothes on the floor) and then be sure that there are adequate shelves/boxes/drawers for a youngster's possessions. It should be a family rule that the room is tidied up once a week so it can be cleaned (by youngster, parent, or cleaning person). This includes changing the sheets, dusting, and vacuuming or mopping. If the room is not tidy for cleaning day, this is an occasion for discipline. (One mom charges her teen ten dollars an hour to tidy and clean it.) How the room looks the remainder of the week is the child's business since the room is her private domain.

❑ **845.** **WHEN TO PUNISH?** As soon as possible, unless your anger is out of control, or the offense is so serious you want to think about it for awhile or consult with your spouse. Sometimes a working parent is told of disobedience at school or hears of it from the babysitter, and so must deal with it after-the-fact. Still, do it as soon as possible.

❏ **846. WHERE TO PUNISH?** Home is best. Punishment in public is difficult and often compounds the problem by adding humiliation. If away from home, you may be able to find a quiet place. If not, you can say "I can't discipline you here, but believe me, you will be punished as soon as we're home." Then follow through on your threat.

❏ **847. WHO PUNISHES?** Unfortunately in many busy families it is no one! Corrections should be made by both parents so that one isn't the ogre and the other the saint. Let kids know that the parent on the scene will do it. None of that "Just wait until your father comes home!" If one parent seems to be more in charge during the week, the other should become the authority figure for the weekend. Be sure to instruct your sitter as to punishments she should carry out, and the infractions that she should report to you.

❏ **848. AT WHAT AGE?** Behavior training starts with babies when you use a pleasant voice and a smiling face for happy times (such as when a baby eats willingly) or a deep and stern voice with a somber face for unhappy times (such as when he throws all his toys out of the playpen). From this point onward, you will be gently correcting and firmly disciplining your youngsters until you are no longer responsible for them.

❏ **849. WHEN PUNISHMENT IS OVER.** When the period of discipline is over, it is over. Sometimes apologies are needed, sometimes not. Teaching children to say, and mean, "I'm sorry" can make others feel better. The parent should give a big hug, forget the incident and not bring it up again at supper, to neighbors, or grandparents. Here are some things you can tell your youngster: "I'm hoping you won't make that mistake again." "I trust you to do the right thing when I'm not watching over you." "I love you too much to let you break the law."

❑ **850.** NO APPEALS. As soon as children are three or four, explain that when a punishment is given, there are to be no appeals to the other parent for leniency. (One family doubles the punishment if kids try this!) Be sure that you have given the youngster every opportunity to talk about what happened before setting the punishment. That way, he will feel that he had a fair hearing. And reassure him that you care so much for him that you can't let him do wrong things.

❑ **851.** ATTENTION GETTING. Preschoolers are often naughty (shouting, kicking, throwing things) in order to gain attention. Firmly set the child down in a safe place on the floor, say nothing, turn away, and walk out of sight. Being deprived of an audience is often sufficient discipline and a child will learn that this behavior was of no benefit.

❑ **852.** BITING. When toddlers bite, some parents try to cure the habit by biting the child in return. This is like teaching a child not to steal by taking him to a store where you steal an item! When a child bites, quickly separate her from the other youngsters. If needed, take appropriate first aid measures for the bitten child. Biting is usually a phase that disappears when kids become more verbal, however, it is distressing and you can help stop it two ways. First, use preventive conversation, spending time with the playmates and giving the child attention, praising her for not biting, and clearly stating what will happen if she bites. Second, use curative measures such as removing the biting child to isolation. Explain simply but very seriously that biting will not be tolerated. Try to find out what triggered the biting and suggest an alternate means of expression. If biting occurs at a party, a park, a friend's home, immediately take the child home, telling her it is because she bit someone. You may have to repeat this process until she understands.

❑ **853.** KEEP IT SIMPLE. For young children who misbehave, don't go into elaborate explanations. One word—"No!"—can be effective. Occasionally it will be followed by an explanation ("because that's not safe"). Teach kids that "no" means to stop immediately, and the question "why" will be answered after the unacceptable behavior has ceased.

❑ **854.** **POWER PLAYS AND TANTRUMS.** Stop this bad behavior as soon as a child starts to use it. Don't appear to be upset (although you may well be). Give the child a choice: "Stop screaming and kicking or there will be punishment—you choose. It's up to you." A parent must remain in control when a child is not in control. Discuss the behavior when you are both calm and then decide on a punishment together.

❑ **855.** **MEAN WHAT YOU SAY.** Ask your youngster if she understands when you say: "If you do that again, you'll get a time-out." Consistency is the basic requisite for good discipline. If you make a threat, you must follow through. Don't say you'll punish when you cannot carry it out. The moment you do, you open the door for kids to behave as they please without paying any heed to your words.

❑ **856.** **ONE CHANCE ONLY.** Some parents give a second chance before punishing. In a case where a child breaks a known rule, this second chance should not be given. Share with kids your decision to be firm about the rules and that ignoring certain rules, especially those concerned with safety, will cause swift punishment.

❑ **857.** **HUMILIATION.** The purpose of discipline is to correct, and humiliation should play no part in it. When you humiliate a youngster, the hurt is what is remembered, not the lesson in how to do better. For example, a parent embarrasses a four-year-old who wets his pants by making him spend the rest of the day in the wet pants. Humiliation is a not-so-subtle form of child abuse.

❑ **858.** **PARENTAL FRUSTRATION.** Sometimes when a child has been naughty, a parent is just so angry that the punishment may be excessive. If in retrospect you feel you have overreacted, sit down quietly with the youngster and apologize. She will be impressed with your honesty! Adjust the punishment if possible. But also explain that a parent wants so much for a child to be good and happy that when a child is naughty, it really hurts the parent. Another time, you might say: "I'm getting angry about this . . ." and that may change the behavior. Don't let kids think parents are always perfect—they'll soon find out otherwise.

❏ **859.** BROKEN CURFEW. One of the most frightening experiences for parents occurs when a youngster doesn't return home on time. Together, establish a curfew and a short grace period. Be very strict the first time the curfew is broken. If the time to return home is 10:45 to 11:00 P.M. be prepared to discipline for even one minute beyond 11:00. If you don't, you'll be taken advantage of on a regular basis. "Campus" a youngster one weekend night for each five minutes late (or portion thereof). Being "campused" means no going out, no phone calls, no TV, no visiting friends. If kids try the old "car ran out of gas" line, investigate the verity of it. Don't accept differences in clocks—tell youngsters that before they leave they should always set their watches in keeping with the family clock.

❏ **860.** NO "GO TO YOUR ROOM!" Many parents think that sending a youngster to his room is proper punishment. It is not. A child's room is his castle—his own precious place—and there should not be bad vibes about it. Besides, there's lots of fun stuff to do there! So, if you must send a child somewhere, send him to your room, or the laundry room, or a corner of the kitchen.

❏ **861.** PUNCH CARD. When taking a youngster out in public, such as to a store, make him a little three-by-five card from a piece of paper. On it draw three smiley faces and three sad faces. Explain that if she's helpful, you'll circle a smiley face. If she is difficult or naughty, you'll circle a sad face. If at the end of the trip there are more circles around the smiley faces, she can choose a treat.

❑ **862.** CHARGE A FEE. If you wish to correct a child who swears, talks in a fresh manner, or whines, here's a good cure. Fill a covered jar with five dollars in quarters. Each time there is an offense, take a quarter out. At the end of the month, the youngster gets any money that is left.

❑ **863.** THE THINKING BENCH. Probably the most common form of punishment for young children, the thinking bench, is also called "time-out" or isolation. The purpose is to stop the wrong activity and give the youngster an opportunity to think about what she did and how else she might have acted. For example, your daughter shoves a friend off a trike and the friend cries. When you've ensured that the friend is all right, take your child to the thinking bench (a real footstool in the laundry room, the second stair tread on the stairway, wherever she can be away from the activity). Put her here and set a timer—the kind that rings a bell. Be explicit about the mistake ("You took the trike, you made your friend cry") and ask her to think about what she did. The timer is set for as many minutes as the child is old, so a three-year-old will sit for three minutes. Early on, explain that if the child leaves the thinking bench, she is put back, and the timer is started again. When the bell rings, return to the child and ask "Since you wanted the trike, what is a better way for you to have gotten to use it?" She may have an answer or you may have to suggest one (asking for the trike, taking turns, offering a trade). Then point out that by being naughty she has missed playtime. Ask if she can now go and play happily and tell her friend she is sorry. Now, this procedure takes your time, but only at first. It will take less time as your child realizes the consequences of wrong behavior and doesn't want to go through this routine over and over again.

❑ **864.** CLEANING UP THE MESS. Sometimes having to clean up a mess—or help to clean it up—is sufficient pun-

nt. (Remember, that playing with numerous toys is
>mething to be punished, it is creative fun. And, pick-
p at day's end is not punishment either, but a
given.") However, if a child spills paint, dumps out a
drawer, throws all the sand out of the sandbox, or tosses
food on the floor, he should clean it up. By the time a child
is five, he should clean up most messes entirely by himself
with only a few suggestions from the parent. Now the parent may be able to clean it up faster, but that's not the
point. Teach the child the consequence of his action and
don't deprive him of the lesson gained from the cleanup.
Show him how to use rags, a pail of water, a scrub brush—
whatever is necessary.

❑ **865.** EVEN STEVEN. Sometimes there is absolutely no
way a child can undo what she has done wrong. Perhaps she
has cut a hole in her best shirt or wasted thirty minutes of
your time by being late when you came to pick her up at the
library. The youngster has used up some of your time need-
lessly—by having to mend the hole or wait in the car. So, she
pays you back your time by doing a special task—this is an
"Even Steven" punishment. She may fold laundry or dust or
weed—any task that can be done alone, in quiet, providing
the opportunity to think about the importance of time.

❑ **866.** WRITTEN REPRIMANDS. It can be very impres-
sive for a youngster to see a parent's displeasure in writing.
Spoken words are said and gone, but written words are
there to read and reread. If the misbehavior is a continual
one, consider writing a note and placing it on a youngster's
desk: "Dear Mark, I know you love Chipper, but dogs truly
need fresh water each day. When you forget, I have to do
your job and that makes me sad. Will you try harder? I love
you, Mom." A child getting such a note is impressed that
you took the time to write—and this often makes it an
effective cure.

❑ **867.** WRITTEN COMPLIMENTS. You reinforce good
behavior when you are appreciative. Perhaps you will men-

tion the child's good conduct to your spouse or your parents (so the child hears). And, you can write a short note to the child and put it on her pillow: "Dear Diana, You really did a spiffy job on the kitchen counters tonight! It made my after-dinner time much easier and I appreciate that! Every minute counts for a working parent. I love you always, Dad."

❑ **868.** LITTLE LECTURES. In our fast-paced society, we often fail to take the time to fully explain the whys and wherefors. Many youngsters respond favorably to reason and, if you are good with words, you can use this talent to advantage. This is especially effective with kids between six and sixteen who have done something thoughtless or dangerous: playing with matches, running into the street, hurting a pet, mistreating a friend, ignoring chores, or failing to do homework. Make your lecture more than a sentence— repeat your message many different ways, which may seem tedious to the youngster but gets the message across. Following the lecture, ask for input as to how to avoid the same mistake again.

❑ **869.** HUGE PUNISHMENTS. Occasionally a child's disobedience is of such magnitude that you must devise a punishment that will be long remembered. You do this in hope that he will *never* repeat the mistake. Such punishment is reserved for occasions where a child has done something to endanger his own life or the lives of others: drag racing, playing with guns, or using drugs. One parent, whose daughter had violated the family rule about going into the swimming pool fenced area without adult permission (and she even fell into the pool), devised a huge punishment that consisted of being confined to the house after school for the first week. She also had to write a research paper on responsibility and safety, including interviews with neighbors, working on it at least thirty minutes a day. The second week she was enrolled in a CPR class. At the end of the second week she read the research paper out loud to the family and gave a CPR demonstration. While this may seem excessive, one of the younger children said, "Wow, I'll never break that rule 'cause I don't want that punishment to happen to me!" There was never any further breaking of the rule.

## DEPRIVATION: A MOST-EFFECTIVE DISCIPLINE

Of all the ways to correct wrong behavior, *deprivation* is one of the best. The word sounds alarming, but it is actually a gentle, persuasive, and thoughtful method. It works with kids as young as three and right on through the teen years.

❑ **870.** A FIRST CONVERSATION. Initiate a dialogue with youngsters concerning society's methods of correcting people: a drunk driver is deprived of his license, a thief is deprived of his freedom. On a smaller scale, if we borrow something and don't return it, we're deprived of borrowing again. Or, if we slurp our juice and wipe our nose on our sleeve, we may be deprived of a party invitation. So, when we lose self-control and behave inappropriately, we lose privileges—we are deprived of them. Make the point clearly: that it is our own choice to act acceptably or unacceptably.

❑ **871.** DEPRIVED OF WHAT? When a child disobeys, she is deprived of something she really likes: a possession or a privilege. So, to use deprivation successfully you have to know what is important to your child. Certainly you know your child well enough to know what is meaningful to her: her bike, use of the telephone, weekend freedom, the car keys, television time, video games, a boom box, the right to spend money, a special toy or collection. Depending on the age of the youngster and the seriousness of the infraction, deprive her of her possession or privilege for a certain length of time—anywhere from a day to an entire month.

❑ **872.** ADVANCE NOTICE. Some deprivations can be known in advance as part of the family rules: If your gradeschooler gets a C minus or less, there will be no weekday TV until the next grading period and an improved grade. If your child disobeys a sitter, he will be put to bed before the sitter comes the next time. If your teen fails to be where she said she'd be, and doesn't phone with the change of place, she's "campused" for a week. If a teen gets a traffic ticket, his car keys and license are taken away. Most kids prefer knowing the rules and penalties in advance.

❑ **873.** BUT IT HURTS! If you have announced the deprivation, don't give in. So it is very important to be sure that you do not make an extremely hurtful deprivation (being forbidden to attend the prom) unless there is a large infraction (driving drunk). You, too, may feel sad when your youngster must miss an important event, but the lesson must be brought home and you can't weaken. So don't say, "If you don't improve your spelling grade you can't be on the soccer team" unless you intend to stick to your decision. And, when you make a concession, make it understood that this is a very special occasion and never likely to happen again.

# ELEVEN

# CAN CHORES BE FUN?

## SECTION 1: WHO DOES WHAT

## SECTION 2: GETTING THE JOB DONE WITH FUN

## SECTION 3: SKILLS FOR INDEPENDENCE

**M**any parents think that they're being kind to their children by not having them do any chores. But really, they are raising kids who later in life won't be able to cope with work around the home. Working together provides opportunity for both conversation and horseplay—and it can actually build positive memories. No child is too old, too young, or too busy to contribute to the family.

# SECTION 1: WHO DOES WHAT

Although I've written about chores in many of my books, in this chapter I've brought the best ideas together so that you can start early to prepare your child to be a functioning adult by teaching what it takes to maintain a home.

❑ **874.** GET AN ATTITUDE! Talk with the family about what makes a good and fair boss since parents are usually the boss when it comes to assigning chores and judging whether the job is done in a satisfactory way. Be consistent but don't be too strict. Unless the queen is coming for dinner, a child's good effort can be as acceptable as a child's *excellent* effort, which will come by example and practice.

❑ **875.** LET ME SHOW YOU. No matter how simple the task assigned, show a child how to do it. You may have to do this several times, but in the long run it will save *you* time. Be strict about the dangers of working around the house: sharp knives in the dishwasher, a hot dryer, running over the vacuum cord, playing with the lawn mower, and misusing a tool. Don't let poorly done work stop you from giving more instruction and more opportunities to do it successfully.

❑ **876.** REPETITION WINS. When first introducing chores, don't change the chores each week—that can come later. Let a youngster repeat the same tasks for two or three weeks until he can do the job in a satisfactory way. Then talk about how often kids want to change their chores: weekly or monthly.

❑ **877.** PUT IT IN WRITING. You may remember everything there is to do, but kids don't. Each week, make a list for young children and have older ones make their own lists of tasks. Be specific. This might be a gradeschool child's list:

Morning: Feed the dog, make three beds.

Afternoon: Set the table, make a salad.

Evening: Wipe the kitchen counters, tidy the family room.

Weekends: Water the house plants, make Saturday lunch, and participate in a project of building bookshelves.

❑ **878.** NO STEREOTYPES. Don't let home tasks get stuck in cement—Mom the cook, Junior the rubbish, Dad the lawn-mowing, and Sis the laundry folding. Dads can bake and make beds, Junior can do laundry and arrange flowers, Mom can wash the car, and Sis can trim the bushes. Giving kids opportunities to do all the chores will empower them when they're finally on their own.

❑ **879.** HOW MUCH TIME FOR TASKS? While preschoolers can work about fifteen minutes a day, older children should contribute thirty minutes. And, over the weekend, a total of two hours of work can be contributed by each family member (except preschoolers who will work about an hour). You can see that with two children, you'll get nine extra hours each week to spend on something special!

❑ **880.** HOW MANY TASKS? AND IS THERE PAY? Helpful things kids can do fall into three categories: routine daily tasks, assigned weekend tasks, and special tasks that are paid for. The first two categories are "givens"—things kids do because they are part of the family. The special tasks should carry a fee. Sit down with the family and make a list of everything that needs to be done to make the house run smoothly, assigning some as regular chores, others as paid work.

❑ **881.** CHORES FIRST, PLAY SECOND. Most weekday tasks should be done before evening fun and television viewing. And when the weekend work projects are finished, there can be a reward: an excursion, ice-cream sundaes, a video, or a later bedtime. Explain when kids are young that they must plan to get their chores done despite their sports practices, parties, and other activities.

❑ **882.** TODDLER TASKS. As soon as a child can walk and understand a few directions, she's ready for toddler tasks—ones you supervise and really express your appreciation for. These are favorites: delivering things to various rooms of the house ("Please put this shirt on Susie's bed"), picking up leaves in the yard, bringing in the newspaper, helping set the table, and of course, picking up toys.

❑ **883.** PRESCHOOLER ASSIGNMENTS. Learning to follow directions and learning to remember two or three things at a time are valuable lessons. Consider these tasks: helping fold laundry and delivering it, smoothing beds and fluffing pillows, emptying wastebaskets, learning the names of tools and how to fetch and carry them safely, opening blinds and curtains, sweeping the patio, and feeding pets.

❑ **884.** GRADESCHOOLERS' WORK. Bigger, taller kids can empty and load the dishwasher, wipe counter tops, bring in the mail, put up the flag, make flower arrangements, select and play recordings, entertain a baby (while adult is nearby), weed the garden, run sprinklers, rake leaves, groom pets, clean lavatories and bathtubs, bake a cake, water house plants, dust and vacuum, polish silver, sew and mend, shovel snow, and help with grocery shopping.

❑ **885.** JUNIOR HIGH JOBS. Although much less supervision is needed, still try to make some chores a team effort with a parent or sibling. Consider: washing the car, making complete meals, painting fences, planning menus, doing repairs, making flower arrangements, sewing clothes, serving as babysitter while parents nap or bathe, running errands on bicycle, taking trash to the curb for pick-up and bringing containers back later, building a fire in the fireplace, reading reviews and recommending movies, testing younger kids on spelling words, reading stories to younger children, and keeping the family scrapbook or photo album up-to-date.

❑ **886.** HIGH SCHOOL CHORES. By this time, little supervision is needed so be sure some of the chores still involve adult companionship. In addition to the preceding list, consider these: changing the car's oil and oil filter, putting up storm windows or screens, building a backyard fire pit or fence, changing faucet washers and light bulbs, washing windows inside and out, doing the grocery shopping, scrubbing floors, mowing the lawn, babysitting, assisting at parties, defrosting/cleaning/reloading refrigerator or freezer, cleaning out closets and drawers, painting a room, setting up the VCR, helping pay bills, and running errands by car.

❑ **887.** PARENTS GET THE LEFTOVERS. Tasks not assigned belong to parents. Don't be shy about listing these to show how much work you are doing. Talk about these jobs and see if kids want to take some of the load off you. If both parents work, the parent's job list should be equally divided between spouses. If there is an at-home parent, the other parent should still accept responsibility for a fair number of chores.

❑ **888.** FAMILY WORK DAY. Occasionally, on a weekend day or a holiday, make a list of jobs that need doing and an estimate of the time required (no more than ninety minutes). Furnish a bell to be rung as each job is completed. Starting with the youngest child, let each choose which task to accomplish, and then all go to work. When one finishes her job and rings the bell, she looks for another worker and helps him. When they finish and ring the bell, they continue to work with others until all the work is done. Then it's time for fun!

❑ **889.** EFFECTIVE ERRANDS. Rather than allotting many weekend hours to running around town doing errands, include kids in these errands when on your way home from school, from sports practice, or other places. Weekend errands almost disappear when you tie them into other trips. And grocery shopping speeds along with good helpers. Divide your list into sections such as produce, canned goods, breads, or paper supplies, and give each mini-list to a youngster. The job will be done in half the time!

❑ **890.** TOOL TIME. Not every member of the family may find the hardware store fascinating, but expose both boys and girls to the wonders of these chock-full-of-stuff places. As you walk about, name tools and other supplies and explain some uses. Our young grandson's first three word sentence was "Go Home Depot" (the name of a favorite hardware store that his handy father takes him to almost every Saturday). By age five, give youngsters their own toolbox and simple, safe tools of their own.

# SECTION 2: GETTING THE JOB DONE WITH FUN

While some youngsters just automatically accomplish their assigned chores, others may need encouragement, especially at the beginning. Here are some ways to get the jobs done without nagging.

❑ **891.** AFTER-SUPPER CHECK. If Fido's bowl is empty and the laundry still stacked and waiting to be delivered to each room, it's best to know about it before bedtime. Not during supper—a pleasant event—but immediately after, ask each family member to check his list and be sure all tasks are completed. Say little to those who scurry off to complete their work, but be full of praise to those who have finished.

❑ **892.** PICTURE CHART. Children who don't yet read can have a picture chart to remind them: a toothbrush picture to remind them to brush teeth, a dog picture means fill Fido's water bowl, a picture of a knife/fork/spoon means set the table, a picture of toys means to pick them up. Explain the pictures so that there is no doubt as to what must be done.

❑ **893.** CHECK IT OFF. Some kids function better by actually checking off the job when it is done. Start with a simple chart with seven boxes for the days of the week. As needed, you can get fancy with stars or stickers or tie the chart into the season or a holiday. Keep the chart somewhere it can easily be seen—on the family bulletin board or refrigerator door. One parent places it right in front of the television screen, indicating that chores come first!

❑ **894.** BE A CHAIRPERSON. Everyone likes to feel "in charge." And you can give kids that feeling of control by putting them in charge of one area in the home and then giving them a title: Chairperson of Pets, Chief Sweeper-upper, Assistant Gourmet Chef, Toy Coordinator, Co-engineer for Maintenance, or Archivist (the one in charge of the family scrapbook and photo album). See who can come up with a catchy title for other chores.

❑ **895.** PICK-UP CHALLENGE. One of the most boring tasks seems to be putting away toys and clothes. For recalcitrant workers, set a timer and issue the challenge: "I bet you can't get everything put away before the bell rings" or "I say this will take you eight minutes—a treat if you can do it in seven."

❑ **896.** CELEBRATION DINNER. On the first weekday of each month, plan a celebration. Be complimentary about all the work the family has accomplished. Ask what new things kids learned while doing chores. If you have been using the star or sticker method to show that a day's work was completed, give a small reward for twenty-five stars (a near-perfect month). And, when there is a perfect month, seat that child at the head of the table and toast him!

❑ **897.** IN THE CRACKS. Teach kids that each task

may require a specified amount of time, but it can take less time if it is done "in the cracks." Some examples: While helping make dinner, set out some of the elements for the next-day's lunch. While walking through the family room, put away one toy. While talking on the phone, brush the dog. While unloading the dishwasher, set the table for the next meal. While picking up your room, select clothes for the next day. While brushing your teeth, memorize a poem taped on the mirror.

# SECTION 3:
# SKILLS FOR INDEPENDENCE

In order to live useful and satisfying lives, young people need to master the "how to" in many categories. Here are a few you can teach by example or with hands-on experiences so kids will know what to do when on their own.

❑ **898.** FOOD NOT GARBAGE. When kids gain that wonderful teenage freedom, nutritious eating often goes down the tubes in favor of snacking and fast foods. This won't happen as often if you include kids in preparing meals at home. Let them plan menus and teach them how to cook. Interest them in the joys and money-saving merits of baking and preserving. Emphasize the importance of kitchen cleanliness and teach the shelf life of perishable foods. During weekends and vacations, give them titles: Salad Chef, Cookie Creator, Vegetable Goddess, Hamburger Hero, and Potato Potentate.

❑ **899.** HOW TO HOST. Help kids to be comfortable when they're entertaining others. Through your own example when entertaining, or in advance of a youth party, show youngsters just how to greet friends at the door, introduce people, announce the rules of a game, award prizes, encourage guests to enjoy the refreshments, mix friends for dancing, be alert to the use of drugs, provide time for conversation, and end the party on a high note.

❑ **900.** REPAIRS. Work together, particularly when repairing broken toys. Teach the names of tools and how to do simple repairs in a safe manner. See if your children can do these things: glue broken china, fix a leaky faucet, repair a garden hose, glue a wobbling chair back, mend a broken door step, oil a squeaking door.

❑ **901.** SHREWD SHOPPING. Whether it's clothes, toys, or food, teach youngsters to look for the best values—not just the cheapest price. As an example, buy two brands of canned pear halves that have different prices. Check to see if the cheaper one has just as many halves of the same size as the more expensive can. Is "heavy syrup" versus "packed in its own juice" worth extra money? Does one pair of name brand jeans last longer or look better than one half the price? How long did a faddish purchase stay in style? If you're comparing two sleeping bags, is the one with the movie logo of better quality so that it's worth more? Teach kids to be comparison shoppers and get the best value for their money.

❑ **902.** PERSONAL CARE. Most parents make all the arrangements for a child's health, dental, optical care—to the point that many youngsters don't know the contents of their own records or the costs of this care. This information is very important when kids are on their own (and possibly without insurance), so let teens make their own appointments, keep their own records, and ask their own intelligent questions.

❑ **903.** HOUSECLEANING. While you may have maid service, this likely won't be the case when kids start out on their own. Be sure kids know there is more to housework than dusting a few table tops and vacuuming the center of the room. Show how to clean bathrooms, baseboards, windows, picture frames, lamps, art objects, refrigerator shelves, ovens, carpets, book shelves, even light bulbs (yes, washing them quarterly when cool will give much more light). And here's an idea for teaching kids how to clean closets and cupboards. Using stick-on notes, put a price on each (twenty-five cents up to two dollars). Let family members sign up on the sticker if they want to do that job within the week. Give good ideas on unloading it, cleaning it, putting down fresh shelf paper, and (unless you choose to do this yourself) returning the contents in an orderly way.

❏ **904.** CLOTHING CARE. As you probably know, you can turn white underwear pale blue by tossing new jeans in the washer with them. Or, you can have green diapers created by a dad who included a small throw rug in with them to save a load. So, to avert disasters, teach laundry skills: sorting, spot-removing, care of wash-and-wear fabrics or wools, and folding. Also teach all children how to sew so that they can create, mend, and properly sew on a button.

❏ **905.** YARD MAINTENANCE. Save money by teaching kids how to mow the lawn and care for the yard (planting, weeding, fertilizing, and composting). Actually, with a power mower safely used, lawn care can be fun. Take kids with you to the garden shop. Teach them the names of some common flowers, shrubs, and trees you have on your property.

❏ **906.** AUTOMOTIVE KNOW-HOW. Teach guys and gals basic car care: how to pump gas, choose the correct gas, read gauges, change oil and oil filter, change a tire, replace car fuses, and wash and vacuum. When you take a car in for service, always take one youngster along. Let him see how problems are described and diagnosed. That way, when a youngster gets her first car, she won't be easily intimidated.

❏ **907.** CLUTTER. Anyone who has visited a youngster's dorm or first apartment realizes that those lessons in housekeeping seem to have been quickly forgotten! Set an example with clutter-free living and help kids to create an environment that is efficient to live in as well as pleasant to look at. Create storage places for items to be recycled and get rid of them monthly. Have a box for out-grown clothing and other items that can be donated to rummage sales or charitable groups. Sort the mail daily and put nonurgent reading and catalogs in a bin for leisure perusal. Provide toy bins with lids so that kids can store similar toys efficiently. Each September, spend time in each child's room—a time to get rid of old clothing, broken toys, and outgrown books, as well as to clear the decks for the new school year. Teach the rule: if it hasn't been used in the last twelve months, give it away so someone else can enjoy it.

# TWELVE
# CHILD OF THE
# TWENTY-FIRST CENTURY

# SECTION 1: YOUR EDUCATED CHILD

This book has suggested many things to do with your child. But concerning his education, here are a few things not to do with your child: Don't do his homework. Don't side with her against the teacher until you know all the facts. Don't overload him with extracurricular activities. Don't force her into classes/careers that were your own unfulfilled dreams.

However, it is important for you to understand basic educational concepts. These differentiate between an educated child and one who has merely "sat through" twelve or more years of schooling. Although the best education begins in babyhood, if your youngster is older, you might want to read and put into practice some of these early concepts, just to be sure you haven't missed encouraging any of them.

❑ **908.** CONCEPTS FOR BABIES AND TODDLERS. A sense of what is important is taught by our responses to his activities—whether we rant and rave about spilled milk or we eagerly help him pick up toys. That we mean what we say is important for our teens but it is taught earlier in our response when a baby reaches out for something he shouldn't touch. Here we're teaching that no means no, not maybe. Caring for possessions is learned when we encourage a child to care for toys rather than destroy them. Unselfishness is taught in simple play when a baby learns to give a toy to another. Patience is learned when little princes and princesses demand toys or attention right now—and parents don't jump to fill the need, instead teach phrases such as "Not now" or "Later." Satisfaction over an accomplishment is learned when you clap for his success with a toy, or smile when he rocks his doll.

❑ **909.** CONCEPTS FOR A PRESCHOOLER. Independence is taught as children learn to be on their own for some activities. Toilet training should be taught but not forced, and a child should learn the descriptive words about it—words you wouldn't mind hearing in public!

Simple table manners should be taught (see chapter 6, section 1) since bad manners can become automatic at a very early age. How to dress oneself using zips/snaps/buttons, tie shoes, and brush hair will require patient parental instruction. Teaching skills such as numbers, colors, left and right, throwing and catching, start in these years. But far more important than teaching a preschooler to actually read is teaching her to love books.

❑ **910.** CONCEPTS FOR YOUNG GRADESCHOOLERS. Before going to kindergarten, it is helpful if a child can print and recognize his own name, know his parent's name/address/phone number, paint and paste, understand how to take turns, and dress himself for cold weather. Some kindergartens have nap time so youngsters need the home practice of resting (pretending to sleep). Other valued concepts are: speaking loudly enough to be heard, sitting quietly and listening, telling time, caring for possessions, handling lunch money, and knowing how to get to school and return whether it be waiting for a carpool or school bus, or walking.

❑ **911.** THE SUCCESSFUL STUDENT. Some students will succeed no matter what school and home support they receive. However, interested and involved parents are one of the biggest elements of success. Parents should provide a place for study and facilities for research so that a youngster can keep up-to-date on homework. The student needs to know how to organize ideas as well as how to write a coherent paper with proper spelling and grammar (there may not always be a computer to do this). A home computer, used for more than games, will be helpful in using school computers.

❑ **912.** THE MOST VALUABLE EDUCATION. If you can teach a youngster to enjoy reading, you have given him the finest education. If he can read, he can do most anything. Start reading to babies so they become accustomed to paying attention to the words and pictures. Make bedtime reading a must—reading to young children, permitting older ones to stay up fifteen minutes later for reading. Keep books in the car and take them into offices where you may have to wait. Let kids read in the bathtub. Encourage listening to books on tape that can be borrowed from the library.

❑ **913.** GETTING AN ATTITUDE. Educated children need to be able to write persuasively: develop an opinion, back it up with facts and reasons, and consider opposing viewpoints. For practice, have kids write out a request (for a later bedtime or to have her ears pierced). Tell them that their essay request should contain the facts, reasons for change, and consideration of the objections. If the paper is well thoughtout, you may accede to the request!

❑ **914.** SILLY COURSES. An occasional lightweight course may have some merit, but set high standards when helping youngsters choose classes. Ask questions such as: "What will you learn in this class? How can you use this information? How will it fit in with other classes?" If kids want to take a course because it is "fun," explain that it must also be practical or physically or intellectually challenging.

❑ **915.** BE REALISTIC. At the beginning of the school year, help kids to set some desired grade standards (such as two As, two Bs, and one C). After the first semester, challenge a youngster to raise one of the grades. Point out that in the real world, excellence comes by accepting the challenge to be a little better each day.

❑ **916.** TWENTY QUESTIONS. The art of asking questions is important in this information age, so teach kids that just being able to answer questions isn't always as important as knowing what questions to ask. Play games with kids that require questioning: the old familiar Twenty Questions and the currently popular Jeopardy.

❑ **917.** FINDING ANSWERS. Parents and teachers will not always be on hand to answer questions. Teach children the resources of a dictionary and encyclopedia—books you should have at home. As they enter school, make the public library a familiar research location. And then introduce them to the Internet—the way a youngster can access the best minds on any subject.

❑ **918.** THE DAY CARE OF YOUR DREAMS. If your baby or toddler must be in day care (as opposed to your care until kindergarten age), choose the best facility with the least number of babies. See that the facility is licensed. Go with your baby and visit and observe the following:

☑ **Staff.** Is there sufficient staff to give personal care? Do they seem calm, interested, and loving? Is staff turnover too frequent to allow for quality care?

☑ **Cribs and diaper-changing area.** Is the bedding clean and the changing surface clean? Does the area have a pleasant odor?

☑ **Kitchen and eating area.** Are the menus posted? Is the food nutritious? Are the high chairs sparkling clean?

☑ **Play area.** Are the playpens clean? Is the floor clean where babies crawl? Are the toys in good condition and stimulating? Are there opportunities for music, book time, outside play?

☑ **Safety.** Is there a full-time staff person with first-aid training? Is there a posted fire/emergency plan? Has there ever been a formal complaint filed against the facility or an employee? (It's your right to ask.) Are you welcome to drop in unannounced?

❑ **919.** PRESCHOOL IS PLAY SCHOOL. A day care for a preschooler is quite different from one for babies and toddlers. This is a venue for learning social skills. Avoid the school that is pushing a child out of playtime years and encouraging early learning, which can bring on academic burnout later. Take your preschooler for a visit and be alert to pertinent points in #918, plus these factors:

☑ **Children's ages.** Are there two or more children the same age as yours?

☑ **Curriculum.** Do the activities support eye-hand coordination, motor skills, following directions, learning to dress self and tie shoes, working with others, increasing attention span? Does the school have a teaching philosophy and a general curriculum? Are social skills (bathroom etiquette, table manners, politeness) taught? Are the educational skills taught without pressure to read or use a computer, but rather with an emphasis on learning to think and express ideas clearly?

☑ **Staff.** Are the teachers well-trained including at least one who knows the various stages of child development? Do they teach at a child's eye level, instead of talking and supervising "from above"?

☑ **Equipment.** Is the outside play equipment challenging and in safe condition? Does the inside equipment encourage both active and quiet play? Is there a large library of quality books? (There should be NO television viewing.)

☑ **Quiet Time.** Does the school have a quiet/nap time? Are the mats clean?

☑ **Atmosphere.** Is the atmosphere a happy one?

❑ **920.** CHECKING OUT A GRADE SCHOOL OR HIGH SCHOOL. As a taxpayer or tuition payer, you should know what you're getting for your money. Go over the following points with your youngster, then make one or two visits to assess the quality of the school.

☑ **Class size.** No more than twenty-five means better learning opportunities.

☑ **Atmosphere.** Upbeat, casual, happy—as opposed to regimented or rowdy. Be sure to inquire of the administration concerning crime at the school.

☑ **Staff.** Experienced teachers of both sexes who are dedicated to teaching—not merely maintaining order; a strong administration that insists on a teaching plan from each teacher; and a grading system that does not simply pass slower students along before they are ready.

☑ **Curriculum.** Solid education in the basics with special classes for reading encouragement when needed; early teaching of a second language; art, drama, music as part of the regular curriculum; and a minimum offering of lightweight classes like basket weaving or hedgehog raising.

☑ **Equipment.** Computers, an extensive library, musical instruments, scientific supplies.

☑ **Physical education.** A rigorous program with both indoor and outdoor facilities; basic safety instruction on drugs and sex taught at appropriate ages and retaught on a regular basis.

☑ **Extracurricular.** Opportunities beyond school hours like science club, spelling bees, speech tournaments, educational decathlons, statewide essay contests, science fairs, and sports teams with competitive team play only for students maintaining a minimum grade average of C.

☑ **Counseling.** Trained professionals who spot problems early and know how to handle them. Counseling for college and career starting in the tenth grade.

☑ **Safety.** A closed campus (no coming and going during the day). A strict and enforceable policy regarding weapons and drugs.

❑ **921.** PROGRESS OR FLUFF? Don't wait for a report card to know how your child is progressing. And don't rely on a youngster's "Everything is fine" response to your questions. Attend all parent/teacher conferences even if you have to leave work early. If necessary, phone a teacher to get a specific question answered. Go over the following questions with your youngster, add to them, and get the answers at your first conference.

☑ Is my child working up to the proper level?

☑ What are her strengths? Weaknesses?

☑ What does the teacher take into account in grading?

☑ Is the homework completed in a satisfactory manner?

☑ Is the youngster self-disciplined, responsible, cooperative?

☑ How does she take suggestions and criticism?

☑ Are her social skills and self-confidence developing?

☑ What can I do to support a good education?

❑ **922.** TESTING TIMES. Ask your child to tell you when there are going to be statewide standardized tests at school. The day before such events should be special for the student (that way you'll be sure to be informed): no chores, dinner of his choice, a long bath before a sensible bedtime, and his favorite breakfast in the morning. These tests show how effective the school teaching is as well as identifying strengths and weaknesses of the students.

❑ **923.** "DO YOUR HOMEWORK!" Your child could probably get a good grade if you did his homework, but that's not the purpose! Homework is the proof of what a child has learned and can put into practice. It is the means of cementing new facts into thought. You can best contribute to good homework by using the PACT System. Let the youngster make the PACT sign that stands for Place, Asking, Checking, Talking. Hang it on the wall near the place he does his homework as a reminder that you have a pact with him to help him be smart, successful, and learn what's necessary for a happy life.

**P IS FOR PLACE.** Research shows that homework done on a bed or with the TV on isn't as thorough or meaningful as homework done in an educational environment. Enlist your youngster's input for making a pleasant place to do homework. It can be a desk or table with a well-equipped shelf in an area that is free from distractions such as sibling play, the telephone, or a view of the yard.

**A IS FOR ASKING.** It's a parent's duty to ask that boring question "What is your homework today?" (Even ask high school kids.) And, it's a child's duty to answer. The question shows that you care about his education, it can be a subtle reminder that there is some homework to do, and it keeps you up to speed on his current learning. Other questions are more specific: "How did your report go?" "Did you have the test today?" "Is your math getting any easier?" "What is the plan for the field trip?" "Did the new band music come?" "Have you been given a long-range assignment?" These questions and answers keep you "in the loop" as far as your youngster's education goes.

**C IS FOR CHECKING.** If you correct math errors in homework, or edit written work, your child will probably repeat the same mistakes. Your job is to make general suggestions ("Problem three is wrong." "The second paragraph could use more exciting adjectives.") For a misspelled word, give a hint how the word begins and let a child look it up in a dictionary. Certainly this takes time, but in the long run it makes for a smarter student. Check on your student during the homework session and offer a snack at half-time.

**T IS FOR TALKING.** Conversation is a great educator. Choose an academic subject you'd like to share with your child—it can be one on which you're already knowledgeable or one you're eager to learn about. You may also find subjects in the newspaper or magazines that relate to school subjects. Talk about your favorite authors, how you got into business, or plans for the future. Let the talk go both ways—listen to your youngster's plans and dreams, have her describe her soccer skills or computer problems. Show your respect for knowledge: look over completed or graded homework and share her successes with all the family.

❏ **924.** MAJOR PROJECT. When assigned a large project, some kids are overwhelmed and just put it out of thought. Because you ask questions and are aware of the project, you can be helpful in many ways. First, talk about it at dinner—you will be surprised at the good ideas offered by other family members. Mark the calendar for the due date and also mark the date two days before (as the date to show off the project to the family). Let the student list the ideas or elements, and together put the work in a logical order. Then, suggest that she work on it only fifteen minutes each day. She'll soon find it's completed!

❏ **925.** ORDER OF WORK. For the majority of students, it is important to do the most exacting homework first while they're most fresh and eager. But the tendency is to do the easy things first. For most scholars, this is the best order: math, writing, nonfiction reading, science projects, fiction reading. Have the student estimate the time required to complete the homework. Then divide it up into twenty to thirty minute segments with a bend-and-stretch time between each.

❑ **926.** PAY FOR GRADES? It's an on-going debate, but nowadays many agree that pay for grades is similar to adult pay for work. The following system works for many families, especially if the pay is sufficient so that a percentage goes into savings. With student input, set up a sliding scale for grades A through C (not C minus). Also set a fee for a grade raised, and a deduction for a grade that falls. Make small bonuses for good character ratings if the report card lists those. Give a small payment for sharing a report card the day it is distributed. Have cash on hand for immediate payment. Do this for each middle-of-term and end-of-term grading period for one year, then discuss the system together to see if it has encouraged better grades.

❑ **927.** THE CONTRACT. When a youngster needs academic encouragement, talk about writing a contract together. It might look like this:

---

THE CONTRACT

Hereby let it be recognized that _____, known hereafter as the Student, and _____, known hereafter as the Parent, have willingly entered into the following contractual agreement. The Student agrees to achieve the following: _____.
In return, the Parent agrees to grant the following: _____. The length of time to complete this contract is from (dates) _____ to _____. The terms of this agreement include no nagging or shouting by the Parent, and no cheating or grumbling by the Student. Signed with love this _____ day of _____, (year) _____.
_____ (Student)
_____ (Parent)

---

❑ **928.** TEACHER AT DINNER. "Oh no!" may be the initial response, but if you start this tradition when children are in grade school, it should go better in the later years. Some teachers detest this idea, others welcome it. If the teacher is married, include the spouse (busy teachers will enjoy not having to cook). Work with your child on planning the food. Allow time to show off his room and time for parent and teacher to talk alone. Don't make it a long event—just a casual time for getting-to-know-you.

❑ **929.** THIS IS MY CHILD. At the start of the school year, write a letter to the teacher describing your young child's interests, her strong and weak points, and including your offer to help. Ask your child what she would like the teacher to know about her. Include your home and business phone numbers.

❑ **930.** IS THIS CHILD GIFTED? Poor grades and apathy can be signs of a child in need of tutoring, but they can also be signs of a bright child not being challenged. While double grade promotions used to be the answer for gifted children, it was found that this often resulted in a child who was socially and physically out-of-step with classmates. In the book *Your Gifted Child* by Joan Smutny, Kathleen Veenker, and Stephen Veenker (New York: Facts on File, 1989), these are the signs of a gifted child:
1. Expresses curiosity about many things with thoughtful questions.
2. Has and uses extensive vocabulary with complex sentences.
3. Solves problems in original and imaginative ways.
4. Has a good memory and can order things in logical sequence.
5. Exhibits unusual talent in art, music, creative drama.
6. Discusses and elaborates on ideas and shows humor.
7. Learns quickly and puts learned concepts in new contexts.
8. Takes initiative, has a sustained attention span, works independently, has persistence in working on challenging tasks.

9. Enjoys reading and can make up stories and tell them.

While the school usually nurtures gifted children, the home environment plays a very important role. Create home opportunities for creativity, effective time management, research, decision making, goal setting, and acceptance of failure and success. Outside the home, provide time for travel, museum visits, and live theater. Hints on raising a gifted child are available free from the Center for Gifted, National-Lewis College, Evanston, IL 60201.

❑ **931. IS COLLEGE IN THE FUTURE?** According to the Bureau of the Census, a college education doubles lifetime earnings and increases quality of life. Starting in tenth grade, work with your youngster and the school counselors to plan a program that will prepare him for several likely colleges. Academic requirements differ from school to school, so it's wise to check entrance requirements a few years in advance. Visits to nearby colleges provide valuable input during the high school years.

❑ **932. NEW SCHOOL.** Take away the fear of the first day at school by making a scouting trip during the summer. Start by going over the route to be walked or driven and determine the travel time needed. (This will help to start the big day on time.) Check out the playground and let kids try the equipment. While you can look in the school-room windows, an inside tour may be available. Youngsters are especially interested in a classroom of their grade level, computer lab, art room, locker location, gym, library, principal's and nurse's offices, and cafeteria.

❑ **933. ADHD?** Not all overly active children have Attention Deficit Hyperactivity Disorder. Some kids just have a less-developed attention span and are more mischievous. Pediatricians say it is normal for three-to-five-year-olds to race from one activity to another when they are overly excited, hungry, or tired. Work with your youngster to develop a sustained interest in books, coloring, play with toys, and conversation with you. For a period of about six months, monitor the behavior. If the child is overly active and unsettled all of the time and in every setting, it can be a sign that help is needed.

❏ **934.** CROSS-COUNTRY CHALLENGE. Most kids have a cousin or friend in another part of the country. In the summer, create a cross-country book reading challenge. Let youngsters choose a book that both would enjoy reading that week. At the end of the week, permit a five minute phone call to discuss the finished book—as well as other bits of news.

❏ **935.** COUNTING GAMES. One grandfather, who lives with his son and family, has started a tradition that helps kids learn to count, and then to learn the multiplication table. After the bedtime story, he and the child start counting toward the magic number, which is 100. They alternate calling the next number. As they get older, they count by 2s to 100, or by 3s to 102, and so forth. When they become proficient, they speed up the counting pace.

❏ **936.** FAST MULTIPLYING. Here's a trick that's fun to share with a younger child who is having trouble with the multiplication table for 9. The trick is to add one digit to the left side and subtract one digit on the right side. So, it's 9 plus 1 on the left (19) and subtract 1 on the right (18). From 18 you add 1 on the left (28) and subtract 1 on the right (27). Once you get the hang of it, it's fast fun.

❏ **937.** MATH WIZARD. The game is called Thirteen. On a table, lay out (face up) a pyramid of playing cards. In the top row place just one card, then place two cards overlapping the lower half of the top row. It is important to reveal only the top half, not the full size of the card. Continue making rows of three, four, five, six, and seven cards, each overlapping the bottom half of the row above. Keep the remainder of the deck face down. Now, start the game with the bottom row. If any two cards total thirteen (for example a six and a seven), remove those cards. (Aces are one, picture cards are eleven.) If no two cards total thirteen, turn over one card from the deck. If it, and a card from row seven total thirteen, remove those two cards. Soon, the *full size* of a card or cards in row six will be visible, and those cards can be included in making matches totaling thirteen. Each player has the opportunity to make a match by turning over a card from the deck. If a match is made, he continues. If not, the card goes to the bottom of the deck and the turn goes to the other person playing. Gradually you will work your way both across and up the pyramid. The aim is to collect as many cards making thirteen as possible—and even all of them occasionally. And while having fun, you'll be learning all the combinations that total thirteen.

❑ **938.** DOMINO MATH. Children enjoy playing dominoes—a game that can be adapted for all ages. Little children count the dots on each of the matched pieces. Young gradeschoolers practice addition, announcing the total number on both matched pieces. And, as older gradeschoolers play their piece, they multiply the numbers on the two pieces. Teens can give the square of the dots.

# SECTION 2: THE ELECTRONIC FUTURE

❑ **939.** EQUALS. Let learning about the computer be a joint experience. Make a comfortable seat next to your own at the computer keyboard and allow very young children to observe how you work. Show the connection between the keyboard and the screen. When old enough, let the child trade seats with you and operate the keyboard. There are a number of clever symbols on the keyboard [such as the happy face (:>) which is seen when turned on its side, or the sad face (:<)]. Even a young child can enjoy these. Let her key in her name and show how to make her own note paper. When a child has some proficiency, ask the child to teach you what he knows. At the same time, share some tips you have found useful.

❑ **940.** CD-ROM. Just like the CD disks you play on your stereo, your child should have available a CD-ROM drive on the family computer. (The letters stand for compact disk read-only memory.) This is one of the most useful learning devices. The drive shines a low-power laser beam onto the recording surface (the side of the disk without a label) and through binary digits or bits that the computer strings together, it produces pictures, text, and video clips on the monitor. Shop together to pick out exciting age-appropriate titles.

❑ **941.** READ UP. There are many magazines geared to computers, some just for kids. Buy single copies of several and see which are most interesting to your youngster. Subscribe to the best one. Then, let her share new things she's learned by reading it.

❑ **942.** SKILLS LEARNED. A creator of video games shared what he believes are the benefits of these toys: enhanced ability to concentrate, increased manual and mental dexterity, and historical input. The first two benefits are valid. The third is only a possibility if you shop wisely. In helping your youngster choose which games to own, try to select some that really do improve the intellect without emphasis on violence.

❑ **943.** FUN, FUN, FUN. Not every experience in growing up needs to be a deep, educational one. Some things should be just plain enjoyment. However, discuss with your youngster just what is meant by "enjoyment." If his idea of fun is playing video games with shooting, torturing and killing, or ones that delve into the world of demons, you will want to discuss how such activities affect his thinking and point of view. It is your parental right to outlaw activities that harm rather than help your child.

❑ **944.** GAME TIME. Computer games come in all sizes and shapes. Because of mass marketing techniques and attractive pricing, games make welcome gifts (especially from puzzled grandparents). Parents and kids should take the time to inspect the games and read the inviting packaging in order to choose wisely. A good game will hold a child's interest over many play sessions. It needs to be sufficiently challenging, but not too difficult. Games to be avoided are those that stress violence, gore, brutality, trickery, and characters acting in bad faith. It should be possible to win honestly. Many of the top selling games may not be the best for your child. If you and your youngster can see the game demonstrated, you will be better able to judge. And, it goes without saying, just because Susie down the street has a certain game is not a good reason for you to buy it and allow your child to play it.

❑ **945.** LEARN AS YOU PLAY. If a computer game has an educational effect, so much the better. Does it teach skills such as spelling, math, history, and so forth? The best of all worlds is a game that teaches as it amuses and fascinates. When purchasing, encourage your child to select a larger proportion of interesting educational games rather than mostly competitive ones.

❑ **946.** ADDICTION ALERT. The addictive nature of many hand-held, so-called pocket games is well known. These games can be carried everywhere and may divert a child from sports, study, even classroom attention. Before—definitely before—you permit or support the purchase of game video equipment, you need to confer with your child about its use and even put a few important rules in writing. How much game play in a day? (A half-hour could be the max.) When is it played with? (After school, but not after dinner until homework and chores are done.) Who pays for it? (Unless it is a gift occasion, the cost is the youngster's.) Can he be deprived of the use of it? (Yes, for breaking family rules or rules concerning the games.)

❑ **947.** VIDEO GAME PARLORS. Every community has one of these noisy places that can gobble up a kid's entire allowance and free time. Many arcade games are addictive and monopolize time without any benefit. Research also shows that most games are inherently frustrating and promote stress and negative behaviors such as aggression, lying, tension, and sullenness. Can this be considered "play"? One psychologist says that the need to score increasingly higher is akin to the chemically dependent person's obsession with "scoring" by using greater amounts of an addictive substance. If video games do not leave your youngster feeling in control, happy, and relaxed, you need to limit their use.

❑ **948.** WWW. The Internet or World Wide Web is continually in the news. Some say this will always be an important part of each person's outreach to the larger world, a way to receive and send information, a powerful research tool in every home. If it lives up to the promises, you will want to encourage your child to explore the Web by looking at it with him. Because it can be fascinating and time consuming, this is a good weekend activity. Start for just fifteen minutes to see what is interesting. Make an hour the maximum if it proves to be an enjoyable learning experience for both parent and child.

❑ **949.** WEB SITES. Help your youngster connect to these World Wide Web sites with programming for families. (You'll need a modem and access to the Internet.)
- CHILDREN'S LITERATURE WEB GUIDE: read favorite books online. http://www.ucalgary.ca/~dkbrown/index.html
- NASA Spacelink: wonderful for space buffs http://spacelink.msfc.nasa.gov/
- KIDLINK: dialogue with kids from more than seventy countries. http://www.kidlink.org
- DISNEY: rather commercial but has the favorite movies. http://disney.com
- AUNT ANNIE'S CRAFT PAGE: learning, problem solving, creativity. http://www.auntannie.com/

- INTERNET PUBLIC LIBRARY: the homework helper supreme. http://www.ipl.org/
- A GIRL'S WORLD: esteem-building clubhouse for girls ages 7-15. http://www.agirlsworld.com/
- FREE ZONE: the hip place for entertaining activities. http://freezone.com/
- FAMILY PLANET: Top-rated one-stop shopping for family activities. http://family.starwave.com

❑ **950.** E-MAIL PAL. Don't permit your youngster to make friends with other folks on the computer unless you have a very good way of checking out the age and background of the person. Rather, encourage an E-mail relationship with a relative or friend. It's so easy to correspond by E-mail and it's always fun to find mail in your own mailbox.

❑ **951.** SAFETY FIRST. Teach kids these on-line facts: Not everything you read is true. People on-line may not be who they seem. Never respond to messages or bulletin board items without parental approval. Report messages that are suggestive, obscene, belligerent, or threatening. Never arrange a face-to-face meeting without parental approval. Never give out identifying information such as name, home address, telephone number, school, or credit card or social security numbers.

❑ **952.** OOPS! Explain respect for the mechanical workings of the computer. Did you know that the most frequent service call for computers is caused by a soft drink spilled in the keyboard? Show how the keyboard and screen need to be carefully cleaned weekly. This can be a regular chore for kids.

❑ **953.** BACKING UP. Early in your teaching sessions, talk about the importance of saving input. Explain how often you need to do so. Then explain how to perform the important function of backing up on a disk. For a responsible youngster, making back-up disks of your work can be a delegated and paid job.

## HIGH TECH LIVING

❏ **954.** THE HIGH TECH HOME.   Some home repairs involve high technology. Discuss the problem with your youngster, guesstimating what a technician might charge. Then consider learning how to do the repair with kid-help. When the parent goes to a store to get detailed information, take the child along to listen and learn. Then discuss how WE will do it. Allow the child to perform a significant and interesting part of it. If the youngster is a mere tool handler, he will learn nothing and quickly become bored.

❏ **955.** AT THE BEEP . . .   The ubiquitous phone answering machine can have a message recorded by your youngster. (This should only be done if the child speaks clearly and can read the manual instructions.) Let her make some calls and listen to other peoples' messages, then write out the brief message, practice it a few times and then record it. When the message needs to be changed, give her the full responsibility.

❏ **956.** GREAT EXPECTATIONS.   Expect your child to lead the way in many new technologies. A parent needs the ability to learn from the younger generation. Ask kids what new inventions he can imagine. Suggest he keep a list of these ideas and see if they are marketed. If he has a truly unique idea, you might want to work together to develop, patent, and market it.

❏ **957.** WEATHER TECHNOLOGY.   Suggest that a youngster keep a weather record for a whole year. Using a maximum/minimum thermometer, let him take the daily readings, record them, and report to the family at dinner each day. Show him how to make a graph of the high and of the low. If he shows interest, you may want to help him purchase more sophisticated instruments and even turn the research into a science fair project.

❑ **958.** AUTOMOTIVE TECHNOLOGY. Farmers' kids know all about the care and feeding of their horses. Do your children know as much about your car or truck? Bring a child along when you take your vehicle in for repairs. Make sure she can see under the hood as the service writer explains the work needing to be done. Let her master the names of some of the automotive parts, and then, on the way home explain (as best you can) what they do. When she's older, encourage her to take an automotive course at school.

❑ **959.** HI-FI TECHNOLOGY. When assembling a hi-fi system, allow your youngster to tell you what to do and how to do it. If he's wrong, figure out the right way together, letting him take the lead. Work together to place the speakers for the very best balance. Let him adjust the treble, bass, and so forth and tell you why this is important. He may want a well-balanced and well-modulated music system in his own room.

❑ **960.** TIMERS. While not new technology, timers are a big convenience in running a home. But they have to be reset for the twice-a-year time change. Show a child how to do this, then let him do it each six months on his own. Find many uses for timers: turning lights on and off, running sprinklers, controlling night lights, adjusting heating/cooling systems, and so forth.

❑ **961.** HIGH TECH CAMERAS. Photography can be an expensive hobby, especially with some of the fancy new electronic cameras. Before buying a camera for a youngster, let him practice taking pictures with yours. Take several rolls of film and critique each picture for subject, lighting, composition, interest, and so forth. Work together to master the equipment and take good pictures. Only then go shopping for the youngster's own camera.

❑ **962.** PASSPORT TO THE WORLD. Short wave radio opens the door to faraway places. Show your youngster how to tune in, and then listen together. See what conversations from other countries you can hear. Find the best times of the day or night to reach the most distant places. Permit radio listening before falling asleep at night.

# SECTION 3:
# A COMMUNITY WITHOUT VIOLENCE

Fear erodes the quality of family life. Families should not have to be constantly concerned with protecting themselves from violence. This section is shared with the idea of giving youngsters the ability to keep themselves from danger, as well as how to act correctly in threatening situations.

❑ **963.** EVER ALERT. When taking a neighborhood walk in the evening, play the AAA Game: Alert/Aware/ Attentive. After passing a few houses, ask youngsters if there were houses with the lights on. Midway in the walk, ask how many people you've passed. See if kids can describe them. Walk silently and ask what sounds are heard: talking, barking, screeching wheels, doors slamming. Near the end of a walk, see if kids can describe the makes of cars that have passed you. The three A's are an important part of safety.

❑ **964.** SAFETY SONG #1. You don't need a tune for this song, just a good sense of rhythm. Again you'll teach the song to include your own address—don't worry if the middle line doesn't rhyme.

> My address has got a beat:
> 4, 8, 7 on Elm Street.
> Aren't those numbers really neat!

❏ **965.** SAFETY SONG #2. Young children often remember facts easily when they're set to music. A simple tune can help a child learn his telephone number. For example, use the familiar tune of "Twinkle, Twinkle Little Star" but change the words to include your own telephone number. It goes like this:

> Ringo, ringo little phone,
> Here's the number of my home.
> It is 5 and 5 and 5,
> Then just 2, 4, 6, and 8.
> Ringo, ringo little phone,
> That's the number of my home.

❏ **966.** SELF-DEFENSE OF YOUR HOME. Since youngsters may be home alone, you want your home to be safe. Let locking up be an every day procedure so that kids aren't alarmed when you do it. The front door should have a dead bolt and a peep hole. For sliding doors, a bar mounted in the middle is a safety precaution. Train youngsters to never open the door to a stranger, no matter what the outsider says. Trim away tall shrubbery from around the house. Put a large dog bowl on the back doorstep, even if your dog is tiny. If you have a security system, have one that sounds a loud alarm. When you're away, call your family regularly, and when you're vacationing, ask a neighbor or relative to check on your house.

❏ **967.** TELEPHONE SELF-DEFENSE. Instruct children to never reveal to a caller that they are home alone. A good line is "Can I have Dad call you back in a little while?" If you have an answer machine, give the impression that a large dog lives at your house by playing a recording of a barking dog in the background of your message. Hang up immediately on obscene calls or when there is just silence.

❏ **968.** NEIGHBORHOOD SELF-DEFENSE. Neighborhood Watch or other mutual surveillance groups are a good protection. Even if you don't know your neighbors socially, see that they have met your children, and let a trusted neighbor know when your children are home alone. Call a meeting of neighborhood adults for the purpose of listing license numbers of cars that belong to each household. Talk about being alert to strange cars and trucks in the neighborhood, strangers going door-to-door, the importance of keeping garage doors closed and porch lights on, and installing motion detector lights all help cut down on crime.

❑ **969.** AUTOMOBILE SELF-DEFENSE. Teach young drivers to approach their parked car with key in hand and eyes scanning the area. They should always lock the car (and use an antitheft device if the car has one), but they still should look in the back seat before entering the car. Once inside the car, immediately lock the doors. Make it a rule that youngsters never give a ride to a stranger—no matter how cute the person looks. Keep purse or briefcase out of sight so as not to attract smash-and-grab incidents at stoplights or in parking lots. Have a phony set of keys in the front seat tray. If approached, throw those keys out the window and drive away while the criminal is picking them up.

❑ **970.** SELF-DEFENSE WHEN WALKING IN A STRANGE AREA. An assertive walk, a good pace, and head up with eyes scanning will make you a less attractive subject. If children think someone is following them, they should turn and shout "What are you doing?" so as to attract the attention of others. And, youngsters should be taught to walk with others nearby or near shops that are open and offer a safe refuge.

❑ **971.** SELF-DEFENSE IN PUBLIC PLACES. If a youngster feels uncomfortable with someone sitting nearby in a movie, she should get up and tell an usher. If wary of someone in an elevator, press every button (in hopes that others will get on) or press the alarm button. And, when using an ATM at night, select a drive-through one, first locking doors, closing windows that don't need to be open during the transaction, and checking your mirrors.

❑ **972.**  SELF-DEFENSE WEAPONS.  Consider carrying a pepper spray or personal alarm. At a martial arts store you can buy a slim poking device to hang on your teen's key chain. And a cellular phone is an ideal defense since 911 can be quickly dialed—even at home when the telephone lines have been cut by an intruder.

❑ **973.**  NO FEAR.  With the media reporting so much violence and because you don't want to raise fearful children, parents have an obligation to balance this negativism with some positive news. Read the first four pages of the daily paper with a youngster—marking pen in hand. Put a green check mark on a positive story, a red check mark on one that reports robbery, murder, chaos, war, and so forth. Talk about the bad things and balance them with items showing how humankind has triumphed.

❑ **974.**  GENEROSITY, AN ANSWER.  While research shows that there is no overall increase in violence in the United States, it is taking bolder forms (overt racial violence, conflict between off-road vehicles and landowners, violence done in the name of environmentalism). One answer is to teach children to be generous, understanding, and forgiving. Encourage kids to put aside surliness in their conversation, in their driving, and in their activities. Setting a good example within the family will help this moderating attitude carry over into the community.

# SECTION 4:
# COMMITMENT TO FAMILY

There is no stronger influence for good than a family that practices what it preaches. Each day, encourage your youngsters to be committed to your family values. (See chapter 9 for descriptions of some of these virtues.)

❑ **975.** FAMILY FIRST. Start with toddlers and continue through the years to instill the importance of the family unit. As much as possible, eat meals together, worship together, do work projects together, have a shared activity each day and a larger joint activity each weekend.

❑ **976.** CHANGING YOURSELF. Effective families don't blame each other for problems or take out their frustrations on one another. They find benefits from considering how one can change oneself. For example, if two youngsters are arguing about what music to play, one can defuse the argument by making a personal change: listening to music in another room, putting on headphones, suggesting that one choose the music for an hour, then switch. Teach kids early to ask themselves "What can I do to change the situation?"

❑ **977.** FIRST THINGS FIRST. Much family friction comes from varied priorities—the family going different directions. Have a weekly family planning session and talk over the week's activities, responsibilities, and opportunities. Prioritize, putting "musts" first (homework, chores, lesson practice) then the scheduled events (the dentist, Grandma's birthday, the big concert). Finally, let the less important activities fit in the cracks around the "musts" and scheduled events.

❑ **978.** LISTEN FOR SUBTLE MESSAGES. When talking with a complaining child, you may not hear the real reason at first. For example, if a youngster says that she hates her little brother, accept that statement by repeating it. (If you start right out with a lecture on how to love a little brother, you'll cut the lines of communication.) Hearing you say what she has said gives her a feeling of validity and will start the conversation with both of you going the same direction. As you continue the conversation, you may hear the real reason: she feels he's getting more attention than she gets. Now you are ready to make appropriate remarks—and even actions— to solve the real problem.

❑ **979.** YOUR WAY, MY WAY, OUR WAY. Disagreements don't have to end with winners and losers. Usually there is a solution that is better than those proposed by the two opponents. A very simple example is this: If your daughter wants the family to go to the movies and you want the group to go cycling, cycle to the movies. Try to help youngsters discover the very best solution—not always their own, but something even better.

❑ **980.** RENEWAL. Families should look out for one another in four very important ways that will give them the energy and skills to continue as a successful group. *(1) Love*—loving oneself, family, and others. *(2) Spirituality*—understanding our moral and religious base that defines our responsibilities as members of the world society. *(3) Intellect*—appreciating it in others and nurturing our own ability to think clearly. *(4) Talents*—using our innate talents to the max—so that we can maintain a strong and healthy outlook. These are not one-time skills but ones that require daily renewal.

❑ **981.** BE THERE. Anticipate the times when you will be needed more than usual: the first days of school, during exams, at the final game of a sport season, at and after the school play or recital, and when any educational, social, or health problem arises. While a youngster may not want to have a long discussion about any of these events, your interest and comfort needs expression. Be there when it counts.

❑ **982.** "RESERVED." Starting when youngsters can read. Make a monthly family calendar showing lessons, parties, and other events for each member of the family. Mark one evening each week and one half-day each weekend as "Reserved." Use the evening for games as well as conversation about the family. Use the weekend time for an excursion. Rarely move a reserved time or excuse a family member from it. If you establish reserved time from the early years onward, you shouldn't have any argument about it as kids become teens.

❑ **983.** GIVENS. In every family there are some things that are not to be argued or compromised. They are part of family tradition. If kids complain, tell them that when they are parents they can make their own list of "givens." Here are some worthy items for your list of givens: personal cleanliness, weekly church attendance, no dating before age fifteen, abstinence from premarital sex, no use of alcohol or tobacco, no drug use, no profanity, no shoplifting or stealing, no cheating on tests, no lying about age, and no use of weapons. This may sound like a lot of "NO" items, but if everyone followed the Givens list, the world would be a very fine place!

❑ **984.** SIBLING SNIVELING. Often, especially when close in age, siblings develop a dislike for one another. While you can't force total peace, you can work toward a truce. Despite their feelings, siblings should agree to these five things: aid in case of emergency, no bad-mouthing outside the family, no trying to get the other in trouble, a respect for the other's individuality, and acknowledgment of something good the other does.

❑ **985.** HELP! Some family members behave like the Little Red Hen who has to do everything herself. Develop within the family the commitment to offer assistance (and mean it) when another needs help. Encourage family members to be alert to the needs, moods, problems, and events that touch the lives of others in the family. Then encourage the offering of help even though it may not be accepted. And, be sure to commend the help when given.

❑ **986.** PARENT QUIZ. Honestly answer these questions and then discuss with your youngster any "no" answers.

▶ Does my day start on a high note and go up from there?

▶ Am I satisfied with my child care arrangements or how my youngster spends after-school time?

▶ Is there at least a half hour each day when I am alone with my child?

▶ Do I set educational and social goals for my child?

▶ Do I set business, social and learning goals for myself?

▶ Am I spending time regularly to make our home an enjoyable family center?

▶ Am I finding the time to keep my other family relationships vital?

▶ Do I arrange after-supper activities so that TV is not the sole highlight of the evening for the family?

▶ Is there a pleasant family event each weekend?

▶ Do I understand the importance of thinking through my own unpleasant childhood experiences as well as my present-day angers and frustrations?

▶ Do I look forward to weekend time with my child, rather than feeling that this time is solely for my own rest and amusement?

▶ Do I take my child to a museum, play, or concert almost as often as to the park or a movie?

▶ Does my child enjoy the pleasure of book reading at least thirty minutes a day? And do I?

▶ As work is done around the home, do I include my child, explain what I'm doing, and let her help?

▶ Do I nurture my child, helping him develop morally, spiritually, physically, and mentally?

▶ Do I know the name of my child's best friend?

▶ Can I name something that really upsets my child and also something that really pleases her?

▶ Do I know what my child really likes about me and what he most dislikes about me?

▶ Do I know what my child likes to do with her free time and what she would like to do more often with me?

► Do I know my child's favorite teacher and favorite subject, and his least favorite teacher and least favorite subject?

► If I could buy my child the gift she most desires, do I know what it would be?

► Am I aware which of my child's accomplishments gives him the most pleasure?

► Do I treat my job as parent with the same integrity and organization that I bring to my career or other activities?

► Am I finding time to grow myself, through reading, classes, activities, or hobbies?

► Do I tell my child each day that I have confidence in him and in his ability to learn, that he is very special, and that I love him no matter what?

► Do I usually go to sleep feeling contented with my day?

❑ **987.** KID QUIZ. Corral your child for this quick quiz, skipping questions that aren't pertinent. Discuss any "no" answers and see how you can help to change them.

► Is it fun to live in this home?

► Do you help with chores around the house?

► Do you have a place for projects that you don't have to clean up very often?

► Do you read, or are you read to, each day?

► Do you know your family rules and what happens if you break them?

► Do you have a relative (grandparent, uncle, cousin) with whom you feel very close?

► If the television set disappeared for a week, could you name ten other things you'd like to do?

► Are you eager to learn new skills and subjects?

► Do you enjoy family meal times?

► Do you know your parents' favorite sport, music, food, and book?

- ▶ Do you know your parents' favorite school subject and least favorite subject?
- ▶ Can you name something you do that upsets your parent?
- ▶ Can you name something your parent thinks is special about you?
- ▶ Do you know what your parent likes to do for fun?
- ▶ Do you remember what was your parent's most favorite family occasion and why?
- ▶ Do you know something that your parent would like to do more often with you?
- ▶ Do you know why your parent works?
- ▶ Do you show your parents that you love them by your words and your acts?

## A FOCUS FOR THE FAMILY

To keep your family strong, take the time to consider together these points that are the basis for living a wonderful life.

## THE FAMILY PLATFORM

❑ **988.** LOVE UNCONDITIONALLY. Learn to show love in varied ways. And if that love doesn't seem to be returned, never give up! Each day, see that you say "I love you" or express your affection to each other. Love can solve anything!

❑ **989.** STRENGTHEN FAMILY TIES. Never let a period of "no communication" get a foothold. Both parent and child have an investment of many years in your family, so keep it going by taking an interest in each person—even at times when your interest may be rebuffed. Come to an understanding or compromise when there is a problem. Plan creative get-togethers and reunions.

❑ **990.** RESPECT DIVERSITY. You don't want clones!

Look for and appreciate the precious individuality of each family member. Try to understand another's point of view, especially when it is different from yours. Realize that each member of your family is one very unique part of creation.

❑ **991.** CULTIVATE COMMUNICATION. Think back at how much you loved your little baby and how you spoke words even before the baby comprehended their meaning. Now that little person may be too big to hold, but certainly can comprehend your meaning. Practice speaking with patience and consideration and provide many opportunities for conversation. For faraway family members, communicate on a regular basis by phoning and writing.

❑ **992.** PRACTICE BOTH GIVING AND GETTING. They're both pleasant! Volunteer. Contribute. Serve. Comfort. Take on an activity: visit seniors, advise a youth group, teach Sunday school or sing in the choir, raise funds for a worthy cause, deliver meals to the elderly, coach a team. The list is endless. Choose one that the family can do together. You'll get great satisfaction from this activity.

❑ **993.** DEVELOP A COMMUNITY AND A CIRCLE OF FRIENDS. Enlarge the borders of your family by establishing bonds with others. A work project with other families such as improving the local park, getting road signs posted where children play, or starting a monthly potluck—these generate a feeling of community closeness. You don't have to be blood relatives to be "family." Don't be an island or a cold fish. Enlarge your circle every year no matter what your age. Even if you think you don't need them, they may need you.

❑ **994.** TRY NEW THINGS. Sameness is easy and can mire the family in boredom. Whether it is what you eat, the music you listen to, the kind of books and magazines you read, the sports you engage in, or the daily routine, remember to try your wings on things that are totally different. You may be in for a pleasant surprise. Remember that no one knows everything. Keep a list of places you'd like to visit. Stop by the Chamber of Commerce for ideas, or look in the weekend section of the newspaper.

❑ **995. BELIEVE IN YOURSELF.** Act with confidence. Mentally make a list of your many good qualities and don't let anyone belittle you. Speak up for what you know is right. If you make a mistake, learn to laugh at yourself and remember it's not the end of the world. Keep your religious beliefs active and listen for guidance—don't always bull ahead with your own ways.

❑ **996. RESPECT THE LAW.** We can't expect to be protected by the law if we cut corners when it suits us. Teach kids to recognize right from wrong and don't support the idea that the end justifies the means. Be law-abiding and just in your thinking as well as in your actions.

❑ **997. BE A GOOD NEWS BEARER.** Share positive ideas, not negative gossip. And don't be a complainer, a judge, or a constant arguer. Sure, every life has some lumps but don't let them overshadow the good. Contrary to much of the evening news broadcasts, there truly are good things happening. Search them out, share them with your family, and think of them through the day and as you fall asleep at night.

❑ **998. APPRECIATE ONE ANOTHER.** A parent can admit to having had in her youth some wild times, strange songs, and odd clothing habits. Thus, when it comes to safe but unusual teen fads, don't judge but rather keep advice to the minimum. Ask questions. Listen and learn. When you approve of something, give compliments. Each day find something you appreciate in each of your family members.

❑ **999. USE YOUR HOME.** Make it the family center, but not the circumference. Plan a party. Invite relatives for a weekend. Make a home craft center. Snuggle up in your warm bed and read magazines. If you get sleepy in front of

TV, turn it off and play a box game with a kid. Share your home with others—don't let it become just a place to sleep, eat, and look at TV. Give it a new look now and then—just rearrange it rather than spend more money.

❑ **1000.** TAKE CONTROL OF YOUR POSSESSIONS. End the clutter. Amassing "things" is selfish. Teach youngsters that things unused deprive others of their use. Give away what you don't need. If you haven't used something in a year or two, pass it on to family, friends, or social services.

# 1001. HOLDING HANDS

You will hold your child's hand through many of the challenges of growing up. But sometimes you won't be there when a little hand-holding is needed, and that's why you teach your youngster the importance of the family bond, for this means you can always stick together in thought even when you are far apart. Hand-holding takes many forms and continues all through life. When you love your child, hand-holding never ends.

When your child is a tiny baby, you let his whole hand curl around your little finger.

When he is learning to walk, you hold his hand as he takes those first tottering steps.

When he is learning to cross the street, he trustingly takes your hand.

When you gather around the breakfast table, you all hold hands for a quiet moment before parting for the day.

When the family goes for a hike, you hold hands in the steep places.

When he leaves for camp, he gives you a brave handshake in front of the other guys.

When he doesn't feel well, your hands lovingly nurse him back to good health and you sit by his bed, holding his hand.

When he has a tough school assignment or trouble under the hood of his car, you give him a helping hand.

When you fall behind with the chores around the house, he gives you a helping hand.

When he goes on his first date, you press an extra bit of cash into his hand.

When he gets his first after-school job, your hands applaud his achievement.

When he graduates, you give his hand a loving squeeze, and then you give each other a "high five."

When he leaves home, your hands touch briefly in a proud good-bye.

Then come hands across the miles. You mentally hold his

hand through the trials and triumphs of learning to be on his own.

And throughout all time, your hand of love will reach out and support your child—and eventually the next generation of little hands.

So at this moment it is up to you to start your own style of hand-holding. Take the hand of your child and go forward together as a family. You can do it!

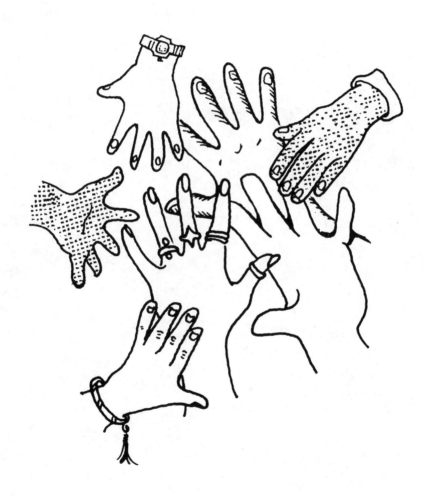

# INDEX

(Activities indexed by item number, not page number.)